Banged-Up Heart

A Memoir

Banged-Up Heart
Dancing with Love and Loss

Shirley Melis

Terra Nova Books
SANTA FE, NEW MEXICO

Library of Congress Control Number 2016959147

Distributed by SCB Distributors, (800) 729-6423

Terra Nova Books

Published by Terra Nova Books, Santa Fe, New Mexico.
www.TerraNovaBooks.com

ISBN 978-1-938288-70-8

To Frank, who never questioned my need to write my truth.

If you haven't already, you will lose someone you can't
live without, and your heart will be badly broken, and
you will never completely get over the loss of a deeply
beloved person. But this is also the good news.
The person lives forever in your broken heart that doesn't
seal back up. And you come through, and you learn to
dance with the banged-up heart.

—Anne Lamott, *Plan B: Further Thoughts on Faith*

Contents

Acknowledgments

I AM DEEPLY INDEBTED TO MANY WHO HELPED ALONG THE WAY:

• My goddaughter and an author in her own right, Gitty Daneshvari, who urged me after reading the first sixty pages to "keep on writing."

• Generous early readers whose comments and questions opened my eyes to blind spots: Philip Metcalf, Diane Norman, Ann Holland, Richard Blair, and Lolly Keefer-Meissner.

• Friends who fanned the flames of encouragement over some six years of writing and rewriting: Barclay Braden, Patricia (Pat) Galagan, Karen Daneshvari, Marilyn McAlice, Barbara Maniha, Melinda and Gary Hall, Carlan and Nancy Tapp, Shamsi Daneshvari, Tori Shepard, Susie Schwartz, Steve Blindheim, Al and Nancy Melis, Titia Ellis, Carol Franco, Kent Lineback, Carol Weston, Robert Ackerman, Naomi Klaus, the Rev. Kim Beach, Michele and Mike Bradshaw, Natalie Van Straaten, Eric (Rick) Carey, Larry Redelin, and Taylor Meade.

• Talented Amiel Gervers, who designed my first website.

My deepest thanks to my husband Frank, who came into my life when I was writing the last chapters, and whose unquestioning support led me to my peerless editor and guide, Morgan Farley. Morgan helped me see the book through new eyes. Without Morgan—who asked the questions that guided me deep inside, who prodded me to tell my truth, and to give more when I didn't know I had more to give—I could not have done this.

Of course, this book would not have been possible without my agent, Liz Trupin-Pulli. Thanks to the Tony Hillerman Writers Conference where Liz selected the first page of my then-first chapter as her favorite during a flash critique session and advised me to finish my manuscript and contact her. Because of Liz's unwavering commitment—she championed my book from the moment she read it—I met Marty Gerber of Terra Nova Books. I am deeply grateful to Marty for his keen editorial eye and sense, enthusiasm, and commitment. For his graphic design ability, among other talents, I owe thanks to publisher Scott Gerber and other members of the TNB team. For their creativity, marketing expertise, and gentle hand-holding as I learned to be comfortable with Facebook and Twitter, I owe much to Mari Angulo and Art Tucker of Artotems.

Banged-Up Heart

Fresh Air

"You're John?" With his easy smile and bright blue eyes, he was a far cry from the forlorn figure I'd envisioned.

"Yes." He was looking down at me, amused by my undisguised surprise. Brown hair shot with silver fell across his forehead.

It was Christmas day. We were standing in the library when John's brother Dick sounded the breakfast gong. The round dining table with its centerpiece of red-berried holly was set for eight. John slid into a seat next to Dick. I sat on the far side between Dick's wife, Kerry, an old friend, and her mother, Gay. I'd been invited down from Virginia to North Carolina so I wouldn't have to spend the holiday alone, and I would also be having dinner with another old friend while I was there.

Dick, Kerry, and I were close friends, but I'd never spent Christmas with them until after Joe died. They knew me well; they had known and liked Joe. Over the past two years, they had watched me attempt to make a life for myself without him. I was still in a limbo I didn't understand, somewhere between my old life and a new one that I could not quite imagine. I would catch myself going through the motions, trying to take care of things as Joe had. I knew I was not succeeding. Would I ever feel more than half-alive? Lately, I had been trying to picture myself in a life that would engage my heart as well as my mind. And now in Raleigh, I would take a step in that direction.

Kerry placed a hand on my arm. "Have you talked with Paul?" She was aware of my date the next night, my first since Joe's death.

"I called him this morning. I suggested he might want to meet you and Dick before we go to dinner."

After sumptuous servings of scrambled eggs and bacon, we exchanged gifts in front of a tree. I had a small gift for John, as part of the family of people I felt close to: an empty leather-covered box purchased a year earlier in Buenos Aires; I couldn't think of what to put in it. That day he didn't give me anything.

With the last of the wrappings whisked away, Dick and Kerry started preparations for their ritual dinner for twenty-five. I knew Kerry had this down pat and didn't need any help from me. Addicted to exercise, I felt the need to walk off a bit of breakfast before sitting down to a big dinner.

"Would you like to take a walk?" I turned to John who had just returned to the living room after retrieving a decanter from a high shelf for Kerry. Everyone else seemed occupied.

"Yes."

"Great! I'll be right back, soon as I change my shoes." I hurried out the front door to the house next door where Gay and I were staying.

John was set to go in jeans and a blue windbreaker, with a Nikon slung over one shoulder. A narrow yellow band circled his right wrist.

"Ready?" he asked.

The neighborhood was old, small clapboard bungalows set back from the street by lawns and large rhododendrons and azaleas. John had a long stride that he seemed to temper so we could walk side by side. I was aware of his height and a slight hunch, which I attributed to years of interacting with people who were shorter. I was only mildly curious about him, anticipating my date with Paul the next night.

It was a big step for me. I had just taken off my rings—wedding and anniversary—and felt nakedly exposed, as though I were sending a message I didn't yet believe in. Until Paul's wife died a few months earlier, I hadn't even thought about dating since Joe's death. But I had taken the initiative; at Sharon's memorial service, I told Paul that I would be in Raleigh for Christmas, and he suggested we get together for dinner. It had seemed reasonable, a sensible way of stepping out of my cocoon. He and Sharon had been family friends, and now he and I were both widowed. We might hit it off.

Setting out with John, I tied my jacket around my hips. "Have you been to Raleigh before?" I asked.

"Yes but not in a long time. I'm surprised it's this warm."

"I've been here but never in December. It looks a bit desolate." Leafless trees cast a lonely pall over the empty street. It had been spring when I visited with Joe—flowers and trees in glorious bloom. I was in bloom. My chest tightened. Joe's death had crushed the bloom, leaving me in tatters.

John hitched his camera more securely on his shoulder.

"I see you brought your camera. Are you a photographer?"

"Yes. I moved to Santa Fe to devote full time to photography."

"What kind?"

"Landscape."

A gray cat darted across the street, disappearing through a dense hedge. I thought about Sami, my failing sixteen-year-old Abyssinian. If Joe were alive, he wouldn't have left Sami for any reason; fortunately, I'd been able to board him at the vet's.

Joe had been devoted to Sami, as to all the cats he ever owned. Because of Joe, I'd become smitten with cats and a host of other animals. I planned to leave money to the animal protection society he'd founded in Chapel Hill, and if I ever owned another animal, I would arrange for its care after my death. Joe had been a powerful force who shaped me in many ways. Intelligent, intuitive, kind—he had loved and supported me through all kinds of experiences. I wasn't sure about finding someone else. In my immediate circle, I couldn't see anyone who even came close.

Slipping the camera from his shoulder, John shot an avenue of skeletal trees.

"You said 'landscape'?"

"Yes."

"How long have you been taking pictures?"

"I was six years old when I took my first photograph."

"Really? What did you photograph?"

"A few stars."

"That's pretty amazing."

"My father taught me."

I thought of my own father who had been such a great support to me growing up. He hadn't shown me how to take pictures, but he thought I could do anything I put my mind to. When he died, just three weeks after Joe, I felt the last bits of me crumble. I could hardly bear it. It was more than his death. His lung cancer had been in remission for nine months when, reluctantly, I called to tell him about Joe. "I wish there were something I could do to help you, Shirley." I heard the tears in his voice.

There was nothing he could do—except not die. I was haunted by a sense that my telling him about Joe had distressed him so much it had brought back his cancer.

For a time, I didn't know who I was grieving for, Joe or my father. In all likelihood, I was grieving for myself. With their deaths, I lost my cheering section. I lost the energy that had been buoying me up all my life. I didn't know what it was like to be without it. My mother had died three years earlier. Suddenly, I was both a widow and an orphan.

John stopped walking to peer at a convoluted rusted metal structure on an empty lot. He lifted the camera and clicked, then showed me the image he'd captured. I wondered why he found the subject appealing. I wanted to ask him but felt as if I couldn't, and anyway, what did it matter? It was all I could do to stay with the conversation.

"You said you moved to Santa Fe?"

"Yes, I took early retirement from Northrop Grumman."

"What did you do there?"

"I was in California, Redondo Beach. I was a physicist and an engineer, mostly in aerospace, but the last two years, I was a Six Sigma Black Belt trainer."

"Black Belt? Sounds like karate."

"Six Sigma trains people to solve problems using mathematics, especially statistics. It was probably the best job I ever had."

I was thinking about the outfit I'd brought for my date with Paul, wondering whether I'd be too warm. It was a wool suit, black, with a red camisole. I imagined Paul's face lighting up when he saw me in it. He was a successful businessman, a professor, and a link to Joe—a concrete and realistic step forward in contrast to my vague fantasies of being swept off my feet and riding into the sunset with some handsome man bent on adventure.

We crossed another street and continued along the sidewalk. "My college roommate was a math major," I said. "When she and other math majors got together, I didn't know what they were talking about." John was one of those, I thought, at home in a world I knew nothing about. Algebra had nearly done me in, and, to my regret, I'd never taken a course in physics.

"My job involved mentoring," he said, "which I didn't think I'd like, but I found I liked it a lot."

"I can relate to that. In my community relations work for the Metropolitan Washington Airports Authority, I mentor middle school students in reading, and I really like it, especially when the students are motivated."

I stopped to retie a shoe. Joe and I had had no children. He'd made clear at the outset that he didn't want a child, and that was all right with me. I had never harbored a desire to be a mother; I wanted a career. We had thrived on being the center of each other's attention. And now, my career was all I had left. My community relations job was the only thing that still engaged me, a welcome distraction from grief. But it was not what I really wanted to be doing.

"You said you retired to do photography. I think about retiring, and what I'd really like to do is write and travel. I lived overseas—in Tunisia—for a year, the year before I went to college. My father was with the State Department. Ever since then, I've wanted to travel. I've done some—I was a freelance travel writer—but I'd like to do more, much more. And I have an idea for a book I'd like to write—interviewing women from sixty to ninety who feel good about themselves."

A couple of young boys raced past us on bikes. I pictured John and Joe as young boys, very different from each other. John active but somewhat introverted, probably attracted to intelligent extroverts as my father had been; Joe physically active—he'd said he used to love to run—and a dynamic leader.

"What's the yellow band on your wrist all about?" He held it out to me, and I could see LIVESTRONG in bold black letters.

"It's worn by Lance Armstrong, who won the Tour de France so many times in spite of having cancer." John swallowed. "I have a rare blood cancer, Waldenstrom's macroglobulinemia."

"Kerry told me. I was sad to hear about it."

"There are maybe fifteen hundred cases a year."

He'd apparently had the cancer for years. I also knew he had moved to Santa Fe with a fiancée who had just died of cancer in the fall. That's why I'd expected him to look forlorn, to be in shock and grief the way I was after losing Joe. Why wasn't he?

"How did you find out you had it?"

"I was playing tennis when suddenly I couldn't run across the court without stopping to catch my breath. I'd always been pretty active—rock climbing, soccer. I thought about my father who was active and energetic well into his sixties, and figured something was wrong. My company offered an executive physical, and I took it. The blood results stumped a lot of doctors. Finally, someone at Mount Sinai made the diagnosis. Most people diagnosed with Waldenstrom's are sixty-five or more, and live on average another five years."

"That must have been scary."

"I thought that being diagnosed at a relatively young age—I was forty—could be a positive. There would be scientific advances I could benefit from, and I have benefited. For the past six years, I've been getting periodic infusions of Rituxan—it's similar to chemo but not chemo—and there's a backup treatment in the wings."

"That's reassuring."

"Yes, backups are good. And I decided a positive attitude was important."

I was struck by John's optimism and lack of self-pity. And when he mentioned the backup treatment, I felt a sense of relief.

John didn't ask questions, but he was an attentive listener. I felt very much at ease as I told him about my earlier career in public relations for life and health insurance associations. "I lost my job as vice president in a big reorganization spearheaded by McKinsey & Company. When they were through, twenty-six positions had been eliminated—mostly in P.R., including all but one vice president. The man they kept was very good at company politics, and he was an avid golfer. I was neither. I was offered a chance to be a lobbyist for one of the big life insurers, but I thought I'd like to try something else. A major P.R. firm, Hill & Knowlton, called me, saying my job loss might be a golden opportunity for them and me, and there was also a P.R. position in a plastics association that sounded intriguing. Neither panned out. I was out of a job for twenty-one months. I worked at Nordstrom, and my husband, Joe, who'd retired years earlier, got a job at Brentano's bookstore."

I waited for John to say something, expecting a comment or question. When he said nothing, I just went on because he seemed to be listening so attentively.

"We were married for almost twenty-eight years, but we were together nearly thirty. He was a lot older than I—twenty-one years—but despite that, I was shocked by his death. He'd had surgery to replace his aortic valve, and seventeen days later, he died. He was staying in a rehab center to regain his strength. He was supposed to come home in two weeks.

"It was shattering. I felt I'd lost my ballast. Almost overnight, I lost fifteen pounds. After Joe died, I made some very unwise decisions—I had no children to advise me or share my grief—but one I felt good about was selling the house and moving into a condo. I did that two months ago."

I had sold the house mainly because there was too much of Joe in it; everywhere I turned, I was reminded of him. A year after he died, I thought I was finally okay. Then my doctor asked a routine question at my annual physical: "How have you been this past year, Shirley?" When I opened my mouth to speak, I couldn't. Convulsed in sobs, I choked out, "My husband died." That's all I could say. I thought the tears would never stop. "Are you seeing a therapist?" she asked.

A few weeks later, I joined a hospice grief group and started seeing a therapist. In the grief group, you told your story whenever you were moved to over the eight-week session. There were eight of us, one man and seven women. When my turn came, I told my story through tears, and when I was through, I felt comforted, embraced by a knowing acceptance of my grief. But it was hearing the others that gave me real solace; their stories actually made me feel almost lucky. Because Joe's death was sudden, I'd escaped the ordeal many of them had gone through as their spouses underwent surgery after surgery, chemo after chemo, in a vain attempt to stay alive. I would not have wanted to go through that with Joe. In a way, I was spared.

Pausing to zip up my jacket, I was surprised to see the rusted metal that John had photographed earlier. We were within a couple of blocks of Dick and Kerry's. I realized I had had no idea where we were—I guess I'd left that to John. I must have felt I was in good hands with him. By the time we got back to the house, I felt we could almost be friends.

That evening, as I entered the dining room, John greeted me with the news that we weren't seated together. I glanced around the room. There were several festive tables, red candles and woven pine on white linen.

"We're not even at the same table," John said. He seemed upset.

"We need to fix that, don't we?" I looked up into deep-blue eyes that seemed locked on mine. I have never considered myself a flirt, but looking back, I was flirting with John—no two ways about it. From the start, I felt relaxed and comfortable with him. He nodded emphatically.

"We can just switch some place cards." I wanted to sit with him. There was something fresh about talking with a relative stranger. It was an opportunity to shed my old grief-worn self and present myself anew. Simply being in Raleigh for my date with Paul, I was beginning to see myself in a new light. I was feeling hopeful. With John, I was glimpsing how it might be to liberate myself from the stale emptiness of the last two years.

"I think you ought to check with Kerry."

She seemed surprised but graciously seated us next to each other. With the best of intentions, she had placed John next to a single spike-haired blonde from California. As guests started arriving, John and I stood near the mistletoe, wine glasses in hand. Now that the seating arrangements had been altered, he relaxed. In my old life, I thought, I would have been kissing someone under the mistletoe. Would I be kissing Paul? Would Paul be kissing me?

I wondered whether I would like Paul in this new context. Joe had known Paul and Sharon since his days in Chapel Hill, and over the years, the four of us had shared brunches and dinners out. Once, Paul flew their twin-engine plane up to Virginia to have lunch with us; we picked them up at a small airport near Leesburg and drove into D.C. We'd spent a lot of time together as couples, but I had never spent time alone with Paul. I hoped we would be a match. I assumed he liked to travel—he and Sharon had taken a number of trips out of the country. What about the chemistry? Would there be any between us? I was hopeful.

Guests decked out in Christmas finery spilled from the library into the dining room. John stepped closer to me. "I'm going to be going to New York in the spring and would like to stop and see you on the way."

His words startled me. Why would he want to see me? We'd just met. "Well, there's a lot to see and do in the D.C. area," I said, purposely noncommittal. By spring, I might be involved with Paul. Who knew?

Over dinner, swept up by conversation with others at the table, John and I talked very little, but I noticed that he seemed to have something to contribute on any topic that came up. He was like Joe in being able to converse about so many things. I liked that in a man. I had a good feeling about him.

"Will I see you tomorrow?" he asked.

"I don't know what Kerry has planned for the day, but I'm having dinner with a family friend."

"May I drive you to the airport then?"

"Yes, thank you," I said, thinking it would be presumptuous to expect Paul to take me.

The following evening, I was changing clothes in the guest bedroom, getting ready for my date, when Gay burst in. "Shirley, I don't know how to say this, but John is crazy about you."

"What do you mean?"

"He's crazy about you!" she repeated, raising her voice as if to convince both of us it was true. "He just told us."

"How is that possible? He doesn't even know me!"

"Well, he just is. That's all I can say."

First Date

A SILVER JAGUAR PULLED UP OUT FRONT. THROUGH THE FRONT window, I observed Paul. He moved with agility despite a slight hitch in his gait. Trim, with a head of thinning gray hair, he was not unattractive in a dark brown leather jacket that was just a little too long. Suddenly, we were face-to-face and embracing. We chatted a few minutes with Gay before walking next door. I had wanted her to meet Paul, and I was eager for Kerry to meet him too. They had known the significant men in my life, including Nikos, the Greek physician whom I once had almost married. I hoped to get their impressions of Paul, although I didn't know when. I'd be leaving Raleigh early in the morning.

Kerry and Dick met us at the front door, and to my surprise, John was with them. After quick introductions, Kerry invited us into the dining room for a glass of wine.

Sitting quietly, tasting the wine, I was struck by Paul's easy affability. What gave me pause was his jacket. What had looked so good through the window was indescribably cheap-looking up close. From across the table, I noted his broad-boned face, well-defined cheekbones, and strong chin. His nose, injured in an accident years ago, was somewhat bulbous with a cleft at the end, but I was not put off by it.

John sipped his wine but was silent. I don't know how he'd managed to sit next to me, but there he was. Earlier when the others were talking, he had said to me, "You look lovely." I was surprised and flattered; I was wearing an outfit I'd bought just for this occasion: a slim black skirt, mid-calf, with a jacket of the same light wool over a red silk camisole. Paul had not commented on how I looked.

He and I stayed just long enough to finish the one glass of wine. Back outside, Paul opened the door of the Jag and I stepped in, sinking comfortably into the leather seat. The sun was setting.

"I know this neighborhood," he said as he maneuvered through rush-hour traffic toward Chapel Hill. "I used to date someone who lived on Glenwood Avenue . . . a lot of years ago."

Trying to picture Paul "a lot of years ago" was a stretch, although I'd seen photos of him in younger years on the walls of his office.

It was to be an at-home dinner. Paul had told me that after Sharon died, his children hired a chef to prepare gourmet meals for him, which he was enjoying. The problem was quantity, he'd explained, saying there was so much delicious food that he was throwing weekly dinner parties. When he'd suggested we share one of his gourmet meals, it sounded tempting.

As we neared Chapel Hill, I recognized the area. Joe and I had driven down from Virginia a number of times for special events—birthday parties, book signings, weddings. Usually, we'd stayed with friends in Durham, but Joe delighted in showing me Chapel Hill, where he'd lived in the late '50s and early '60s. I liked what I'd seen. Residential areas were heavily wooded for the most part, with many houses camouflaged by large trees and, in the spring, blooming azaleas and rhododendrons. I'd liked the fact that it was a university town where, I assumed, people talked about more than politics. A political junkie by virtue of living and working in the D.C. area, I knew there was more to life than politics, and I longed to taste it. In addition to his work as the Blue Cross public relations director for North Carolina, Joe had written a column for the *Chapel Hill Weekly* and reviewed theatrical productions by the Carolina Playmakers. Maybe if we moved to Chapel Hill, there'd be opportunities for me to use the experience I had gained dealing with business writers for insurance associations. At the very least, I might read more than the *Washington Post* and *New York Times*. I might read books. I might take classes at the university. I was hungry for good nonpolitical conversation, which Joe said he missed in the D.C. area. With his encouragement, I'd tried to get a job with the Blue Cross plan in the Chapel Hill area. But I didn't succeed. Probably just as well, as his former wife lived in Chapel Hill and worked at the university. She'd asked Paul for advice—perhaps the name of a lawyer—when Joe told her he wanted a divorce.

As Paul pulled into his driveway, I was hopeful that we might be a match. I wanted to know him better. Joe had liked Paul, although he'd described him as consumed with work and neglectful of Sharon at times. But that was years ago. Paul had spoken movingly of Sharon at her memorial service, and I suspected a softer side. I was hoping for Joe's sensitivity and charm, someone who loved animals, someone who enjoyed music and theater.

He led the way up a wooden stairway to the wide front door. Like the rest of the house, it was made of dark wood. As I remembered from the times Joe and I had visited, even on the brightest day, the interior of the house was dark except for the atrium.

Paul switched on a light, revealing a small kitchen table set with two placemats hugging one corner. The overhead lighting was aimed toward the table, the rest of the kitchen in semi-darkness. "Have a seat." Paul pointed to one of two straight-backed chairs. I sat down, noting the old flooring and dark cabinets, unchanged since I'd first set foot in the house, while Paul went to the fridge and came back with a decanter of chilled white wine. He offered me some (though he was not drinking alcohol for health reasons), which I accepted. Then he got two small glass bowls filled with several large peeled shrimp and wedges of lemon from the fridge, placed one on each mat, and sat down.

"The cook couldn't come yesterday because of the holiday, so we're eating what she made last week."

Visions of a delicious gourmet dinner suddenly gave way to images of stale, dried out food, tasteless and worse. Was it my imagination or were the shrimp ultra-chilled, the lemon wedges flabby? Why hadn't he suggested going out for dinner? As soon as we'd gotten through the shrimp, Paul stood up and cleared the empty glass bowls from the table. A buzzer sounded, and he reappeared with Tupperware containers filled with steaming side dishes that he placed on the table. A buzzer went off again as he made another trip to the microwave, returning with a plate that had a single thick fillet of beef in the center which he placed in front of me. After he returned with a steak for himself, I easily cut into the tender fillet and closed my mouth on a piece that was absolutely chilled.

"I'm sorry, Paul, but my fillet is cold."

"Oh, I can fix that." He jumped up from the table. "I'll just put it back in the microwave."

He did not offer red wine to accompany the steak, so I continued to drink the white. Except for the on-again, off-again buzzing of the microwave, it was quiet. Paul, a presumed music lover, did not have any music playing in the background.

"I'd like to hear more about your new real estate project."

"I'll tell you about it as soon as I reheat these fillets."

The residential development would feature hangars for airplanes instead of garages for cars. I'd found the concept intriguing when I'd first heard about it, probably from Joe. In a few words, Paul gave me an update, ending on a positive note.

"We've sold a few lots. I think the project is viable."

This real estate venture was in addition to his consulting. For as long as I'd known Paul, he'd done consulting, and had continued since retiring from the university.

"Say," he said, cutting into his reheated fillet, "whatever happened to that fellow named Richard, the one I met at Joe's birthday party? I sort of figured you'd be seeing a lot of him."

I swallowed hard. Richard, a few years younger than Joe, had been Joe's best friend, and a good friend to me too. When his wife was alive, the four of us had seen a lot of each other, taking weekend or longer trips together, and after her death, Richard had been like a member of our small family. To celebrate Joe's seventy-fifth birthday, he'd taken the three of us to New York City for a long weekend of Broadway theater, caviar, and champagne at Petroussian, steak at Smith & Wollensky, and dinner at the Russian Tea Room. At Joe's seventy-ninth birthday party, which Paul and Sharon had attended, Richard had given a moving tribute to Joe. And he'd helped me in countless ways when Joe died.

"Richard moved back to Ohio."

I had not been happy with his decision to return to Ohio, where many of his relatives still lived. But I thought I understood in part why he had moved. "You know I love you," he'd said to me shortly before he left, about a year after Joe's death. I had suspected he might, but at the time, I was incapable of reciprocating his feelings, and I think he knew that.

"Tell me," Paul said, as though mentally ticking off a list of must-ask questions, "why haven't you retired?"

"Well, I'm a bit dubious about my financial situation."

"Tell me what it is."

Without hesitating, I proceeded to give him a general picture.

"You could easily arrange for a fixed annuity that would pay you a certain amount each month, and you'd be fine."

I assumed that Paul, with his various business interests, was an effective money manager, and made a mental note to ask my financial adviser about this type of annuity. (When I did, I found it was actually not in my best interest.)

Paul started talking about there being no good reason for me not to retire.

"There's another reason I want to work, at least through the summer," I said, interrupting what was becoming a rant on the subject. "I've arranged for a recently discovered young relative in Prague to fill a summer internship at the Airports Authority where I work."

"Does he need protection?" asked Paul, somewhat derisively.

"He's never been to the United States. He'll be staying with me, and I want to help him as much as I can."

"I'm planning to take a cruise this spring," Paul said, abruptly changing the subject, and, without outright inviting me, started in again about the desirability of my retiring right away. As he talked, I looked at him intently. Ever aware of eyes, I found Paul's bright gold-brown eyes a bit small for his face, and his wide smile marred by nearly nonexistent lips.

"I've met a lot of women in the last few months, but none of them appeal to me." *Appeals,* I thought, almost saying it aloud: *"None of them appeals to me."* I couldn't help it. I was a demon for correct use of the English language, much as Joe had been.

While I was mentally correcting Paul's grammar, he moved his chair closer and turned, pushing his face inches from mine.

"Well, Shirley Nagelschmidt, why did you want to have dinner with me?" Taken aback by the question, I sat back in my chair and thought for a few seconds.

"The possibility of a romantic relationship had crossed my mind."

Paul grinned, his thin lips stretching wide. "I'd like to fly up to see you again on Valentine's Day."

"Oh, that might be nice." On the other hand, I thought, it might not be. Paul's manner coupled with his apparent assumption that a microwaved week-old dinner in the kitchen was an appropriate dinner date wasn't computing as Valentine-worthy. Suddenly, he kissed me hard on the mouth, his lips closed. Surprised, I blanched and stood up, excusing myself to use the bathroom. This wasn't even close to a match, I thought, as I looked in the bathroom mirror to repair my lipstick. Why had I thought it might be? Joe was right. Paul had the charm and sensitivity of cardboard. I should have insisted on going out to dinner, then he could have just taken me back to Raleigh. Now what was I going to do?

When I walked into the dimly lit living room, I heard sounds coming from the kitchen. I supposed he was cleaning up. He had that 'everything in its place' way. It would be so easy to just walk out the front door, but then what would I do? Feeling trapped in a situation of my own making, I sat down on the long upholstered sofa. Within seconds, Paul walked in and sat beside me. Without reaching for my hand, or pausing to talk, he kissed me again. I tensed, inwardly recoiling.

"Paul, would you play the piano for me?" I asked, hoping to put some distance between us.

"Sure," he said. "Whadaya wanna hear?"

"How about show tunes and jazz?"

An accomplished jazz pianist, he had played at Joe's birthday party not that many years ago. As he started, I could feel the tension in my body start to ease. What a talent, I thought, wishing there were other aspects of Paul I could appreciate as much. He must have played for thirty minutes, maybe longer, when I stood up, purse in hand.

"I'm sorry but I need to be getting back."

"Okay," he said, getting up from the piano bench and putting on the leather jacket.

"I enjoyed your playing," I said, following him out to the car. Paul said nothing as he opened the door for me. It was pitch black, a moonless, starless night. He had just driven onto the highway heading to Raleigh when he announced, "I can't get an erection because of the prostate surgery I had," then went on to describe it in some detail. Joe had told me about the cancer. It was serious, and we'd been concerned about Paul's survival. His erectile function, or lack thereof, had never crossed my mind, at least not until now. His voice rose: "It's been seventeen years since I've been inside a woman!" I said nothing, not knowing where this clinical confession was going. "But I'm taking treatments to correct the condition, and . . . I'm doing this just for you!" I could feel my jaw drop. For me? Why me? Why not for himself, or for Sharon who'd had a vested interest in the relationship? As if nearing the finish line of a race, he went on: "Rest assured, I have no trouble finding the G-spot!" I really didn't want to hear this, any of it, not on a first date, maybe never! Nonetheless, my curiosity was piqued.

"What are the treatments?" I asked, thankful for the cover of darkness. He explained that he was getting injections directly into his penis. In fact, he said with notable enthusiasm, he had recently experienced an erection improvement, describing the angle as a mathematical percentage. Suddenly, I found myself feeling sorry for Sharon for so many reasons, Paul's physical complaint perhaps the least of them. I couldn't wait to get out of the car, away from this man.

"Can I give you a ride to the airport in the morning?" Paul asked, pulling up outside the house in Raleigh.

"Thank you, but the family's planning to take me," I said, opening the car door. I gave Paul a perfunctory hug and then got out. Fighting the urge to run, I closed the car door and turned toward the garden gate. Opening the front door of the house, I let out an audible sigh.

It was 10:30. Gay was in the living room, sitting in an easy chair, ostensibly reading the *Times*.

"My date with Paul was less than stellar," I said, taking off my shoes and falling back onto the sofa near her chair.

"Oh?"

"Did you notice his leather jacket?"

"Yes," she said knowingly.

"Well, my evening with Paul was a lot like his jacket—cheap and a little too long. But to his credit, he plays wonderful piano."

I told her about the microwaved dinner and his asking about Richard.

"I'm sorry, sweetheart. I know you were looking forward to your date."

I didn't talk about the drive-home conversation. I felt it too crass to share with her.

"He wants to fly up to see me on Valentine's."

"Oh?"

"I'm not going to let him do it."

Email Courting

"WOULD YOU LIKE SOME BREAKFAST?" GAY WAS STANDING IN THE doorway.

"Coffee and a toasted bagel would be good. Thank you."

I didn't have a lot of time. Fortunately, I'd packed the night before. Practiced at putting on makeup, I dressed in a matter of minutes. I left my bag at the front door and sat down at the dining table as Gay placed orange juice, coffee, and a bagel in front of me. I had just bitten into a lightly buttered bagel when the doorbell rang. I looked at my watch. Eight o'clock. "We should leave for the airport at 8 a.m.," John had said two days before when I'd accepted his offer to drive me. I got up to open the door and there he was. A blue linen shirt with sleeves rolled above his wrists hung out over loose gray pants. On his feet were a pair of sandals.

"Ready?"

"Yes, soon as I brush my teeth."

Without another word, he picked up my suitcase and carried it out while I hurried into the bathroom. Wrapping my wet toothbrush in a Kleenex and stashing it in my purse, I grabbed my coat and hugged Gay goodbye. From the porch I could see Kerry's neon blue VW Beetle in the driveway. The passenger door was open. I hurried down the steps and across the lawn to the car, tossing my coat onto the back seat next to my suitcase. John was nowhere to be seen. He must have gone back next door for something, I thought. When the door on the driver's side opened, John got in, folding his long legs under the steering wheel, his right hand clutching a piece of paper. Looking over his right shoulder, his left hand on the wheel, he backed out of the driveway.

"This is the first time I've driven to the Raleigh-Durham Airport. I asked Dick to draw a map for me this morning." Ten minutes later, our speed slowed. I sensed John was looking for a landmark he didn't yet see. Our 8 a.m. start had been closer to 8:15, and I hadn't seen any signs to the airport.

"You can just drop me in front of the terminal," I said, trying to put him at ease. I didn't want him to think he had to take time to park and then go into the terminal with me. John looked again at the map and turned onto a highway. Within seconds, we picked up speed. I sat back, relieved that John, not Paul, was driving me to the airport. The evening with Paul still fresh in my mind, I silently castigated myself for having put so much stock in it.

At the terminal, John double-parked. I looked at my watch; I was cutting it close. I got my coat from the back as he picked up my suitcase and carried it through a crush of people to the curb. I was right behind him when he turned to face me.

"Thank you," I said. Impulsively, I raised my arms and wrapped them around his broad shoulders. In a nanosecond, I felt his arms around me.

"I hate to say goodbye," I said, overcome by a sudden feeling of loss. Loss of what I couldn't have said. Our encounter had been so brief. Was it simply the contrast between John and Paul that had given our chance meeting a fleeting poignancy I didn't understand?

"We'll see each other soon," he replied, "because I'm going to explore consulting options in the D.C. area."

"Really?" I dropped my arms and backed up to look at him.

Reaching for my left hand, he placed a small card in my palm. I looked down. It was one of Kerry's place cards, and on it were many numbers and an email address.

"This is my contact information. I hope you'll send me yours when you get home."

"I will," I said, looking up at him.

*   *   *

During the flight home, I mused over my little-more-than-forty-eight-hour Christmas in Raleigh. Not at all what I'd expected, on any front. My first date since Joe's death, an utter disaster. What was I doing? What had I been thinking? I really had no idea. Granted, I'd been intrigued by Paul, but I supposed that was more the fact that I'd considered him a friend than anything else. Or maybe it was just wishful thinking. Paul had been a link to Joe, not a complete stranger, and we'd both survived the recent death of a spouse. Hardly a sure-fire formula for romance, as it turned out. But what *was* the formula?

Intelligence, for one thing, and curiosity.

Joe, who had never gone to college, was highly intelligent. After joining the Navy in World War II, he'd been distressed to find he wasn't on the roster shipping out on the USS *Juneau* with the other enlistees. "Sailor, your I.Q.'s too high. You have to go to school," the Navy clerk had told him. Joe said the test had shown an I.Q. of a hundred seventy but that he didn't believe it. I thought it possible, though. He was a voracious reader. When we met, he'd already given away two libraries of some two thousand books each. While we were together, he read the daily *New York Times* and *Washington Post,* the weekly *New Yorker,* and all kinds of books—novels and nonfiction, especially memoirs. Before he was sixteen, he'd read and annotated all of Shakespeare's plays. And after graduating as valedictorian from a good public high school on Long Island, he'd edited and written for three Long Island newspapers.

"Why didn't you go to college?" I asked.

"All I ever wanted to do was write. I didn't see the connection between going to college and writing. And besides, my parents wouldn't have had the money to send me." Joe's father was a supervisor in a large post office on Long Island.

A sense of humor was another prerequisite. Joe had a good one. He was a punster who could also tell clever, complicated jokes, something I never could do well. He met people easily and got along well, sometimes better than I did, with my relatives, friends, and colleagues.

And a keen sense of justice. Unlike me, Joe had been an activist in the civil rights movement during the '60s when he was living in Chapel Hill. I'd been in college in the early '60s, comfortable in my ivory tower, immune to politics and the social issues of the day. And after graduating, I'd lived in Greece, deeply distracted by foreign affairs of the nonpolitical type.

"Joe is a gentleman," my Vassar roommate, Ann, once said. Yes, I'd thought, and a gentle man. He couldn't read about cruelty to animals or children. "I can't bear it," he'd say. In Chapel Hill, he'd founded an organization dedicated to finding homes for animals abandoned by college students and others. After his death, I found a cardboard box in a closet filled with obituaries from the *Times* of everyone who had died in the attack on the World Trade Center.

An adventurous spirit, not to mention a love of travel—another desirable trait.

Before marrying, I had lived with a sense of adventure. Marrying Joe had been an adventure in and of itself, and in our early years together, I'd thrived professionally and personally. But in his last decade, his life grew narrower because of physical limitations, and I had adjusted my own accordingly.

I fantasized that I might meet an adventurously spirited man on a trip to Africa or some other foreign destination, but I was sure such travel wouldn't occur until I retired, and I was not about to stop working anytime soon. Meanwhile, the thought of registering with Match.com or eHarmony held no appeal. I liked the idea of meeting someone serendipitously, caught up in memories of the bygone years before AIDS, when eye contact at a party might lead to a coffee date and more. But now I was leery of meeting total strangers.

I also thought that Joe probably had spoiled me for other men I might meet. Certainly, those I knew at the time seemed to pale by comparison. He would have been appalled, as I was, by Paul's boorish behavior. But he might have been even more appalled by my instigating the dinner date in the first place. I didn't think he would have considered Paul a suitable successor.

Back home, I took a few minutes to unpack and then went into my office. I retrieved the place card with John's contact information from my purse and placed it on a paperweight next to the computer. There was something about this man that I found utterly appealing. Perhaps it was his self-confidence, tempered by a gentleness or a sweetness altogether missing in Paul. I thought he'd said he was staying another few days with Kerry and Dick. Today was Sunday. I typed out my contact information and clicked Send.

When I got home the next evening, I dropped my workout bag in the hall and headed straight for the fridge, where I knew I'd find a chilled bottle of chardonnay. Glass in hand, I walked into my office to check email. Among the various impersonal messages was an address new to me. I recognized it at once. It was John. Catching my breath, I set the glass down on my desk. I hadn't expected to hear from him, not this soon. Was he back in Santa Fe?

Good morning, Shirley . . . . I expect you are on your way to work by now. Just wanted to drop you a quick note before I leave Raleigh. It was a joy to meet you and to get to know a little about you. I came to Raleigh expecting to have an enjoyable holiday. Meeting you has made it much more wonderful than I could have anticipated.

He described a meal he'd had in Chapel Hill at Crook's Corner, a restaurant founded by a local icon of southern cooking, Bill Neal.

"His signature dish," John wrote, "is shrimp and grits. Not bad at all with a little Tabasco added." The image of this slender man chowing down shrimp and grits with unabashed enthusiasm was endearing.

But it was John's second paragraph that riveted my attention:

I was thinking last night—you will learn that this is occasionally dangerous, but I shall press on regardless. Is MLK Day a holiday for you? I could fly out on Friday 2 weeks hence, and we could spend the weekend together. In the meantime (more thinking), I am going to contact several people I used to work with and explore consulting options in the Washington area. If nothing else, there is a large Northrop Grumman sector headquartered in Reston. This and the group I worked for were the two pieces that made up the aerospace part of TRW before NG acquired them three years ago.

The trip back to Santa Fe should be good. The weather looks great for flying, and I don't have to change planes, so I will just sit back, get a drink, and settle in for the duration. Hope your week goes well. I will call you from Santa Fe in a couple of days. Affectionately, John.

Swallowing hard, I reread his second paragraph. Oh my god, he wants to see me, to spend time with me, and soon! Taking a deep breath, I placed my fingers on the keyboard.

"Yes," I typed, "MLK Day is a holiday for me, and I would be delighted to see you," adding that for me, our meeting in Raleigh had been a "surprisingly wondrous encounter." Why did I say *that*? Looking back, I was getting ahead of myself, way ahead. My very positive response was hardly in synch with my psyche. Granted I was surprised by his clear-eyed, upbeat appearance—but "wondrous encounter"! I must have been carried away by the contrast between John and Paul, sending vibes to John that I wasn't even aware of.

With the same ease I'd felt talking to him during our walk together, I kept on typing, telling him about a plethora of messages I'd found on my phone after returning from Raleigh, including one asking me to call to schedule a delivery of flowers. I explained that my brother and his wife in Houston had sent a reportedly fabulous bunch of flowers, "which I may never see because I'm never here to receive, and the florist doesn't know he can leave anything and everything (under fifty pounds) with the concierge! As the call-back number, the florist, whose name I can't make out, gave *my* number!" Finally, I hit Send.

While still at the computer, I printed out John's email, including images of concrete sheep he'd photographed in North Carolina. I picked up my wine and walked back to the kitchen. A pad Thai was in the freezer. Dinner would be easy.

Sitting at the kitchen table, my thoughts raced ahead two-plus weeks. I'd been in the condo two months, but it was hardly ready for prime time. Much of the living room's oak flooring was covered with unopened boxes awaiting delivery of special-order bookcases. And in the midst of the boxes sat a brand new wide-screen HDL TV that was slated for the top of a cabinet separating the two bookcases. And then there was the nonexistent sofa that I hadn't yet ordered. I let out a deep sigh.

The next evening, another email from John described frightening turbulence on his flight back to Santa Fe:

"It sure woke everyone up . . . . I guess I needed a little drama to end the trip. It just puts an exclamation point on what is a sure candidate for best Christmas ever. At least until now anyway. I am looking forward to sharing many more with you." In his closing paragraph, he said, "I hope you get all your deliveries, especially the flowers. Did you call yourself and try to arrange delivery?" I liked his wry sense of humor but found his "looking forward to sharing many more" Christmases alarmingly premature. Why was he moving so fast? It made me uneasy. Was I communicating *Yes* when I meant, Yes, let's get to know each other and see how things go? Or was John on automatic pilot?

Wednesday evening, he called to tell me he'd made flight reservations for the MLK weekend and would email the schedule. In his email he said, "Shirley, it was delightful to talk to you tonight. Here is my flight schedule. I'll send you a couple more pictures tomorrow. I have to go out and buy some groceries. The cupboard was pretty bare when I went looking for dinner tonight. Hope your day goes well. Love, John."

In his now-daily emails, John often noted the weather in Santa Fe, e.g., "gorgeous day—a little wind and temp around 50"; described attached photos; and mentioned the high or low lights of his online poker playing, which I'd asked about: "It's truly an international game. I think I play on a par with the best at the low limits I tend to stay with, but I can tell there are some flaws in my game that need work before I get to where I am betting serious money. Most of it is discipline in deciding what hands to play and when to get out of a hand that may be losing. I am slowly improving. Experience at the table is a big part of becoming a good poker player." He'd talk about other things in his life such as identifying items for his taxes; his cleaning lady's failure to show up ("when I get back, the mice will be complaining about the dust balls"); and food he'd prepared or which I'd described, e.g., "Cold coffee on vanilla ice cream—that is something I would have never thought of . . . . I am going to have to get some vanilla and try it. I certainly always have coffee around."

Less than a week after meeting John and endorsing his visit, I panicked. In his emails, he described his job search with intimations of moving east. "Ideally, it will be part-time or consulting, although I won't pass up the opportunity for a great full-time position for at least a little while. I am finally committed enough to the photography that I could work full-time and still keep it going. There will be many opportunities to take pictures while I become familiar with Virginia. It will be a new experience, and I will have you to share it with." On New Year's Day, he ended his email with: "Hope you are having a good day and a good evening. The first day of the new year—I wish I could share it with you. It will be a wonderful year for both of us." There he went again, sweeping me off my feet. Too fast, too soon.

Here I was, dipping a toe into the dating pool, with one date permanently underwater, and here was John talking as though we were on the verge of living together! While I liked what little I knew of him and was looking forward to our weekend, I felt he was way ahead of me. He'd jumped over all kinds of getting-to-know-you steps. Breathing rapidly, I called his brother Dick and told him of John's seemingly rash behavior, wondering whether this was typical of John. "No," Dick said, "this is not the John I know." Tense, brow furrowed, I emailed

John, asking, "How can you be so sure [of us]?" He replied, "How can I be sure? I don't know if I have a great answer but here goes. It just feels right. Maybe it is a case of 'irrational exuberance,' to use Alan Greenspan's famous phrase. I will admit that I generally tend to take an optimistic view of things. If it does turn out that we are a match, that will be a great thing. That does seem to leave a lot riding on our weekend. I am not sure if that is a good thing, but I don't have any other great ideas on how to find out. And I like you well enough that I cannot envision not taking the chance. Independent of any other considerations, we are just beginning to get to know each other, and it is possible our relationship will not work. But I would like to think it will. I really enjoyed being with you in Raleigh—you are a wonderful person, and I want to get to know you better even if our relationship turns out to be friendship rather than romance." I liked his response, and my anxiety subsided.

In another email, thinking about Sami, who was ailing, I asked John how he felt about cats. "I love cats!!!" He said he'd had two Maine coon cats—Tana and Chablis—who lived to age eighteen, and two more later. Whew! I was relieved and pleased. After telling John more about Sami, and his near-euthanization a year earlier, I was heartened by his reply: "Sami sounds like a real good cat. It is always interesting how much we will do for pets. My first cat Tana (short for Ventana, a vineyard in Northern California) took a fair amount of attention (and $$) her last few years. But I think I would do the same in a heartbeat. Maine coons are real people cats, and Tana and I were definitely best buds." Unknown to John, Joe and I had looked at maine coons, as I was quite taken by the longhaired creatures with their tufted ears. But we had tabled any thought of acquiring one because of my cat allergy; Abyssinians' relatively short hair was definitely in their favor.

As the long weekend drew nearer, I was filled with anticipation but wary. Who was this man who seemed so comfortable in his own skin and so sure of a future with me? I had many questions, and, surely, I thought, he must have questions of me too.

Three days before John's arrival, the bookcases and cabinet were delivered. I called Comcast to arrange for hookup of the TV. Two days before his arrival, I was still unpacking.

"I'm afraid I won't have the books unboxed before you arrive," I said, my voice revealing my dismay.

"I am sure everything will look wonderful when I'm there."

With adrenaline pumping, I unpacked the last of the books the night before he got there. Despite the absence of a living room sofa, I declared the condo "ready," or as ready as it was going to be before his arrival.

"He's going to stay in *your* condo?" Verdella's brown eyes opened wide.

I had just told the receptionist at my office about John and his imminent weekend visit.

"Verdella," I said, "at my age, I don't have time to take it slow. There are some things I need to know up front. If things don't work on that level, chances are they aren't going to work on any other."

"Oh, Girl, you are something," she said, winking.

If I were ever open to the possibility of a committed relationship, the absence of sexual intimacy would be a deal breaker. Paul's matter-of-fact admission had been a wake-up call. If he had been someone else, someone I liked or grew to love, could I have overlooked his erectile dysfunction? Not likely. Over the years, I'd enjoyed sex, perhaps too much. It had figured prominently in my betrayal of Joe. "I wish our relationship had been more sensual," he had said months before he died. I wished so too. Any relationship I might entertain now would have to be far more than platonic. I needed to know at the outset whether John and I were sexually compatible. Staying in my condo would make it fairly easy to determine.

A Weekend of Firsts

DULLES WAS LITTLE MORE THAN A TEN-MINUTE DRIVE FROM MY condo in Reston, but rush hour traffic on a Friday night, especially before the long weekend, was worse than usual. I pressed down on the accelerator, fear of being late momentarily pushing away thoughts about how the weekend might go. I knew what we'd do—dinner in Town Center tonight, tomorrow a tour of Reston, which was a planned community, followed by dinner and theater in D.C., and on Sunday, my neighbor Marilyn would join us for a glass of wine in the condo. But would I like him? I already liked him, but would I *really* like him? Would I know after just one weekend?

I parked near the main terminal. Inside, I searched the flight information display: On Time. My pace quickened as I used my Airports Authority badge to get through security and onto the "mobile lounge" shuttle to Terminal C. I'd told John that I'd meet him at the gate. I tapped my foot impatiently while two minutes ticked by before the shuttle left. Fortunately, it was a short ride. Walking quickly, I paused to glance at the flight display: Landing. The plane was landing. I hurried on, breathing hard as I envisioned the real possibility of John's arriving ahead of me. How embarrassing. I should have given myself more time.

At the gate, the door to the jetway was open. A few passengers were coming through. I scanned the crowd expectantly. Suddenly, I tensed. What did he look like? For the life of me, I couldn't picture his face! Seconds later, he emerged from the jetway and my body relaxed. There was no mistaking him: the easy smile, the rimless, nearly invisible glasses, the thatch of brown hair streaked with silver falling over his forehead, and the direct blue-eyed gaze—how could I have forgotten his face? He was even taller than I remembered. A black camera bag was slung over one shoulder.

"Hi," he said, his arms surrounding me in a gentle embrace.

As we walked toward the baggage claim, John reached for my hand. It felt natural although I'd rarely held hands with anyone before, not even with Joe. In fact, he'd taken issue with my not wanting him to hold my arm when crossing a street. Why had I objected? Maybe it was a feminist thing. Maybe it was my discomfort with public displays of affection, mine or anyone else's. Thinking back, I'd held hands with Nikos or tucked my hand in the crook of his arm as we'd walked through the Plaka in Athens. Of course, I was much younger then, my feminist side less developed, and I'd been passionately in love.

I'd met Nikos while I was living in Athens writing newspaper columns for the *Tahoe Daily Tribune,* but mostly working as a lifeguard and swimming instructor at the Athens Hilton. One day when I was sipping coffee at an outdoor cafe in Syntagma Square, he leaned over to ask what I was reading. That was the simple start of a four-year relationship that brought me within a hair's-breadth of immersing myself permanently deep in that male-centric culture—and married to a philanderer to boot.

He had been a doctor, but one problem after another was keeping him from practicing again. Visiting him on his home island of Crete a few months after we met, I was powerfully smitten. Back working in Athens—as a live-in governess (probably my least favorite job ever), then in the marketing division of a major international company—our lives became more powerfully entwined. There were reasons to think he was unfaithful, but I ignored them as we continued moving closer to a married life together in Greece.

My feeling of commitment never wavered during a year and a half working and studying in the U.S., but when I returned to Athens, the signs of his cheating became impossible to ignore—as did the true meaning of his delays for our wedding plans. I had run out of patience; I told him it was over. After returning to L.A., I moved to San Francisco and made a new life. Looking back, I feel so lucky to have escaped being trapped by Nikos's hold in a world where my wings might have been irreparably clipped.

It was dark as John and I drove from Dulles. Stepping into the condo, I switched on the foyer light and led him down a short narrow hallway to the guest bedroom that also served as my office.

"You can leave your suitcase here," I said, turning on a floor lamp. "And there's room in this closet if you want to hang some things."

"I'll unpack later."

"Would you like a glass of chardonnay and a tour of my spacious new condo before dinner?" At fifteen hundred square feet, it definitely felt small compared with the thirty-five-hundred-square-foot house I'd sold.

"Yes."

John seemed most impressed by the two balconies and their views of Market Street, the commercial center of Reston, now lighted by street lamps. I'd been in a frenzy to get the bookcases in place, the books unpacked, and the TV connected when, if I'd known John better, I could have waited. He couldn't have cared less. At least not that weekend.

It was nearly 8 p.m. when we caught the elevator down to the lobby with its marble floors and crystal chandeliers. I was aware of a chill in the night air, but as we walked, holding hands, I felt warm inside. Clyde's would be a good place for talking, especially if we were seated in a booth. As if reading my mind, the hostess led us to a brown leather booth in a room with large model airplanes suspended from the ceiling.

John took a small box from a pocket. "This is for you. It's a belated Christmas present because I didn't have anything for you in Raleigh."

I lifted out an exquisitely crafted silver pin, a roadrunner with a turquoise eye. "Oh, it's wonderful! Thank you. I'll put it on right now." It would be a long time before I realized that the speedy roadrunner was John.

His unexpected gift reminded me of Joe, who had given me a gift of jewelry not long after we met, some thirty years earlier. I was living in San Francisco, he in Washington, D.C. I remember my surprise, after three months of letters and visits, when I opened the package from D.C. to find a sterling silver bracelet engraved with my initials, S.A.M. (Shirley Ann Melis). In jest, he would sometimes call me Sam. The gift touched me deeply. It signaled Joe's serious interest in me.

I hadn't planned to talk about Joe, but John gave me that road-runner, which I hadn't expected—a sign of his serious interest. My eyes darted back and forth across John's face. It was almost as though Joe were there, but it was John, not Joe. Yet Joe—and the absence of Joe—still were defining me.

Now, as we lingered over dinner, I found myself telling John about Joe's unexpected death nearly two years earlier, and as I did, I seemed to be reliving it, the scenes flashing through my mind.

* * *

I remembered hurrying home from work and heading over to see him at the rehab center. Two weeks after heart surgery, he was back to his daily crossword puzzles from the *Times,* but physical therapy was another matter: He hadn't gotten started yet.

That evening, as I rushed down the corridor of the rehab center, a nurse intercepted me.

"I told Joe that if he didn't get with the program, Medicare wouldn't pay. Today," she crowed, "he got with the program."

Heartened by the P.T. news, I entered Joe's room.

"Where did you get that coat?" His tone was querulous.

I was wearing a stunning faux fur. "A colleague in the office is selling it. What do you think?"

"If you want it, you should have it, but maybe you'd better take it off. The nurses will be jealous."

I noticed he was on oxygen, something new.

"I want to thank you for making arrangements for my care."

His words caught me by surprise. Granted I'd taken time off work to accompany him to appointments, but I wouldn't have considered not doing so. Nonetheless, I was touched.

Joe seemed tired. "I did physical therapy today, not much but some."

We talked a little more, but I didn't stay long. I kissed him good-night and told him I'd see him the next day. Now that he was doing P.T., he'd be home soon.

I remembered the moment when the phone rang. I was in my office at National Airport the next morning a few minutes before 8. A woman said, "Your husband had a cardiac arrest. We're rushing him to Reston Hospital." I started trembling. I managed to call Richard. Then I told my boss, who arranged for someone from airport security to drive me to the hospital.

In the car, I was too dazed to talk. My chest was tight. I could hardly breathe. After an interminable time, we pulled up at the E.R.

I rushed in, only to be brought up short when a receptionist told me Joe wasn't there. "I don't understand," I stammered. "Someone at the rehab center told me he was being taken here. Nearly an hour ago." I stood staring at her. I didn't know what to do.

"Would you like me to dial the facility?"

"Yes. Thank you."

A wave of relief washed over me. Joe must be okay. The cardiac arrest must have been a false alarm, I thought, regretting that I'd sent the driver back to the airport. She handed me the phone. My husband was not in the E.R., I said. An officious voice on the other end replied, "Oh, didn't you know? Mr. Nagelschmidt died earlier this morning."

I stood there motionless until two strangers guided my halting steps to a chair. Someone placed a paper cup of hot tea in my hands. I couldn't speak. I was still holding the full cup when Richard appeared. I knew the truth from his red-rimmed eyes. How could this be? I had just seen Joe and talked with him the night before. He had survived surgery and would soon be coming home.

After driving me to rehab, Richard led me to a room that wasn't Joe's. Maybe a mistake had been made? But when he opened the door, it was clear there was no mistake. Joe was on a narrow bed, a sheet pulled up to his bearded chin. His eyes were nearly closed. He was still warm to the touch, but his mouth was open, his tongue upraised as though he'd been gasping for breath.

Alone with Joe, my eyes were strangely dry. I kept saying, "I'm so sorry." My hand caressed his arm. I stayed for some indefinable time and walked away with a feeling of unreality and overwhelming sadness. He had died, I was told, at 8 a.m.

*   *   *

Tears streamed down my cheeks as I came to the end of my story. John's eyes had never left my face. Now he reached across the table and took my hand.

I felt a weight lift from my heart. I had entrusted my sadness to this man, and he had offered me his hand, a simple gesture of understanding. I had never told my story to anyone. I must have wanted John to know me, to know that this grief was part of me. He hadn't shrunk from my telling. I pressed my fingers against his and he responded, holding my hand tighter.

Back at the condo, I flicked on the living room lights, sliding the lever to dim. Within seconds, we'd shed our jackets and wrapped our arms around each other. He held me close, but not suffocatingly so. With my cheek pressed against his chest, I could feel his heart beating. I wanted to feel more. I wanted to feel him, all of him, around me.

"Shall we go to bed?" I asked.

"Yes."

I led him to the bedroom, enveloped in the soft glow of bedside lamps turned low, still on from the earlier tour. I tossed the pillow shams onto the floor and pulled back the lavender comforter. John disappeared, presumably into the guest room where he'd left his bag. As I walked into the bathroom, my limbs were tingling. How would he look? Feel? Would he prefer my right side of the bed? It had been almost two years since I'd spent the night with anyone in my bed. How would he feel about me? Would he be put off by my unbridled desire? Would he find me wanting in some way?

Slipping into a nightie of lavender silk, I took a deep breath and stepped into the dimly lit bedroom. John was already in bed. He wasn't on my side. I smiled. He was sitting up, a pillow between his back and the headboard, his chest and long arms exposed. He had nothing on. My body tensed ever so slightly as I slid into bed.

Within seconds, I was enveloped by arms and legs. His body was warm, almost hot, although the sheets were cool. As I caressed the length of him, his skin was smooth to the touch. He had very little body hair. He was lean, his legs and buttocks well muscled. His chest, which appeared somewhat concave when he stood fully clothed, was not at all concave as he lay in bed. He had broad shoulders and narrow hips, the declension between hips and rib cage dramatic.

It was a night of firsts. Our first probing kiss lasted for a very long time, as did our first deeply intimate moments. Peering down at him, I detected a scar under his diaphragm on the left side. With the index finger of my right hand, I traced the arc of lighter skin intersected by evenly spaced stitches.

"My spleen was removed, not long after my diagnosis," he said.

A visible sign of an invisible organ, I thought, oblivious to the significance of that absent organ. Oblivious to the gravity of his illness.

John was loving and lovable, and I found myself responding in ways that were natural and yet utterly new for me. Quiet John was an astute and generous lover; he seemed to enjoy making love as much as I did.

Finally, we kissed goodnight.

"I'm sorry. I sleep on my left side," he said, turning away. With his back to me, his right hand found my left. He pressed his fingers gently into my palm before pulling his arm away.

I lay still, feeling the warmth of John's body next to mine, and closed my eyes. More than sated, I felt safe, as though after enduring a storm at sea, I'd awakened to find myself in a protected harbor.

Late the next morning, we awoke and made love again before getting up to shower. After breakfast at a French cafe in Town Center, I gave John a tour of Reston. I wanted him to know who I was, or had been. First, I drove to the house Joe and I had built twenty years earlier, a two-story soft contemporary with cedar siding and a heavy wooden front door set inside an entry of river rocks. Berms planted with white-blossom dogwood trees, lavender rhododendrons, and fuchsia azaleas grown large shielded the house from easy drive-by viewing. The new owners were out front, so I stopped. They offered to show us the house, which pleased me. I must have felt that the condo wasn't a true reflection of me, or rather, that it was a reflection of a new me whom I didn't yet know.

That evening, with tickets to *Les Miserables* at the National Theater and dinner reservations at Brasserie Les Halles, we drove in to Washington, D.C., some twenty miles from Reston. Months earlier, a friend had asked me to join her for a theater date, as her company had purchased a block of tickets to *Les Mis* and her husband wasn't interested. "Let's go," I'd said, and offered to make dinner reservations at a nearby restaurant. When John's arrival became imminent, I'd told her I'd have to give up my ticket. "Oh, I'll gladly give up mine for you," she'd responded, "if it means you're going out on an honest-to-goodness date!"

"I don't know what you'll think of this," I'd told John on the phone, "but I have tickets to *Les Mis* on Saturday night with dinner reservations at Les Halles."

If he wasn't obviously thrilled by the prospect of seeing *Les Mis*, he was ecstatic about Les Halles. "That's my favorite restaurant in New York," he said. "It's one of Anthony Bourdain's, the chef who wrote *Kitchen Confidential*. I go there with Dick whenever I'm in the city. They have great steak tartare!"

Before we left for D.C., John suggested we take photos of each other on the balcony. Beneath his gray sports jacket, he was wearing a blue shirt the color of his eyes and a stunning silk tie imprinted with a jazz musician motif. I'd selected the Burton Morris when he asked me to choose between the two ties he had with him. In the photo, I'm smiling broadly; my black velvet dress sets off my blunt-cut blonde hair. John, wearing glasses, is looking directly at the camera (at me), his gaze thoughtful and intent. He exudes a quiet, trusting confidence.

At Les Halles, John ordered champagne cocktails followed by a bottle of full-bodied French burgundy to accompany his escargots and steak tartare and my filet mignon. For dessert, we ordered espresso and shared a crème brûlée. Enjoying every tasty morsel, we were actually late for the theater and had to wait to be seated.

"I think we're a very striking couple," John said as we stood at the end to leave. "Oh, you think so?" I was startled by his statement, and thought it was very forward of him. I hadn't thought of us as a "couple," a term with the ring of a certain permanency. I didn't know him well enough. Granted we'd been intimate, but intimacy, to my mind, was not license to assume we were a couple. I felt we were just getting to know each other. In retrospect, my actions in having him stay with me and sleeping with him belied my inner ambivalence. Though not as far as I was concerned, in John's mind, my actions may have spoken loud and clear without a hint of underlying uncertainty.

The next morning, Sunday, we slept in late.

"There's a yoga class at 10:30 if you'd like to go," I said.

"Let's do it. We can go somewhere for brunch afterward."

I'd been doing yoga on weekends since Joe's death. I was delighted John wanted to join me. I may have mentioned the class to him on the phone, because he emerged from the guest room wearing a pair of loose pants and a T-shirt perfect for yoga. During class, I noticed that he assumed the child's pose instead of doing a challenging sequence of movements. At the time, I saw this as indicating only that he was out of practice and needed to build up his yoga endurance. But I later realized—as he continued over ensuing months of yoga to revert to child's pose—that his strength must have been irreparably compromised by the cancer.

When we left the restaurant after brunch, the weather was still cool but sunny. Walking back to the condo, I suggested we keep on going toward Lake Anne—the original heart of Reston. I knew John belonged to a hiking group in Santa Fe. He'd emailed photos of startlingly beautiful rock-strewn landscapes, so different from the lush green of northern Virginia. But during this walk, he was without a camera.

We followed a curving asphalt path through a densely wooded area. The trees were stark, the absence of leaves giving them a skeletal appearance. The sun shone through, unimpeded by summer's canopy of green.

"Did you really help put things in outer space?"

"Yes, I was involved in putting some things in space that are still out there. I feel good about what I did in that arena."

"That smacks of so much math and science. To me it's mind-boggling."

"Just think of the math and science as something odd that I do in my work. I'm interested in a lot of things."

I was struck by John's lack of self-importance. His college roommate, Ron, later told me he thought John had aced every math course he ever took. "Those equations actually mean something to John!" Ron, like me, had been a history major.

"When I was seven or eight years old," I said, "I was playing with dolls, reading Grimm's fairy tales, and bicycling on country roads while you at that age were taking photos, reading physics, studying the stars, and doing fractions in your head for older friends."

"But those are the things I understood." He was matter-of-fact.

"We're so different from each other."

"I think the differences are what's interesting. I can't imagine being involved romantically with a scientist."

Nearing the lake, we crossed the dark wood Van Gogh Bridge and continued as the path curved around several townhouses before emptying onto brick-covered Lake Anne Plaza. Designed to emulate the Italian coastal town of Portofino, the plaza hugged one end of the lake. The water was dark and smooth except for ripples from a geyser-like fountain out in the lake.

I led the way toward a bench with its back to the lake. Seated on it was a bronze sculpture of Reston founder Robert E. Simon, so life-like that I'd often do a double-take from a distance because Simon, who had been a dinner guest of ours when Joe was alive, still lived in the high-rise on Lake Anne Plaza. In front of the bench lay rows of personalized bricks with names and dates, and some with sayings. I showed him the one I'd bought after Joe died. It read: "Joe and Shirley Nagelschmidt, Est. 1978" (the year we'd moved to Reston).

"There's a binder in the Reston Museum with stories written by those who've purchased these bricks. I feel bad that I've never written a story for the binder."

"You can still write it." John's words warmed my heart. He was right, of course. But more than that, he was encouraging and not at all dismissive of my feelings.

Walking across the plaza to a coffee shop, we sat at a wrought-iron table outside and ordered two cappuccinos. It was mid-afternoon, still cool but not cold. Sunlight slanted through winter-naked vines in the trellis overhead. From our vantage point, we could see the sculpture on the bench and the lake fountain spewing in the distance. I remembered the conversation we'd had earlier in the day. Before leaving the condo, John had assessed my library.

"We have at least one book in common."

"What is it?"

"*Ex Libris* by Anne Fadiman."

Fadiman's essays about books and language had been a seventy-ninth birthday gift to Joe from a friend whose love of books, like his, was lifelong. Many of my books had come from his library, which was heavily weighted toward biographies, memoirs, and novels. John's homing in on Fadiman suggested that he too was a reader.

"What do you like to read?"

"Mostly nonfiction, although I like complicated mysteries, especially British spy thrillers. Occasionally I read novels because I think I should."

He told me he had hundreds of books in storage in Santa Fe—on the Southwest, water (and its lack in the West), history and politics, art, religion, and sports. He also had some two hundred fifty cookbooks, and mentioned one of his out-of-print favorites: *Who's Your Mama, Are You Catholic, and Can You Make a Roux?*

"You must like to cook."

"Yes. My ex-wife and I belonged to a gourmet group when we were in Southern California. Each couple took a turn hosting dinner. The hosts would decide on the menu. They were responsible for the entree and the wine. The others would prepare appetizers, side dishes, and dessert based on recipes given them by the hosts."

"Sounds like a big production."

"It was. It was a fun experience."

He said he had a number of books on Picasso, Jackson Pollock, and other creative geniuses.

"Are you a genius?"

"I don't know. I never knew my I.Q. I did start reading at a young age, before going to school. One year—I think I was eight years old—I received a medal from the library in Laramie because I'd checked out so many books."

Monday, after a late breakfast of O.J., cereal, and bagels, we walked across the street to Barnes & Noble. It was quiet—almost library quiet—despite the presence of a number of people. Soundlessly, we went our separate ways. When he found me, he was carrying a Barnes & Noble plastic bag.

"I see there's a Starbucks next door. Would you like a coffee?"

"A cappuccino would be great."

We were sitting at a table near the entrance when Dave walked in. A former Reston neighbor, he now lived in California but returned once a month to do consulting for the Pentagon. After quick introductions, Dave got a coffee and joined us. I told him that John had worked for Northrop Grumman and was interested in part-time consulting in the D.C. area. John talked sparingly about his work in aerospace and his recent stint as a Black Belt Six Sigma instructor. They discussed John's high security clearance, which would be useful to an employer.

That evening, I prepared dinner at home, fettuccine with garlic, olive oil, and parmesan, and a salad. John opened a red he'd bought at a local wine shop. I set the table in the dining room and lit candles.

We talked about his seeking part-time consulting work. I thought the chance meeting with Dave had been serendipitous, and my neighbor Marilyn, who'd come up just the night before to meet John over a glass of wine, worked in Northrop Grumman's corporate office and had offered to put his resume in the right hands.

"There's something else I might consider," he said. "I've taken enough courses in business that I could teach it."

"Really? There are a lot of universities around here."

"I'd like to explore the possibility."

I was struck by his self-confidence.

As he refilled our glasses, John talked about creativity and how important it was to him. He said he had a talent for discerning patterns, whether in statistics, economics, politics, or nature. He viewed his photography as a creative outlet, but more than that, he enjoyed thinking about things in unusual ways. He confessed, however, that during dinner with his parents one evening (I think he was doing graduate work in astronomy at the time), he told them he was greatly troubled because he was beginning to think he wasn't creative. After dinner, his father gave him a copy of a letter in which a professor at the University of Wyoming, had written, "John is the most creative student I've ever had in class."

We were lingering over ice cream.

"In my school partnership job for the Airports Authority," I said, "I beat the bushes for judges for high school science competitions. If you worked for the authority, I'd be after you in a heartbeat. Did you enter science competitions in high school?"

"Yes. In one when I was paired with a girl from my school, part of the test called for mixing a concoction using a three-meter-long stick. There was no stick like that nearby, so I grabbed a broom and started mixing with the handle."

"Resourceful," I said.

"She had a fit because I wasn't using a three-meter ruler. I told her 'This is approximately three meters long and will get the job done.' We won the competition."

John and I were cleaning up the dinner dishes. It was our last night. He was leaving in the morning.

"I'd like to come back to see you."

"I'd like that."

"Perhaps in a couple of weeks."

"Yes, that would be good."

My initial wariness had all but disappeared. I was intrigued by this man whose demeanor was so remarkably calm. He struck me as being a good listener, not uncomfortable with silence. In this respect, he was in stark contrast to Joe, who had tended toward anxiety and was notably verbal and voluble. I liked John's holding my hand when we walked together or were just standing in the condo elevator. I liked his dry wit and obvious intelligence. He was a reader; like Joe, he would get through the *Times* and *Post* in short order. Having worked closely with reporters in Washington, I had a high regard for the fourth estate and an abiding respect for the *Times*. I could not envision a lasting relationship with someone who didn't care about what was going on in the world.

I liked John's physicality, his slender six-foot-four frame and broad shoulders, his long arms and strong legs from hiking and cycling. I liked the way he looked at me when he sat across the table or when we embraced and then stepped back a little to gaze at each other. His eyes seemed at times to be lighted from within. He had expressive hands, visibly veined, with remarkably long fingers that easily enclosed mine. His breath was sweet any time of the day or night—he was not a smoker—and I found his natural aroma intoxicating.

There was a familiarity about him. From the moment we met, I felt as though I'd known him in some sense for a very long time. I could be myself with him without fear of arousing anger, impatience, or disapproval. Nonetheless, I wondered about his working in the area. He seemed to be serious about finding a job there. Would I want him living so close? I didn't know. I knew only that I wanted to see him again. I liked him, but one weekend was hardly enough time to get to know a near stranger. There seemed to be so much to him; I suspected I'd only scratched the surface.

Tuesday morning we said goodbye, and I left early for my office. He would take a taxi to Dulles.

A couple of days later, Dave called to say that John should have no trouble reinstating his security clearance since he'd been retired for only a year. His words were reassuring, a positive omen, I thought, until I heard his closing advice: "Shirley, you have plenty of time. Don't jump into the deep end of the pool."

I didn't like hearing this. I didn't like Dave's intruding on something so new and fragile. I wasn't jumping into the deep end. I was just getting to know John. He was the one who was talking about working in the area—although, granted, I wasn't discouraging him. I felt our relationship was promising. Dave's words gave me pause. Had he seen something I'd missed in his brief meeting with John? Clearly, he had reservations, but I wasn't going to ask him to elaborate. I would make up my own mind about John.

Once More with Feeling

THE AIR WAS FRIGID INSIDE DULLES TERMINAL C. THIS TIME, I knew what he looked like. He'd emailed the photos we'd taken of each other on the balcony, and I'd printed them on one of the office color printers.

"He's handsome," my secretary said.

"Really? I don't think so."

"Oh, but he is. Look at those broad shoulders, those blue eyes. And his smile." Listening to her, I looked again. My idea of handsome had been Nikos, the Greek with chiseled features and fierce eyes beneath a head of thick, tousled, salt-and-pepper hair. Maybe John *was* handsome. I didn't know. What mattered more than looks was the person himself. I felt an overwhelming need to spend more time with him, to know him as well as he felt he knew me. What if I fell in love with the wrong person? Nikos had been the wrong person, but I hadn't acknowledged it until almost too late. I'd escaped the situation by the skin of my teeth. Joe had been the right person, but ultimately, I'd been unfaithful. My anguish and guilt about that had been real. I couldn't allow myself to become seriously involved with someone unless I was sure I'd be faithful. How would I know? Maybe, given enough time with John, I would know.

My breathing was shallow as I stood at the gate, anticipating the sight and feel of him. I watched intently as he maneuvered through the crowd, making his way to me. I wanted to feel his arms around me.

"Hi." He was smiling, his eyes fixed on mine.

Before wrapping our arms around each other, we kissed. It was a soft kiss, not passionate, but our embrace was strong. My desire to be as physically close to him as possible was fierce.

After depositing his luggage at the condo, we walked to Paolo's at Town Center for an Italian dinner. Seated side by side at a lacquered wooden table away from the noisy bar, we ordered wine and pasta. I liked sitting close as we talked about plans for the weekend. We would have three days since I'd arranged to take Monday off.

The next morning, the sky was overcast. Snow was predicted.

"What do you think?" I asked.

"I don't think a little snow will hurt a tour of Virginia wineries."

John had researched wineries in northern Virginia on the Web and was eager to check out a few. He not only knew wines but also drank them with gusto, especially French reds. He'd become a wine aficionado at an early age. "Dick and I learned to drink wine at home, with our parents when we were in high school."

"If we stop at the wineries we discussed at dinner last night, we could end up at the Red Fox Inn in Middleburg for lunch. It's a really nice place, especially on a cold day. If memory serves, there's a good-sized fireplace."

"Let's plan on it."

As I drove out of Reston approaching the toll road, John slapped something against my windshield.

"Oh my god, it's an E-ZPass!" letting drivers pay without stopping at the toll gate on many roads in the Northeast.

"Now you can drive to New York and back without stopping to pay tolls."

"Well, thank you. This is wonderful. I can drive wherever, anytime."

"Yes. Of course, I'll know where you've been."

I glanced at him; he was smiling. What a great gift! Not conventionally romantic but very thoughtful. Before moving into the condo, I'd rarely used the toll road. Now I was using it more often and forever trying to keep enough change on hand. That must have registered with John on his earlier visit.

Our third winery stop was the proverbial charm. After our tastings, John decided to buy several bottles—all reds. While he was discussing wine with another customer, I checked out some other items for sale and found a set of English-made placemats with a grape motif.

"These would be great in the kitchen."

"Put them on the counter with the wine, and I'll get the lot."

It was snowing when we left the winery and drove into Middleburg. Spotting the Red Fox Inn just off the main street, I pulled in and parked. There were few people in the restaurant, but it felt cozy nonetheless. We were seated at a dark wooden table. Behind John, a crackling blaze filled a large fireplace. Through the windows, we could see the falling snow.

"Tell me about your winery. When and how did you get interested in starting a winery?" I'd heard about this venture from Dick and Kerry but not in any detail.

"I'd completed graduate school and defended my dissertation when I was offered a job in Santa Rosa, in the California wine country." (His dissertation, "Picosecond Spectrophysics of Semiconductors," was rated "Distinguished," although John never told me this himself.) "I spent off-hours playing soccer and tasting wine every chance I got. I'd help out with tastings at local establishments and meet other people who liked wine. It wasn't long before I decided, with three friends, to start a winery."

"Where did you find investors?"

"Friends. My parents put money in."

"Where *was* the winery?"

"In Petaluma. We called it La Crema Vinera. It was the first winery since Prohibition to operate within the city limits of Petaluma."

"I've heard of La Crema. I'm crazy about La Crema chardonnay. Did you produce that?"

"Yes, along with pinot noir and cabernet sauvignon. We won awards for the chardonnay and cabernet."

"What happened to the winery?"

"We went bankrupt."

"Oh, no."

"Kendall-Jackson bought us out. At the time, I was the only partner who had a well-paying job, so I was dunned by the IRS for the full amount owed in taxes."

"Did your partners pay you back?"

"Eventually."

"Losing the winery must have been a big disappointment."

"Yes. I felt largely responsible. Other partners were making the wine; I was supposed to be watching the finances. I was working full-time, I'd just gotten married, and I was commuting nights to U.C.-

Berkeley for an MBA. Many nights I'd end up sleeping at the winery. My ex-wife got really pissed, so I cut back on time at the winery."

"How did your parents feel about losing their investment?"

"They got a tax write-off." He didn't elaborate. John's easy dismissal of his parents' investment loss struck me as strange and more than a touch unsympathetic. Getting a tax write-off was a far cry from losing one's investment, not to mention one's hopes for a son's success in the competitive glamor wine business. Only later did I equate John's seeming lack of empathy with his steadfast refusal to dwell on missed opportunities. I think it was his way of coping with disappointments, the biggest being his cancer. By not dwelling on the downside he was able to let go of dreams and move on.

We lingered over lunch and wine for more than a couple of hours. When we pulled away to head back to Reston, the snow was coming down thick and heavy.

That afternoon while I washed my hair, John, without my asking, installed a new phone system that he'd helped me select, and assembled a desk chair that had lain in a box unopened for several weeks.

The next day, we took Metro to D.C. to see the Cézanne exhibit at the National Gallery; he was one of John's favorite artists. For lunch, we found a table in the small picturesque cafe there where we sat for a long time.

That evening, handing me a scotch, John said, "We have to talk, you know."

"Yes, but I don't know what to say." I sat down quickly on the two-person sofa. He sat next to me and looked me in the eye. "What next?"

"I don't know. I don't see myself remarried." I looked away, momentarily blinded by the setting sun. Talk about jumping ahead! John had never mentioned the word "marriage." Though I may have sensed that was his direction, I knew it wasn't mine. Or maybe by saying the word aloud, I was inadvertently forcing myself to contemplate the possibility. My eyes found John's. "A friend offered an unsolicited bit of advice the other day. 'Shirley,' he said, 'you've got plenty of time. Don't jump into the deep end of the pool.' What do think about that?"

John laughed, obviously amused. "I think things are going so wonderfully that I ought to come back for longer than a weekend, say ten days, while you're working, and we'll see how it goes. If anyone asks, we'll say we're in the shallow end of the pool. An extended visit also might give me an opportunity to meet with some people to discuss work possibilities."

I don't know what I was expecting, but it wasn't John's suggesting a stay of ten days. That was way more than a long weekend! And why would he want to see me in work mode? I was such a drudge during the week—up early, work, athletic club, Sami—and I really couldn't vary it, even for a special guest. On the other hand, maybe it would be good. I'd have a chance to know him in a context other than weekend fun and games. Much later, it occurred to me that even roadrunners are capable of forethought and strategy.

"All right," I said, laughing, jumping into the deep end.

In the Shallow End

IT FELT LIKE NO TIME AT ALL BEFORE JOHN WOULD RETURN. THE next morning there was an email from him when I arrived at the office.

> The house I'm selling has been inspected. There appear to be only two issues, which I'll check out in the morning after reading the full report.

> I've registered for a workshop with the Santa Fe Photographic Workshops for the first week in April. It's focused on editing software for digital photography. The book I purchased at Barnes & Noble in Reston has caused me to think a little more seriously about the editing and printing of my photos. One outcome may be the purchase of about $10,000 worth of high-end computer equipment. I am going to wait until the seminar before I buy anything because I will get a chance to try out a high-end Macintosh system there.

> Will go out a couple times starting next week to look at potential future housing possibilities. Next big event is to start looking at my taxes. That will be a thrill.

> Thinking of you, a lot. Wish I was there. At least it is only two more weeks (give or take a day). Love, John

"Why?" I'd asked when he told me he'd decided to switch to digital despite owning a complete setup for film photography, including a darkroom and multiple film cameras.

"I like the challenge."

He seemed so laid back. "Have you ever struggled to do *anything?*"

"I was once criticized by a supervisor for making my work seem too easy."

Apparently, he was not one for pretense even if it might have been in his best interest.

"When I took written exams, I was often the first to finish. After sitting another hour or so, I decided that sticking around was pointless."

Most of my exams in college were essays. I didn't recall ever feeling I'd finished, even when the exam time ended.

"I bet you aced every course you ever took in school."

"I got a D-minus in world history once," he said almost proudly. "My view of things didn't mesh with the professor's."

The day before John's return, I received an email: "Hours to Go and Counting!"

> I've checked in (online) for my flight, so when I get to the airport all I have to do is check my bag. This morning was a visit to the dentist . . . . Now my task is just waiting for the day to end. Who knew that even one day could seem too long? All my love, John.

I couldn't get over John's unabashed feeling for me. It still struck me as being too quick, too certain. I loved him too. But how much? I didn't know, not yet.

The evening he arrived, we decided we'd begin Day One of our ten-day marathon by going to the Smithsonian Crafts Show. Once we got there, we parted company to explore on our own. Back together, I described unique silver earrings designed by a Japanese artist in New York.

"I want to see them." John bought them for me on the spot.

"I want to show you a coffee table I like," he said, leading me through the crowd. When we arrived at the exhibit, I spotted it immediately—a stunning table made of walnut with five square insets of burled wood aligned along the center. "It'd be great in Santa Fe," he said. In a matter of minutes, he had purchased the table and arranged for it to be shipped home. I liked his decisiveness and his taste, not to mention his generosity.

When we got back to my condo, I told John I was going to try taking a nap for a half-hour or so. I went into the bedroom and crawled under the comforter. Close to thirty minutes had passed when John walked in and gently let himself down, pinning me under the comforter. Soon, it no longer separated us; we were thoroughly relishing the closeness.

"There's a jazz concert at the Birchmere dinner theater in Alexandria Thursday night," he said that evening after skimming Sunday's *Washington Post.* "I could take Metro and meet you at National. We could drive from there."

"That sounds fun. I've heard of the Birchmere, but I've never been there."

John liked all kinds of music, from classical to jazz to dissonant contemporary. One summer after he and his brother finished college, they camped all over Europe tracking Formula One Grand Prix races and taking in as many concerts as they could along the way. Both had a profound love of classical music fostered by their parents, primarily their father. Dick, who played clarinet in the high school band, had won first prize in a statewide Mozart competition. John, who said he couldn't have played the clarinet or piano with any success because he was so strongly right-handed, had played the trombone. I had also played a brass instrument in my high school band, the baritone saxhorn, but my first love was piano.

That evening, after playing a Chopin étude, I got up to check my email. When I returned, John was sitting at the piano playing.

"I didn't know you played."

"I don't, but I taught myself to play this one of Bach's inventions." He was using just his right hand.

When my workweek started, John insisted on getting up when I did at 5 a.m. to prepare breakfast and drive me to the bus stop. This also let him use the car during the day unless for some reason I needed it. That first morning, I arrived at my desk to find an email from him:

> It feels strange and different and wonderful to be at home
> here, knowing that I will still be here when you come home
> tonight. I hope Sami doesn't get too discombobulated with
> me being around and running in and out. I have a few

things I want to do and a couple that need to get done. I
will let you know if anything interesting happens, and since
that is not the most likely occurrence, I will let you know
some of the uninteresting stuff as well! I will plan on being
at the bus lot at about 5. Lots of love for your day, John

The first time I got off the commuter bus and spotted John parked
there in my car, my heart raced, as it did every day when I'd find him
waiting for me.

While I spent my days working on community relations for the
Airports Authority, John explored Reston or drove through the Virginia
countryside with camera at the ready. In the evenings, I'd come home
to a dinner he'd prepared—pasta with meat sauce and spicy sausage or
something a bit more complicated such as chicken with Indian spices
and yogurt or a roasted boneless turkey breast with savoy cabbage.
When Joe was alive, I'd done the cooking. It wasn't unusual for us to
eat the same meal two or even three nights in succession, especially a
casserole. A large scotch and soda was our predinner ritual. John did
not enjoy eating the same food two nights in a row, and he liked a variety of ethnic foods. He was not keen on casseroles. Unlike me, he
didn't mind shopping for groceries daily, usually at the nearby Whole
Foods, Harris Teeter, and sometimes the Wine Cabinet, which I'd introduced him to on his first visit.

Before dinner, we'd relax on the new ivory sofa and watch the sunset as we sipped a finger or two of single-malt whisky, which John had
purchased along with two Riedel crystal whisky glasses. I'd go through
my mail and we'd talk or just sit quietly, listening to jazz C.D.s he'd
brought with him from Santa Fe. These were a treat. A jazz novice, I
quickly developed a strong liking for Jamaican jazz artist Monty
Alexander. After sipping the last of my scotch, I'd prepare a salad and
set the table in the dining room. John would select wine, light the candles, and serve dinner. On rare occasions, we'd eat in front of the TV
to watch pro basketball, particularly the Washington Wizards.

I found John's wide-ranging interests fascinating, even sports. Joe
had had almost no interest in sports, and the sports section of any newspaper was automatically discarded. John not only read the sports section but also enjoyed watching professional basketball, soccer, tennis,
Formula One car races, and the Tour de France. Joe had almost insisted
on my being interested in whatever he found compelling. John did not.

Nonetheless, I found many of his interests tantalizing, windows onto worlds that were wholly new to me. By the same token, I'd been delighted when he joined me for a yoga class during his first visit.

I never knew when I'd come home to discover something new in the kitchen such as a Henckels slot-knife holder with a set of new sharp knives or a bagel slicer. One Saturday morning, John suggested we walk across the street to Williams-Sonoma to check out both coffee makers and grinders. He quickly targeted a Braun coffee maker and a Breville grinder. "These should serve the purpose," he said. Since Joe's death, I'd become a regular subscriber to Gevalia ground coffee; I considered it a step up in flavor from the Folgers or Maxwell House that Joe and I had drunk. John told me that the best coffee in the world, as far as he was concerned, was Peet's, which he'd discovered when living in California; in fact, he'd brought a pound of the beans with him from Santa Fe. With the new coffee bean grinder and coffee maker, he converted me to Peets in short order.

"In past relationships, I've usually improved palates for coffee and wine."

I caught my breath but had to laugh. "I'm sure you have!" John was consistently forthright. Momentarily offended by the realization that I was not the exclusive beneficiary of his culinary predilections, I appreciated his matter-of-factness. I knew he would never intentionally hurt someone's feelings, mine or anyone else's.

Subtly, I realized on reflection, the roadrunner was pulling me into his sphere of preferences, be they hand-crafted coffee tables, wine, liquor, art, music, or coffee. Bit by bit, he was decreasing the distance between us. By openly sharing himself with me, he was inviting me into his exclusive, private club. He wasn't asking me to pay dues, not yet. As I found out, they would come later.

A Letter to Remember

"WOULD YOU LIKE TO TRAVEL TO AFRICA TO SEE THE ANIMALS?" I asked out of the blue. I was putting our breakfast dishes in the dishwasher. John was in the living room, reading the paper.

"Absolutely!"

Over the remainder of the weekend, the last of our ten days together, we pored over safari information that he pulled from websites, plus Abercrombie & Kent brochures I'd collected. Late Sunday, as we sat on the sofa sipping scotch, we focused on an A&K trip described as "semi-independent."

"This will ensure we're not with a large group," he said. "And we won't get lost." We agreed that the October dates looked good.

"I'll book our reservations when I get back to Santa Fe."

I was thrilled he'd answered yes to Africa without the slightest hesitation. It was a dream trip of mine. Who knew I'd meet someone who would want to share my dream?

"I called A&K this morning," John said when he called from Santa Fe the next day. "All the semi-independent safari trips are sold out through October, so I booked the first available in November."

"That sounds great!" My heart was flip-flopping.

I picked up my glass of chardonnay. He'd said he was going to and he'd done it. He'd booked our reservations. We were really going to go!

In a matter of days, books on southern Africa started arriving, many of them from England. One contained breathtaking photos of animals in the wild taken by Frans Lanting in Botswana's Okavango Delta, where we would be going. When I commented over the phone about the sudden influx of books, John said, "It'll be good for us to know something about the area before we get there."

A few days after booking the trip, he emailed a proposed itinerary of travel from Santa Fe to Reston, three trips—each two weeks or more—over the next couple of months:

> Let me know how this works, or do I need to tweak days one way or the other? It looks like airfares are reasonable for all of the times. We also need to start thinking about NY in mid-June. I will call Ricardo and ask for hotel recommendations. And last, but certainly most important, I want to tell you that I love you. John.

> PS. I am finally sending this off before I change the dates even more. The more time I spend thinking about being with you, the shorter the stays in Santa Fe become.

I was delighted. His itinerary accommodated at least three events we'd discussed: an open house celebrating my new condo (which I would call "Open Sesame," at John's suggestion), a weekend retreat at an ashram in Virginia with my favorite yoga instructor, and his niece Jacqueline's high school graduation from Marymount in New York City in June.

For his birthday in March, I sent John a silver picture frame. "Your love is the only present I need," he said in an email thanking me.

Later I discovered that he'd put a photo of me in the frame, one he'd taken on the balcony. I'm wearing a fuchsia turtleneck under a light blue cotton shirt. I'm looking at him intently, my lips closed in a smile.

"Carla [one of his friends] can't believe your age. She said she hopes she looks half as good when she's your age."

"How does she know how I look?"

"I showed her your photo."

Oh, no, I thought. He'd not only shown her my photo but also told her how old I am. I rarely disclosed my age to anyone. I was less than thrilled that he'd revealed it to a total stranger. Carla was in his hiking club, but to me, she was a stranger, a stranger I might meet one day. I was eight years older than John. With Joe, who was twenty-one years older, I'd been ever-young. But now, with John, I'd lost my chronological youthful edge, and I was vain enough to care.

A couple of days later, John wrote:

> Darling Shirley, I awoke again this morning missing your presence next to me and everything that means. I know I keep trying to sound like the time until I see you is short, but it will always be too long if I am not with you. I long to feel your body against mine, our arms wrapped around each other. I long to kiss you . . . . But most of all I long to be with you, whether we are touching or separate, talking or quiet, making love or sleeping. My life changed the instant I met you. Nothing before that moment meant as much as you mean to me now. I treasure the memories of our togetherness—our first kiss, the first time we made love . . . the touch of your hands, the sweetness of your lips, the melody in your voice. Those things delight me when we are together and sustain me when we are apart. You are the center of my universe and occupy most of the rest of it as well. As long as I have you nothing else matters. My love for you is complete and unreserved and forever. It will keep me going when we are apart, until I can see you and hold you and kiss you again. The days until we are together again are too many. They will pass slowly, one by one, until finally they are gone. And then we will hold each other and express in words and deeds all of the feelings that we have had. I long for that time to come, so I shall think of you and my love for you will continue to grow without end. I love you with all my heart, John

I must have read his email a hundred times or more. That John loved me I knew. That he cared so deeply touched me to the core. I loved him too. I could not, however, have said to him what he had written to me, for a number of reasons.

He reminded me of Joe, who had never doubted his love for me. But on occasion, I had doubted mine for him. The thought that I might have married Joe on the rebound, after ending my tortured relationship with Nikos, crossed my mind more than once.

While my marriage with Joe had not been as physically passionate as my love affair with Nikos, I had assumed that I would be sexually faithful.

Then several years after Joe and I married, I was in the Canary Islands on a travel-writing trip courtesy of Iberian Airways. The itinerary included a visit to the underground home of a Spanish architect on the island of Lanzarote. That evening, over cocktails and dinner, I met a man from Barcelona, one of the architect's engineering colleagues. He had shoulder-length brown hair streaked blond by the sun, and flashing brown eyes. As we talked, I found him charming, intriguing, and irresistible. Standing together—he wasn't much taller than I—I was completely absorbed by his presence, wondering how it would feel to be kissed by him and have his body against mine. When he walked me to my hotel room, I didn't turn him away at the door. That night we made love fervently and repeatedly.

"I am sorry that I am not a teen-ager any longer when I had more stamina," he said.

"I think your stamina is superb."

After our night of passion, we parted, and I continued my Iberian journey. He too was married. Although I luxuriated in the memory of how I had felt that night, I was surprised by my behavior—not that I had been drawn to the man from Barcelona but that I'd been sexually unfaithful to Joe. I knew couples who had "open marriages." ("He does what he wants, and I do what I want," a friend in Washington had confided about her relationship with her lobbyist husband.) But this was not the nature of my marriage to Joe. I saw myself as a hypocrite of the first rank. Although we had never discussed it, I assumed Joe was faithful to me, and that he assumed my sexual fidelity as well. I loved him and did not wish to sow any seeds of discontent between the two of us. Certainly, I did not want Joe to discover my indiscretion, and I felt confident that he would not.

A year or two later, though, I became involved with a Washington politico on Capitol Hill. Also married, he actively pursued me, and eventually, after several lunches and an occasional dinner, I let myself be caught. I liked him a lot. He was an admirable man. Like Joe, he had been a civil rights activist, even enrolling his children in black schools in the '60s. He had a number of qualities I admired. He was brave, intelligent, socially conscious, and unpretentious. I suspected that he'd had numerous affairs before meeting me. Occasionally, we would meet in his office on Capitol Hill. Once, in the throes of passion in the back seat of his car, we were accosted by a Maryland state trooper who backed off after warning us about the "obvious implications" of our actions.

Initially, I had not anticipated that our relationship would be anything other than a short-lived romp, but unlike my affair in Spain, this was more than a flash in the pan and continued for a couple of years.

Joe, highly intuitive, must have sensed my affair. "I will do anything to keep you from leaving me," he said one night.

His one-sentence plea was a wake-up call. I knew instinctively that I would never leave a man with whom I shared so much—things like love of the English language and writing, love of animals, theater, and music. At six-foot-two with white hair and close-cropped beard and mustache, he was tall and distinguished looking. My attraction to him was multidimensional and powerful, with physical passion a secondary consideration.

"I'm not going to leave you."

* * *

Despite my earlier assumption about being a one-man woman, I now realized that I had the potential not to be. I had shared this with John during our ten days together, telling him how remorseful I'd felt at times, and how threatened my feelings for Joe had been by extramarital affairs. In my mind and heart, I equated fidelity with depth of love, and I wasn't yet sure of the depth of my love for John.

Also, there was my tendency to act rashly. After Joe's death, I'd plunged into one thing after another, blithely oblivious to the possible consequences of my actions. Impetuously, I had hired a house painter who not only did a poor job but also later sued me. More recently, I had made a substantial down payment on a yet-to-be constructed condo, only to discover many weeks later that none of the rooms would accommodate my baby grand piano. I'd gotten my deposit back by the skin of my teeth.

With this modicum of self-awareness, I pondered where my feelings for John were going. One thing was certain: His feelings for me were unwavering, and his certainty made me feel wonderful. True, I was in love and found the prospect of a trip together to Africa utterly thrilling, but I was comfortable taking it all one day, or one trip, at a time. And I appreciated John's not pushing me to go beyond this.

During our five-week separation, I knew he was dealing with a host of issues swirling around the sale of his house in Santa Fe. The first week of April, he was taking the long-anticipated photo workshop.

Contrary to his original intention of trying out the high-end computer system at the workshop before deciding whether to invest in it, he'd made the purchase and installed both the computer system and a large fine art printer in his Santa Fe house before the workshop: "I figured that having the computer system and printer up and running, I'd be able to maximize what I'll be learning in the workshop by practicing at home between classes." Was he impetuous also? Or just wildly enthusiastic? Or was he aware that time might be running out?

On my birthday in April, John wrote:

> Happy birthday to a very special person. I hope it is a good day. I look forward to celebrating it with you in person in about fifteen days. I long to be with you—I am thinking of you all the time and can't wait to tell you in person how I feel. All my love on your birthday and forever. ILU John

A few days later, he wrote:

> Darling, One more day in the week and then one more week and a couple days. Can't wait . . . . I am tired this morning—I stayed up until about midnight playing on the computer. I printed out a couple pictures using some of the things I have learned this week. Plus I tried something new in the printer selection. It seems to have done the trick. Hope your day goes well. It is windy and cool this morning. Hi to Sami and a big kiss to you. All my love, John

Despite the daily emails and phone calls, I missed John acutely. I missed seeing him, being with him. With increasing frequency, I was taking Sami to the emergency vet in in the middle of the night or on weekends. It hurt me to watch him so obviously declining.

In response to an ardent email from me, in which I described my longing for tangible proximity, John wrote:

> Darling, I feel the same—thinking about you takes up most of the day, and the nearing of tangible proximity is not making it any easier. But I am sure we will make up for being apart when we are together again. Call me when you get home. I will be waiting. ILU John

A few days later, he wrote:

> Today and tomorrow . . . and then I will be with you. I am
> counting down the hours. The biggest problem will be tak-
> ing time away from thinking about you to actually get ready
> to leave here. I find my thoughts about you are more fre-
> quent and more intense the closer I come to being with you
> again. I can't stand not being with you. In many ways I find
> that to be a wonderful feeling. My flight is American 1720,
> arriving at 5:23. Thinking of you continuously and missing
> you intensely. Love, John

When at last John returned to Reston, we agreed that we'd never
again be separated for as long as five weeks.

Epiphany

It was the Friday before Open Sesame. John placed a toasted bagel in front of me and refilled my coffee cup.

"Are you going to be all right without the car today?" I asked. Usually, he drove me to the bus stop in the morning and picked me up there in the evening. But I had a memorial service to attend that afternoon.

"Yes, I have things to do on the computer and the latest *Economist* to read."

"I'll probably be home later than usual. I'm driving straight from the office to Maryland for the memorial service, assuming I can find it!" The service was for the husband of a former colleague. Donna and I had become friends and remained in touch by phone over the years, occasionally meeting for lunch. But she'd married since we worked together, and I hadn't known her husband well.

John held the door open. "I'll have dinner ready whenever you get here."

"I won't argue with that!" Coat in hand, I paused to give him a quick kiss before catching the elevator to the garage.

Late that afternoon, driving home under an overcast sky, I was still feeling the effects of the service, which I'd found deeply moving. Donna's husband was sixty; the husband of a Vassar classmate whose memorial service I had recently attended was only fifty-nine. Both were so young, not like Joe whose death at age eighty-three had been shocking only because of its suddenness. *What if John should die?* He was fifty-seven. I wasn't afraid of his cancer, but people I knew were dying prematurely.

Crossing the Potomac back into Virginia, I was overcome by an intense desire not just to be with John but to be *married* to him. If anything should happen to him, I thought, I would want to be able to speak not as the girlfriend or significant other but as his wife. Suddenly, the prospect of John's continuing to travel back and forth from Santa Fe was not enough. I wanted him to be an intrinsic part of my life, day in and day out. Two months earlier when he'd poured out his heart in that amazing email, I hadn't been able to respond in kind. Now, because of the memorial service, I felt that I could—and I wanted him to know. Impatient to tell him, I pushed down on the accelerator.

Looking back, it was more than the memorial service, more than crossing the river in the dusk. In a remarkably short time, only four months, John and I had crossed a number of bridges. He had led the way but now—after all the emails, phone calls, confessions, and exploratory time together—I had caught up. I was not merely in love but committed in my bones. The attraction between us was fierce. I knew I would never betray him, as I had betrayed Joe, and that was my criterion for marrying again.

John was standing in front of the stove with his back to me as I walked into the kitchen. He turned around, holding a wooden spoon. Every muscle of my body tensed.

"What are you making?"

"Potato-leek soup." He stared at me. "Why are you looking at me so strangely?"

My eyes riveted on his. I could hardly breathe. "Would you want to marry me?"

"Yes!"

"But I feel sort of strange asking."

Dropping the spoon on the counter, he pulled me close, his lips against my ear.

"Will you marry me?"

"Absolutely!" My brain filled with bright lights, I relaxed into John's embrace and felt his heart thumping. Or was it mine? "Who should marry us?"

"I don't care who marries us." He sounded almost giddy.

I inhaled deeply, trying to slow my still-rapid breathing. Oh my god. We were getting married. But who would make it happen? The decision was mine, it seemed. And when I decide to do something, I really want to do it. After a long, jubilant embrace, I tore myself away, went to my office, and looked in the Yellow Pages. Ethical Culture? I found nothing, although someone from the Ethical Culture Society had married Joe and me in Washington, D.C. Unitarian Universalist? I didn't want the minister in Reston who had presided over Joe's memorial service—too sad a connection. Being married in a church struck me as more than a mite hypocritical. But what were our options? Within minutes, I was talking with a Unitarian minister in nearby Loudoun County. She sounded nice on the phone and could meet with us almost immediately.

I found John still in the kitchen. "We have an appointment tomorrow morning at 10."

"Good." Open Sesame wouldn't start until 4.

We met the minister at a Starbuck's—"my office," she called it. Moving her coffee aside, she pulled a calendar from her purse and started flipping pages. "I can marry you three weeks from today."

I looked at my calendar. "That would be May 20." The date fit John's travel schedule, and May meant we'd miss the full brunt of Virginia's summer heat and humidity. Sipping my cappuccino, I looked across the table at John, who nodded yes.

"Where?" I asked.

"In a log cabin. If you have time, I'll show you."

I liked the looks of the cabin, but it was in the wilds of Loudoun County. The logistics of getting people there seemed complicated. Finding a caterer would be another matter. There was no kitchen. The only aspect that didn't trouble me was the three-week window. In my work for the Airports Authority, I was accustomed to handling special events and tending to myriad details. I knew I could pull it off.

We Will It So

"Oh, Shirley, what great news!"

I had just told Debbie, my caterer for Open Sesame, that John and I were getting married in three weeks. "Is there any chance of your catering our wedding out in the wilds of Loudoun County?"

"Yes." She responded on the spot, without checking her calendar.

I felt a bond with Debbie. She had catered the reception after Joe's memorial service two years earlier. Seeing her again that afternoon triggered memories of the service and reception for Joe. I remembered wishing he could have been at both, if only to witness the affection, gratitude, and respect he had inspired. A few years earlier, he had said, "When the time comes, you probably shouldn't hold a memorial service for me. So many of my friends are dead, and I would hate for there not to be a crowd." There had been a crowd, some hundred twenty people.

It was Debbie's manner, in addition to her professionalism, that I liked. She had inspired trust and confidence at a time when I felt incapable of giving much, if any, direction. Without being asked, she had brought lovely flowers for the living room. She had not objected to the presence of Joe's beloved Sami when he broke free from his confined quarters upstairs to join the crowd, deftly maneuvering among assorted legs and feet. Sami, like Joe, had loved being part of the action.

When my friends Pat and Philip arrived for Open Sesame, I pulled them aside. "John and I have decided to get married."

"Great! You can do it at our house," Philip said without a moment's hesitation. "We can ask Kim Beach to perform the service." I had met Kim, a former Unitarian minister, the year Joe died. In fact, with Pat and Philip, I had spent my first Thanksgiving after Joe's death with Kim and his wife at their vineyard farm in Madison, Virginia.

After the open house, John was folding up the large map of Africa that he'd placed on the piano to show guests where we'd be going in November. "Sweetheart, when I told Philip and Pat we'd decided to get married, Philip offered their place for the wedding. And that's not all. They have a friend who might be able to perform the service."

"The problematic logistics are history," he replied. John was right. And we were able to keep the original date and still use Debbie for the catering. When John's best friend Ron and his wife in California said they could make the wedding, I knew the date was a good one. Granted, I hadn't realized what a whirlwind I'd be caught up in—getting invitations printed and mailed, finding a dress, flowers, rings, and musicians—but if I had, I wouldn't have cared.

Later, John would tell friends, with pride and amazement, "We did it in three weeks!" Looking back, it wasn't rational, this feeling that we had no time to waste. How did we know?

John lost no time in presenting me with an engagement ring, an heirloom diamond set in platinum that had belonged to his grandmother. In his lifetime, the one-carat beauty had been worn twice before: by his ex-wife and his late fiancée. "You're not getting this back from me," I'd said, only half-joking, when he surprised me with it. "You won't have cause to." I couldn't imagine ever divorcing John.

I found my wedding dress at an exclusive boutique in Washington, D.C. It was made of sheer white silk imprinted with small leaf-like patterns of lavender and pink. Swaths of silk pulled on the bias hugged my torso to hip level before cascading to the floor in two slender tiers. But it was too pricey. Looking elsewhere, I found a two-piece outfit in lime green, but I didn't buy that either.

"Does either show off your figure?" Kerry asked on the phone that night.

"Yes, the expensive one."

"Get it, Shirley!"

With less than three weeks until the wedding, I suggested to John that he look for a suit at Nordstrom because I felt sure it could deliver the goods in time. He wanted me to go with him. I called ahead to make sure we would get an experienced suit salesman, and when we arrived, he had pulled some possibilities for John to see. After trying on a dark blue and a gray that both looked good on him, John asked me to choose. I was about to say "the blue one" when he surprised me: "I'll take both. I'll probably need a second suit if I'm going to be spending time in Virginia."

The night before the ceremony, the wedding party gathered in my condo. I remember listening for the doorbell. My heart was beating in my ears. I would be introducing John to some of my closest friends. I wanted them to like him. I wanted them to believe I had made a good choice, that I hadn't gone off the deep end.

When I opened the door, it was the minister. I took a deep breath, relieved that it wasn't anyone else arriving early.

Kim had met with us at the condo three weeks earlier. It was then that the idea of a wedding party had taken shape.

"There is really no such thing as a Unitarian Universalist wedding," he had said. "The religion is noncreedal, and members hold a wide range of spiritual and religious beliefs. Your ceremony can be as secular as you wish." The three of us were on the same page from the start.

"What would you suggest as a ceremony?" I had asked.

"I brought some poems and other readings for you to consider. Maybe you'd like me to read one or two during the ceremony." After ruffling through a folder of papers, he began to read a poem aloud. I felt a tingling sensation across the back of my neck. It was our story, John's and mine. My eyes found John's and held steady.

"I think that's it," I said when Kim had uttered the last word.

"I agree." John was on board.

"I'll leave a copy with you, along with some others, and you can give me a call after you've had a chance to look them over. Will you want to exchange rings?"

"Yes," we said in unison.

"Will there be others in the wedding party?"

"If my three oldest friends can make it," I said, "I'd like to have them stand with me."

"I'll ask my brother Dick to be my best man."

"And I'll ask mine to escort me."

I was startled out of this memory when the doorbell rang again. There they all were, bursting into the condo, arms embracing and voices talking at once. I didn't have to introduce John to anyone. One minute he was standing behind me smiling, and the next everyone was hugging him. My heart thumped happily in my chest.

"Al, you don't know who I am, do you?" Ann said to my brother.

"I probably should but I don't."

It had been more than forty years since they had seen each other at Ann's and my graduation from Vassar. Later that evening, Ann pulled me aside. "Remember how gorgeous Al was, to-die-for gorgeous . . . . and now he's not!" We laughed.

"Forty years ago, he was seventy pounds thinner!"

John and I shared the sofa with Al while others pulled up chairs to form a circle in front of the bay windows. His back to the windows, Kim told us how the ceremony would flow. He had worked out where each of us should stand on the balcony, overlooking the guests on the patio below.

As Kim spoke, I gazed at my three old friends in the circle. They had laughed when I dubbed them my Matronettes. Ann had been my college roommate all four years, her dark hair now shot with silver. Barclay, my friend since age ten in Colusa, California, had attended Joe's and my wedding at the Madison Hotel in Washington, D.C., thirty years earlier. Karen I'd met when we were in our twenties in Los Angeles; years later, when her daughters were in their thirties, she had asked me to be their godmother.

"The exchange of rings will follow my reading of the poem." Kim paused to look at me.

"We have one small problem," I said, feeling sheepish. "It's my knuckle. John won't be able to slide the ring onto my finger unless someone sprays my knuckle with Windex seconds beforehand."

"You're not serious." Ann was chuckling.

"I am. My knuckle's a doozy. The jeweler is the one who recommended Windex. Ann, would you spray my finger?"

"Yes, I'd be honored," she said with a wink.

I got up and went into the kitchen, returning with a large bottle of Windex which I handed to Ann.

"Ann, you can't carry that!" Karen was aghast. "I'll find something smaller."

I told them how I saw the details unfolding: "Nanoseconds before John and I exchange rings, I'll hand my flowers to Karen, then I'll swing my unencumbered left arm back so Ann can spray my finger. With a bit of luck, no one below will see."

The next day, Ron and his wife drove us to Pat and Philip's white clapboard house in McLean. White streamers and balloons fluttered in the breeze. Suspended from the brass door knocker was a sheer white ribbon tied in a bow. Pat was smiling when she opened the door. Embracing her, I peered beyond the oak foyer, looking for the Matronettes. I had less than an hour to get ready. John had dressed at the condo; I was the one who needed time. My shoulders tensed.

"Let me do something to help." Ron's wife must have felt my anxiety. Without hesitating, I handed her a brown envelope filled with forty place cards and a seating plan of the tables set for dinner. What a godsend! Why had I ever imagined I would have time to handle this important detail?

"Can you figure this out?"

"Of course. Don't worry."

"The flowers just arrived," Pat said. "Let me show you your bouquet and get John's boutonniere." The Matronettes joined us in the foyer. When Pat returned, I gasped. The combination of whites, pinks, and lavender in my bouquet was perfect. I had given the colors of my dress to the florist over the phone and placed my order sight unseen.

"I can't put this on myself." John fumbled with his boutonniere.

"I'll help you." Ann reached up and pinned the flowers on John's lapel. Inwardly, I winced. The boutonniere looked great, but the pins attaching it were showing! No time to fix it, I thought. I needed Ann's help to dress. Weeks later, when we reviewed the wedding photos, I grumbled in dismay about the visible pins. "Oh, I can Photoshop them out," John said.

The Matronettes followed me into the guest room. I tossed my blue jeans and cotton shirt onto the bed.

"The tailor sewed a long-waisted bra into the front of this dress, and there's no way I can fasten it in the back."

"I believe we can handle this, Shirley." Karen's lips were parted in a wide smile.

Barefoot, I held my breath while Karen closed each hook down the back of the bra, then zipped up the strapless dress. Camera in hand, Barclay recorded the action. Ann held open the silk shrug while I inserted an arm into each tapering sleeve.

Taking the shoebox from the bed, I lifted out strappy three-inch heels. Because I had splurged on my dress, I felt no compunction shelling out top dollar for these glamorous shoes. Bands of sparkling crystals criss-crossed just behind my toes, with one strap meeting the other above the ankle. My pedicured toenails gleamed pale pink. I wore no stockings.

I stood up and took a few steps. I was not accustomed to heels as high as these.

"You look beautiful." Karen clasped her hands together and beamed. Ann and Barclay nodded their approval. My eyes misted. The three old friends who had seen me through so much were with me once again. All three had been at the memorial service for Joe, one of the saddest days of my life. And now they were back, for one of the happiest.

At Joe's service, Ann and Barclay had sat on either side of me in the front row of the Unitarian Universalist Church in Reston, holding my hands. I remembered gripping their fingers hard as the musicians played the "Adagio for Strings." I had survived the shock and pain of Joe's death. And now, with the support of these enduring friends, I was beginning a new chapter.

Checking myself in the bathroom mirror, I noted how the dangling crystal earrings I had found days earlier caught the light. I had decided against wearing a necklace. Too much going on, I thought. Keep it simple.

"I want Shirley and the Matronettes in the hallway." Ron stepped into the guest room, his camera hanging from a black strap around his neck. When he was satisfied, we walked into the living room. John's brother and mine were standing in front of the fireplace. John was nowhere to be seen.

"Let me get your flowers, Shirley." Pat disappeared into the kitchen and returned with the bouquet.

It was 5:30, time to marry.

The sliding glass door to the balcony was open. I could hear the trio of musicians—two guitars and a sax—playing softly. The living room emptied. Suddenly I was alone with my brother. In a dark blue suit with a striped silk tie, he looked rather distinguished and reminded me ever so slightly of my father.

"Do you want me to give you away?" he'd asked when I phoned to tell him I was getting married.

"Give me away? I don't think so," I'd laughed. "Maybe you can present me." But here he was, in effect, giving me away.

"I wish Mom and Dad were here." He looked away, his voice wistful and solemn. "They would be very happy."

I supposed they would be. Al had met John less than twenty-four hours earlier. Apparently, he liked him. I was pleased. He had liked Joe too, until Joe threw him out of the house. But that was a long time ago.

"It's time for you and Al to go." Pat cued us from the hallway.

I placed my right hand in the crook of his arm and we walked across the oriental rug, past the fireplace, the black Eames chair, and through the doorway onto the balcony. There was John, handsome in his dark blue suit and blue silk tie. He looked at me and smiled in a way that told me he liked what he saw.

I inhaled deeply. It's really happening, I thought. I'm getting married for the second time in my life, and it feels right. The first time, thirty years ago, had felt right too. I thought of Joe, how shattered I'd been by his sudden death and how, when I could feel again, I'd wondered whether I would ever stop feeling sad. Joe had been like a symphony—strings, brass, wind, and percussion—largely agreeable, occasionally discordant, and always provocative. We had shared so much, and through it all, Joe had always been there for me. Without warning, the symphony had stopped, and the resulting silence was deafening. I had felt bereft.

I looked out at our guests on the patio below. Their faces, dappled by shafts of sunlight through leafing trees, were upturned and smiling. Almost everyone there, with the exception of John, had known Joe. They knew how stricken I had been after his death and, three weeks later, the death of my father. They knew I had tried, not without mishap, to put one foot in front of the other until I thought I could make a new life for myself. If they were surprised by the suddenness of my decision to marry John, they didn't let on.

I stood on the balcony, my left hand holding a bouquet echoing the colors of my dress: deep pink and white roses, lavender freesias, and a singular white stephanotis peeking past lilacs. Their delicate scent wafted through the air. My fingers tightened on my brother's arm. My eyes were riveted on the minister as he read the poem John and I had selected, "The Ivy Crown" by William Carlos Williams. I remember fighting back tears, mindful of my makeup helper's warning, "Whatever you do, Shirley, don't cry!"

> *Daffodil time*
> *is past. This is*
> *summer, summer!*
> *the heart says,*

and not even the full of it.
No doubts
are permitted —
 though they will come
 and may
before our time
 overwhelm us.
 We are only mortal
but being mortal
 can defy our fate.
 We may
by an outside chance
 even win! We do not
 look to see
jonquils and violets
 come again
 but there are,
still,
 the roses!
At our age the imagination
 across the sorry facts
 lifts us
to make roses
 stand before thorns.
 Sure
love is cruel
 and selfish
 and totally obtuse —
at least, blinded by the light,
 young love is.
 But we are older,
I to love
 and you to be loved,
 we have,
no matter how,
 by our wills survived
 to keep
the jeweled prize
 always

> *at our finger tips.*
> *We will it so*
> *and so it is*
> *past all accident.*

This poem was my heart speaking. With more of my life behind than ahead of me, I did not regret the passing of spring. It was in the spring that I had been mesmerized by Nikos. I had not seen clearly the pitfalls of loving someone who was not trustworthy, of living in a centuries-old male-centric culture, of being far away from close, sustaining friendships. When I married Joe, who was all that Nikos was not, I grew up, becoming someone better than I had been—more accomplished, more self-confident and kinder. Despite our difference in age, I was not prepared for his death. Like an arrow, it had pierced my heart, emptying it of joy. "Remember, Shirley, *you* are alive!" a woman I barely knew said to me nearly two years later. Her words rattled my brain. Did I want to do more than survive? Yes, as improbable as it felt, I wanted to love, perhaps more than to be loved, but the path was unclear. One afternoon, alone in my bedroom, I took off my wedding and anniversary rings and placed them in Tiffany boxes in the back of a dresser drawer.

Ringless, I would tell the world I was ready to move on, but I felt naked and hypocritical. My scarred heart still longed for Joe. I was not ready. I was not ready the day John walked into my life. When I was younger, he would not have appealed to me. Too quiet, too nondirective. So different from Joe. But I was older now, more self-possessed and self-directed. In the summer of my life, I found myself appreciating John's many qualities, including the quiet, nondirective ones. Like a budding rose, my heart had slowly opened until I found myself capable of loving again. By loving John as I did, I was able to step away from the grief that had run through me like a raging river, its currents swift and unstoppable. Granted, I did not know John fully, but given time, I would. Given time, I would come to know his shadow, and I would love that darkness in him too. I harbored no doubts. My unspoken vow: I love you past all accident. I love you forever.

As Kim read, I thought of John's courage—his determination to live and love despite the cancer diagnosis, the divorce, the death of a fiancée. Against all odds, we had survived to reap the joyous reward of discovering one another. We were astonished that at our age, we could be so deeply in love. The words of the poem Kim had read came back to me: *We have, no matter how, by our wills survived to keep the jeweled prize always at our finger tips.*

Ours was a bold marriage. We had been together only thirty-two days over a span of five months when we pledged the truth of our very beings to one another.

Safari Honeymoon

"DARLING, WILL YOU HELP ME THINK ABOUT RETIRING?" WE were home, sipping our usual two fingers of scotch before dinner, when I popped the question.

John set his glass down on the coffee table and looked at me. "Do you want to do it before we go to Africa or after?"

"Before. Working doesn't make sense anymore. I want to travel with you without having to figure out whether I can take time off. I'd like to spend more than a long weekend in Santa Fe. I want to write. I've looked at our finances, and we'd have enough with my pension and Social Security and your consulting and sales commissions from *Le Verre Fluoré*" (a glass and optical fiber company based in France).

He never questioned my decision. I felt as though he had been waiting for me to make it.

It's a rare person who retires from the Airports Authority without a party. Mine was scheduled to coincide with my last day of work.

"It begins at 4," I'd said when John dropped me at the bus station that morning.

"I'll be there."

I was looking forward to John's being there. He had met my closest friends at the Airports Authority, but there were other people I liked whom he had not met. I wanted to show him off.

When the receptionist announced his arrival, I hurried out to the lobby, my heart doing flip-flops in my chest. Wow! This man, who liked nothing better than to wear blue jeans and hiking shoes, was wearing a gray herringbone sports jacket with a blue shirt, gray flannel pants, and black loafers. Yes! We embraced warmly before catching the elevator to the board room.

In one photo taken at the party, we are standing in front of a wide expanse of glass overlooking the airfield at National Airport. John is leaning across me, shaking hands with the president of the Metropolitan Washington Airports Authority, Jim Bennett. I'm beaming. I was touched by the presence of so many people I had worked with over fifteen years, everyone from airport management and the public safety division to school principals and teachers. But the icing on the cake was John's presence. He was the reason I was retiring. As I told everyone in the room, "A year ago, this man wasn't even a gleam in my eye, and now I can't imagine living without him! We plan to do a lot of traveling. I'm going to write while John concentrates on photography." It was a joyous leave-taking.

Joe had wanted me to retire early. Although he had forged a post-retirement life for himself, he wanted company—my company. At the time, I didn't think I could afford to retire. Joe kept saying I could find a part-time job in Reston. But why would I give up my relatively well-paying full-time job for a part-time job that probably wouldn't pay much of anything? In addition, more than the money or lack of it gave me pause. Joe was such a commanding personality that I sometimes feared I couldn't be my own person if we were together 24/7. John was different in that respect. He gave me space to think and to feel.

Our trip west four weeks earlier had been the first time we were apart since the wedding. We had driven from Santa Fe to Sedona. Then I went to San Diego with John's friends while he drove to Canyon de Chelly for a week-long photo workshop.

"John called," a friend in California told me. "He'll try again later."

I could feel my face flush. It had been four days since we parted in Sedona. We had not talked about calling each other before reuniting at the airport in Albuquerque. I had imagined his being completely absorbed by the workshop and out of cell phone range. That he had been thinking of me enough to call warmed me through and through.

"This is for you. I found it in a shop at Canyon de Chelly." We were standing at the airport baggage claim when I unfolded the white tissue paper and gasped.

"I've never seen such a beautiful turquoise! And I love the small coral beads on either side." It was a necklace with a silver "can't lose me" clasp.

"I thought the length was right, but I wasn't sure."

"It's perfect. Thank you, sweetheart."

"This is for you too." Inside a small Ziploc bag lay a pendant, a polished red-brown stone in the shape of a bear. I knew that for Native Americans, the bear symbolized health and strength. Later I would wonder whether the bear related more to John's health than anything else. If I had worn it every day, would it have made a difference?

Still in Reston the month after the retirement party, we were sitting in the living room one Sunday reading the papers.

"Here's a job that might be interesting." John handed me a page from the classified section of the *Washington Post*.

I sat up. "But it's full time. What about your photography?"

"I'm committed enough to my photography that I could work full time and still keep it going."

I swallowed hard. John had not mentioned seeking any kind of job, full or part time, since our wedding. And I was impressed by his photography. His passion for it was hardly fly-by-night; he had nearly given up graduate school to study photography. Together we had visited galleries in Virginia seeking opportunities for him to one day display his landscape photography. "I want to be able to sell prints for as much as $400 or $450 each," he had said. "It might take several years, but I know I can do it." Already a couple of friends had asked to buy prints of *Dog Tracks,* one of John's recent photos. A tawny dog with a regal presence had stopped while crossing railroad tracks and turned his head to look back at the camera.

"I don't know why you feel you have to work," I told him. "You're still earning income as the rep for Le Verre Fluoré. You have investments, and after you sell the house in Santa Fe and downsize to a condo, you'll have even more." My reaction surprised me. Why did I care? If John wanted to work, he should. Before we were married, I had been 100 percent behind his polishing his resume and finding work in Virginia. What had changed? I think it was my growing appreciation of his photography coupled with the realization of how important it was to him—important enough that he had bought a Mac computer system and a quality Epson printer for Reston to mirror what he had in Santa Fe. He had retired early to do photography. Why go backward?

"All right." His voice was calm. "I won't answer the ad, but if something interesting comes along, I'll consider it."

Whew! I breathed a little easier. I couldn't tell whether he was concerned about his income or motivated by something else. Perhaps he missed the challenge. Later, I wondered if he had been trying to gauge my feelings about his not working. Northrop Grumman had called two or three times asking him to consult in Texas and elsewhere. He had rejected all the offers, saying, "I won't accept any consulting job that requires my being away from you for more than a week." My heart had melted. I didn't want to be separated from him either. Since our wedding, the sense that we were an indivisible unit was intensifying. Not that we couldn't be apart from one another for hours, even days at a time. But together or apart, I sensed an invisible force binding us together.

* * *

Five months after our wedding, we boarded a South Africa Airlines flight from Washington to Johannesburg. When John made our reservations back in March, before we had even thought about getting married, we had no idea that this trip would turn out to be our honeymoon. For me, it was even more than a honeymoon. It was celebrating our marriage and also my retirement, a dramatic change in my life.

A few hours before landing, the flight attendant handed us forms to complete.

"Now that I'm retired, I don't know how to describe my occupation." I looked at John.

"You're a writer," he said matter-of-factly. I glanced at his form. He had described his occupation as photographer. Simple, straightforward. Not physicist-engineer or consultant. I smiled to myself. Separately, we had shed our workaday identities, choosing new ones to follow our passions. And we were following them together. Incredible! John planned to hire an expert to design a website for us. "We can promote my photography and your writing," he said. Although I wasn't yet sure how much of my writing would relate to John's photography, his vision of our working in tandem filled me with joy.

Fifteen hours after taking off, we landed in Johannesburg, sleepless and bone tired. I took comfort in John's having arranged with A&K for us to stay an extra night in Johannesburg to rest up before flying north to Botswana.

The day's layover gave us the opportunity to visit the downtown. While waiting for our driver outside a museum, I photographed John as he stood with one leg propped against the low wall behind him, his arms resting atop the wall. He was wearing dark blue Dockers, my favorite blue linen shirt with the sleeves rolled up, and on his right wrist, the yellow LIVESTRONG band. His face and arms were tanned. He looked relaxed, his lips open in a broad smile.

"Do you think you could show us where Nelson Mandela lives?" We were cocooned in the back seat of a black Mercedes-Benz. The driver told us that Mandela's house was near our hotel. I looked at John and squeezed his hand. Imagine seeing where the great man lived! I peered out. Wide empty streets fronted nearly invisible houses shielded by high walls of earth-toned stucco. "Oh, John, look! The jacarandas are the color of my wedding dress!" We were driving under a canopy of blooming trees. Fallen blossoms carpeted the streets in lavender. I pressed my fingers into John's, transfixed by a vision of dancing together through the blossoms, me in my wedding dress, John in his dark blue suit. Truly wishful thinking, as John didn't dance. And Joe hadn't either. It had been my misfortune to marry men who didn't dance.

"This is where Nelson Mandela lives," the driver said, nodding toward a distinctive wall on our right. Built into its mustard-colored exterior was an obvious security station fronted with glass. Visions of men armed with guns eclipsed my vision of dancing in the streets.

"I need to lie down for a while," John said when we returned to the Saxon Hotel. "I want to explore the hotel grounds before it's dark, so don't let me sleep too long."

"I won't. While you're napping, I'll check out the spa." I had slept well the night before and wasn't tired. I assumed John had jet lag—or was it something else? I wondered. His oncologist had talked about John's needing a Rituxan infusion.

"If we weren't going to Africa, I'd probably be getting the infusion now," John had told me.

"Will you be all right?"

"Yes. I asked my internist for an antibiotic to take with me in case I feel an infection coming on. He prescribed Cipro."

I listened without truly comprehending. The infusion was to treat the blood cancer. I didn't understand why there was concern about infection. I assumed that if John got an infection, he would get over it. It didn't seem real or threatening. He looked so healthy. He acted healthy then. I had heard the oncologist suggest a gamma globulin injection to bolster John's immune system before departing for Africa, and I knew he had done it. I had asked him a gazillion questions about his life but very few about his health, and nothing about infection. Was I naive, or perhaps willfully blind? I was not looking for reasons to be concerned about John's health. He seemed to be on top of his cancer.

That evening we dressed—A&K had suggested taking one set of "good clothes"—before making our way to the bar. We *are* a striking-looking couple, I thought, glimpsing ourselves in the mirror over the bar. I was wearing my long crinkly Babette skirt and black top. John sported a navy blazer and gray pants, his gray hiking shoes the only discordant note. "I'm not taking more than one pair of shoes," he had announced when we were packing.

John believed in having the right stuff for whatever endeavor he embarked on, and camera equipment was not the half of it. Well before our trip, he had introduced me to REI, the only place, apart from bookstores and camera shops, where he enjoyed shopping. He was proud of his notably low REI membership number, since he had joined when he was in school in California. At REI, he had helped me find the clothes he thought I would need for the safari. And his selections, from drip-dry pants and shirts to shoes, proved to be right on target.

"What am I going to do? They don't have my size," I'd said after looking through the women's section for pants and shirts.

"Try the men's. I'm sure a small will fit you."

All but the bras and shoes we found in the men's section.

"Let's go out on the patio," John said after his nap, ordering two single-malt scotches from the bartender. It was still light as we sat in cushioned rattan chairs overlooking a large infinity pool. Beyond it stretched an expanse of bright green grass setting off the largest fuchsia azaleas I had ever seen. They seemed to be crawling up one wall of the hotel.

"Here's to us." John's voice was soft, intimate. His eyes met mine as we clinked our glasses.

"Yes, to us." I was drinking him in, my heart thumping happily, barely aware of the throngs of well-dressed Africans coming and going behind us.

The next morning, we walked into the dining room shortly after it opened at 6:30, but we were not alone. Seated nearby was Oprah Winfrey, with two others at her table. She greeted us with a friendly "good morning" as we passed en route to the buffet. We knew nothing about her impending launch of a school for young women in South Africa.

"Oh, no," I said, sitting down with my plate of exotic fruits. "I wanted to photograph that striking tree over there, and now I can't do it without looking like I'm trying to take a picture of Oprah."

"I wouldn't do it," John said. Joe would have egged me on.

Warned but not put off, I positioned myself away from Oprah on the other side of the tree and took my shot. Nothing. The light was too dim and my flash too weak to capture the tree, let alone anyone in the room.

Dressed in drip-dry beige safari garb, we boarded our van and were delivered to an airport waiting room throbbing with a rainbow of travelers, many in brightly colored native dress. Eventually, we heard a muffled announcement over the din alerting passengers traveling to Maun, Botswana, to board the bus. Deposited on the tarmac, we walked to the stairway propped against the eighty-seat jet and climbed in, claiming window and aisle seats. A half-hour later, flying over Botswana, my nose pressed to the window, I was struck by the parched bleakness, endless sand, and low-lying scrub, a world far removed from bustling Johannesburg.

We stepped off the plane into a blast of hot air. It was early November, the beginning of summer in southern Africa, with temperatures nearing a hundred degrees. In the terminal building, two ceiling fans moved slowly without effect.

"Can you believe this heat?" I could picture mascara running in rivulets down my moist cheeks. Even John, who did not easily break a sweat, was perspiring through his shirt.

"I hope we can grab something to eat before we leave Maun," he said, seemingly oblivious to the heat.

I looked at my watch. It was well past noon. I didn't know when we should expect to arrive at Chief's Island, our first game camp. What I did know was that when John said he was hungry, it was not an idle comment. He had to eat, to ward off the effects of low blood sugar.

Fortunately, John was carrying a supply of Clif bars, as our MachAir pilot, Matt, convinced us there was no time for lunch. "Your plane was late, and I'm on a tight schedule. You'll find plenty to eat when you reach camp," he said. Bags in hand, we followed him to his six-passenger, two-engine Cessna prop, part of a line of small planes leaving the ground like a swarm of orderly mosquitoes bound for safari camps throughout northern Botswana.

As we and the other couple aboard made our ascent and leveled off, the noise of the engines precluded conversation, letting us concentrate on the terrain below, an endless sun-bleached savanna dotted with islands of gray-green scrub and palm trees. Occasionally, oases of green softened the arid landscape. Etched into its sandy surface were delicate tracings leading to now-dry water holes, temporary trails created by water-seeking animals. We were arriving at the start of the rainy season. I was thinking of Precious, the female detective in Alexander McCall Smith's mystery novel set in Botswana, *The No. 1 Ladies' Detective Agency,* when John placed a hand on my knee and pointed out the window. Below us, several giraffes were on the move, and a little farther on, three elephants, nearly invisible against the beige landscape. Our first game sighting! My jaw dropped.

Thirty minutes after leaving Maun, we landed on a strip of white sand in a clearing surrounded by scrub. The loud drone of the engines at once gave way to an extraordinary silence. "This is Chief's Island," Matt announced. Parked a few feet off the airstrip was an open-sided Land Cruiser. A passenger got out and walked with his luggage toward the plane, accompanied by the driver, who introduced himself to us as Rogers. He too was dressed in khakis, solidly built with a slight paunch. A stiff-brimmed hat sat low on his forehead above a round, solemn face. "I will drive you to Chief's Camp on the island."

During the drive, John and I looked at each other and smiled ear to ear. We were in the Okavango Delta, on the verge of something completely new, and we were thrilled. We were also very hungry.

Despite arriving close to 2 p.m., we found that the camp manager's wife had saved lunch for us, a tasty meal of roasted and fresh vegetables, meat, and fruit. While we ate on the veranda, she explained that we'd just have time to find our tent and freshen up before afternoon tea and the game drive that would follow.

Our "tent" was one of twelve elevated thatched-roof huts with canvas walls, complete with private bathroom, plus an extra—outdoor—shower. Within minutes, we spotted wildlife from the balcony: two baboons crossing a grassy area not thirty feet away. With little time to spare, I hopped into the indoor shower to cool off while John said the outdoor shower would suit him. When I emerged, I found him still standing under the outdoor shower, fully clothed and sopping wet!

"What are you doing?"

"I figured I might as well wash what I'm wearing, considering how hot I've been all day." As I watched, agape, he stripped off everything, wrung it out, and hung it to dry over the shower walls. I laughed in disbelief and delight. He had a wonderfully refreshing way of experiencing the world.

Dressed in clean safari clothes and sprayed with insect repellant John had found in the tent, we returned to the veranda for tea. John was wearing his long-lensed Nikon suspended from his neck and carrying a tripod, which he figured he could use as a monopod to help steady his camera in the Land Cruiser. Hanging from my neck was a small point-and-shoot Nikon that John had helped me select in Santa Fe. Over tea we learned that Rogers, who joined us, would be our game-drive guide and that we would share the Land Cruiser that afternoon with a couple from Canada. Rogers explained the rules of the drive: "Do not get out of the vehicle; do not stand up; and speak quietly." If we did not make ourselves stand out, he said, the lions would perceive only the large mass of the Land Cruiser.

That afternoon, every sighting seemed extraordinary—from the slender mongoose with its black-tipped tail to numerous honey-colored impalas. With the start of the rainy season increasing the supply of food for the young, pregnant impalas had begun "dropping" their babies. Ever alert to possible predators, these graceful, delicately boned creatures scampered away as soon as they caught sight or wind of us, leaving us staring at the black "M" markings on their rears. "We call them Bush McDonalds," Rogers said with a rare smile.

Easily traversing the uneven terrain, the Land Cruiser rounded thickets of acacia trees whose thorny branches more than once made contact through our thin-sleeved shirts, but we hardly noticed as we searched for wildlife left, right, and all around. Rogers, with his trained eye and acute ear, spotted animals and birds long before the rest of us, but soon John was spotting them almost as quickly. As we stopped to observe, several giraffes, their long necks moving gracefully from treetop to treetop, ate without interruption. From the start, Rogers took his lead from John, pausing long enough for John to shoot and then, when he raised his head from the camera, moving on.

It was still daylight when the Land Cruiser stopped in an open area and Rogers transformed the back of the vehicle with an array of beverages, including scotch and South African wine, accompanied by cheese crackers.

Looking toward the horizon, I was struck by the vastness of the sky and the light that softly washed the beige-green landscape as far as I could see.

"The quality of the light is different from the American Southwest," thicker with dust, John noted. He was sipping scotch and chatting with Rogers and the Canadian couple. The man was using a video camera, planning an African video party for his grandchildren when he got back home. I stood next to John near the Land Cruiser, saying little. As I sipped my scotch, I was momentarily overcome by the feeling that I was dreaming. Was I really here in Botswana with a man I loved?

Back on the move, Rogers took us in a new direction. Without warning, we found ourselves in the midst of a moving herd of cape buffalo—two hundred fifty of them, he said—reputedly the most dangerous animal in southern Africa. While most of the herd walked around us, several buffalo stood motionless no more than ten feet away, their expressionless gaze unwavering as John shot them head-on. "If you ever find yourself chased by a cape buffalo, Rogers warned, "try to run up a tree or hope you are running with someone who is slower than you." Feeling more than a little tremulous, I was reassured by John's seeming fearlessness.

That night we slept soundly in our tent until awakened by screeching baboons in the overhanging trees. A couple of hours later, we were reawakened by "Knock, knock!" It was 5:30 a.m. and pitch-dark outside. Peering through the mosquito netting draped over our four-poster bed, we greeted the knocker, a tall woman who stood briefly in the doorway before entering with a tray of strong black coffee and orange juice. Anticipation overrode our groggy state. We pulled on our clothes and drank down the prebreakfast coffee and juice.

A few minutes before 7, we were heading out of camp, cameras at the ready. Rogers stopped the Land Cruiser and pointed up. A giant eagle owl, pale gray with distinctive pink eyelids, was roosting on a branch some ten feet overhead. Rogers drove on, stopping once again, this time to let a female baboon carrying a baby on its back pass in front of us. We had been out for less than an hour when I spotted them ahead of us—two young male elephants feeding on the leaves of thorny acacia trees. Unfazed as we watched from about seven feet away, they continued to pull down and break off branches with their trunks, eating only the delicate leaves before discarding the thorny limbs. John and I both got striking elephant photos.

It was Rogers who spotted the black-maned lion lying on the ground ahead of us, and stopped beside him. Flies hovered above the lion's outstretched body, and I wondered aloud whether he was alive. Rogers assured us he was simply sleeping. A hundred feet away, we discovered the alpha male's pride. Rogers, who told us that this pride was rarely seen here, drove into the middle of the group, where we counted twenty-six lions. Several females groomed each other while others lay sleeping on their backs, their big paws pointing to the sky. "They haven't eaten in a while." Rogers indicated the lions' concave stomachs. One young male walked to the back of the Land Cruiser and lay down behind the right rear wheel to sleep. If we hadn't been warned not to, it would have been tempting to lean over and pet him, he was that close.

Later in the morning, we returned to the site to find that the leader of the pride had joined the others lying in the shade of a few trees. John was able to capture a head-on close-up in which the lion's gaze is so direct he almost seems to be communicating with John, as if he were a kindred spirit. The battle-scarred lion was young, Rogers said, perhaps twelve, but one day soon, he would not be capable of defending his alpha role any longer.

By 11:30, we were back at camp, with a half-hour before lunch. Walking to our tent, I spotted a feather on the pathway and stopped to pick it up. Barclay had asked me to bring her "a bone, a feather, something distinctly African." While John transferred photos from his camera to a digital viewer, he suggested I ask Rogers to identify the feather. Rogers held it close. "Yes, I can identify this." I listened expectantly. "It's an ostrich feather . . . from a feather duster." We all had a good laugh, although I was more than a little crestfallen.

That afternoon, Rogers spotted a leopard draped over a branch in a tree near camp, and we tracked a solitary male cheetah—John's favorite animal in the wild—who posed long enough for a stunning portrait that John called *Esquire Model.*

From Chief's Island, we caught a small plane to Baines Camp, this one much smaller with just five bungalows constructed of soda cans enmeshed in wire and covered by white plaster. Ours was at one end of a long wooden walkway over a sometimes-swampy area. It was here that we were awakened one morning by loud rumbling, shrieking sounds right outside our door.

"John, what *is* that?"

He got up and strode to the door, opening it enough to see beyond the walkway. I hovered behind him. "It's a bull elephant, and he's not happy. He's trying to break through the walkway." As we watched, three

Africans appeared with a fire extinguisher and sprayed him with it until he went away. It turned out that a few days earlier, the elephant had broken through the walkway because it separated him from the fruit of a date palm. Fearing a repeat performance, the management had cut down the tree—but without anticipating the elephant's angry response.

During our stay at this small camp, John and I were driven to another area to spend a morning with three "tamed" wild elephants that lived in the bush but were tended by humans. Guided by an eccentric American from Oregon who lived there with his wife and had adopted the three, we received a crash course in "elephantology." After walking alongside them for nearly a mile, we were allowed to touch a female— to feel her sandpaper-rough skin, tail hairs like pieces of black wire, and her breast, which was utterly smooth and soft. John took some remarkable photos of me with the elephants; one shows me standing with an elephant's trunk on each of my shoulders and another atop my head—just as they had been trained to do. The weight of their trunks, almost imperceptible, was like a lover's gentle caress. In a sense, I felt as though John too were caressing me with the tantalizing promise of more rapturous intimacy to come. But later that day, he confessed that he had experienced a visceral repulsion when he touched the elephant's breast. As happy as I was that he felt he could share this with me, I was disappointed by his revulsion. It suggested limitations as a lover that bothered me. Did he sometimes find caressing parts of me revolting, or was I reading too much into it?

That night, we slept outside in a four-poster bed covered with translucent mosquito netting. Before retreating behind the netting, we stood on the veranda, our eyes riveted on the countless stars. John identified constellations by sight while I wondered whether he would want to touch me. Early the next morning, we made love for the first time since arriving in Africa. Despite the pre-dawn cool, I was on fire. Luxuriating in the afterglow, our limbs entwined, I half-expected to peek out from the netting to find the rogue elephant staring back, drawn by our mating sounds! Sated by John's generous lovemaking, I was reassured.

After one more game camp on the Chobe River and a small-plane flight to Victoria Falls in Zambia, we returned to the bustling city of Johannesburg. It was our last night in Africa.

"I've started taking Cipro," John said without preamble. "I feel a sinus infection coming on."

A Taste of Santa Fe

WITHIN DAYS OF OUR RETURN FROM AFRICA, JOHN BEGAN HIS first outpatient treatment in Virginia. In one of several small rooms in the doctor's suite, he reclined in a light gray leather-covered EZ-chair, reading material on his lap while the antibody Rituxan began dripping into his bloodstream. Based on his earlier treatments with it, he had warned the oncologist, Dr. David Heyer, and me that during the first in the series of four treatments, he would invariably experience a severe reaction. "Shake and bake" is what he called it. He described a fever of such intensity that he would seem to be burning up, sweating profusely, and when the fever broke, he would become so cold that his teeth would chatter. Heyer looked skeptical, saying this type of reaction was usually limited to the first-ever infusion. But, as John had predicted, that's what happened. The infusion was stopped, then restarted after a time when the effects abated. Six hours later, he called and I picked him up. Back home, he slept for a couple of hours, then woke for dinner and a Wizards basketball game on TV. The worst was over, I thought.

"Life interferes with plans, but it's important to have plans." That was John's motto, which I understood and easily adopted. God knows we had plans, many of them made well before the Rituxan treatments began. The construction of his condo at the Zócalo development in Santa Fe, which John had monitored impatiently all summer, had been completed while we were in Africa. We were eager to see it and to furnish it, the upper level as a photography studio for John and writing space for me. Within a week of the first infusion, we flew to Santa Fe.

In early December, it was cold in the condo since the heat had not been hooked up yet—we were wearing jackets over sweaters. Standing on the gray concrete floors of the future photo studio, I took in the bare eggshell white walls and the uncovered windows looking out onto a narrow patio off the living room below.

"Oh, no! There's a crack in the concrete!" I stared in dismay. A long crack ran like a wavy river across the floor of the studio. "I don't remember seeing this when we checked on construction last summer."

"The floor is still settling. Why don't we wait awhile, let it settle completely, and then fill it with a colorful grout? It'll be a work of art."

"Oh, what an idea!" Captivated by his suggestion, I was no longer upset and couldn't wait for the curving crack to complete its growth spurt. This was not the first time I was struck by John's ability to recast a seeming negative into a positive. I came to realize that, as a rule, he did not allow himself to be put off by perceived negatives, his or anybody else's. His bent was solving problems by using his imagination and other natural gifts.

"One thing's for sure, sweetheart," I said. "These floors have to be grouted before we can move in a stick of furniture." The expanse of concrete on both levels was scored at regular intervals as part of the design.

"I don't know why. They look fine to me."

"Because dust and grime will settle into the scored areas."

"A vacuum cleaner would take care of that."

"Perhaps, but *I'm* not going to spend time vacuuming all these crevices!"

"All right. But we don't need to hire someone for this. I'll do the grouting. It's relatively simple. We do need to see someone about covering the windows." John wanted to be able to shut out light from the large window in the photo studio to protect not only the prints he would display on narrow ledges built into the walls but also his high-end Macintosh system and the large fine art printer that would sit on the floor.

"Let's hang the paintings before I show you what's in the storage units," John said.

"Oh, yes!" That morning, we had stopped at a storage unit just long enough for John to pick up a tool box before driving to the Niman Fine Art gallery to pick up paintings purchased two months earlier.

I remembered the unexpected purchase during my first trip to Santa Fe with John.

"I want to show you a gallery I like." We were finishing breakfast at Cloud Cliff, one of John's favorite restaurants for its pancakes and ditzy staff.

"All right." I was curious to see what he liked. Twenty minutes later, we were in the Niman gallery just off the Plaza, standing in front of three landscape paintings hung one over the other. Looking at them, I was mesmerized by the large southwestern skies, the intensity of color suggesting sunsets and an early morning sunrise.

"I've admired Dan Namingha's work for a long time. I'm going to buy one of these."

"I don't think you can get just one. These three belong together. Let me contribute."

John asked the gallery to hold the paintings for us until we returned to take possession of the condo. It was a significant purchase, and not only because of the cost. My artwork was in Reston; John's, which I had not yet seen, was in storage. These paintings would be *ours*.

"Our first footprint in our new condo." Hammer in hand, John stepped back to admire the three paintings hanging vertically on the living room wall.

"They're wonderful!" I could feel my face flush. The paintings on the wall helped me to envision the look of our new condo, tasteful and sleekly modern.

That afternoon, John showed me his three storage units, intending to transfer some of the contents to the condo. Oh my god! Where did he get all this heavy oak furniture? Beneath the protective sheeting, which he lifted for viewing, loomed not one but several oak bookcases and an enormous oak desk that looked like it weighed a ton. A captivating round copper dining table with leather chairs caught my eye. I remembered our small rectangular dining alcove. If we could even get it through the front door, which was highly doubtful, the table alone would be too big.

"What is *this?*" I asked, pointing to a dark-stained high-backed chair, a solid piece of oak without arms or legs.

"A pew from a church. My ex-wife's sister gave it to us. I've always liked it. It could be an extra chair."

"Really?" I swallowed hard, saying little. Apart from the walnut coffee table John had bought with me in D.C. and the walnut desk he had had built after graduate school, there was not one piece of furniture in storage that I would ever want to see in the new condo. How would I break this news to John? Could I?

With little more than an hour before it closed, we found the window coverer we were looking for and made our selections, arranging for installation while we were back east. An appointment with California Closets the next day would conclude our to-do list for the trip. Because the coat closet would serve as a wine cellar—more than five hundred bottles of wine were waiting in the air-conditioned storage unit—we wanted California Closets to re-configure the bedroom closet.

Later, leaving the hotel to meet friends for dinner, John picked up the safari photo prints and the portfolio he had brought from Reston.

We were driving along Bishops Lodge Road when I looked at my watch. "You know, we're going to be about fifteen minutes early."

John pulled off the road and stopped the car, his upper body falling heavily against the steering wheel.

"Oh my god, are you all right?"

"I feel like crap. I think I'm getting another sinus infection."

"Let's go back to the hotel."

"No." John's tone was adamant.

"Darling, you have to tell me when you're not feeling well." I was upset that he hadn't said something earlier, and concerned that I'd noticed nothing amiss.

That evening, John talked with enthusiasm about his photographs and answered all Dee Ann's questions about digital cameras. Before we left, she ordered a print of *Dog Tracks*. Neither she nor her husband, Scotty, had any idea John was feeling below par. It made me wonder how he was really feeling a lot of the time. He could tough it out so it didn't show. He would let me know when he had to, but he didn't want to be perceived as someone who was ill.

Returning to the hotel, John took a dose of Cipro left over from the trip to Africa. "Once this kicks in, I'll be fine."

He spent much of the next two days resting in bed, going downstairs only for meals. I had not seen him flat out before. I was concerned but not alarmed, because he said he would be all right.

Captive in the hotel, I mentally reviewed what I had seen in the storage units. We were sitting on the bed, leaning against the headboard, reading the paper we had picked up at breakfast. Rather, John was reading. I was fixated on the bed I had seen in the storage unit: king-sized with a Tempur-Pedic mattress.

"Darling, I think the bed may be too large for the condo."

"It should fit. It's a quality bed, especially the mattress."

"Did you purchase it for the house here?"

"Yes."

"You said Diane died in the house. Did she die in that bed, on the Tempur-Pedic mattress?"

"Yes."

"Oh my god. Even if the bed fit, I wouldn't sleep on it! How could you even *think* it would be okay?"

"We'll get a new bed," he said, his voice calm, effectively ending the discussion.

By the time we left Santa Fe, John was feeling much better, and so was I. The disposition of his furniture, apart from the bed and mattress, had been relegated to a back burner.

Back in Reston, John had his second antibody treatment. Afterward, he walked home, about a mile. A few days later, we flew to Cabo San Lucas to spend some time with my brother and his wife in their new time-share house on the side of a mountain.

The four of us were in a taxi leaving the airport when I told them about the Waldenstrom's. I wanted them to know that John, still somewhat weak, was not inclined to do anything rigorous.

"What does this mean?" Alarm rang in my brother's voice.

"It means that one day, I will die," John said, "like everyone else."

Returning to Reston, he received a third infusion before we drove to Raleigh for our second Christmas with Dick and Kerry. He took short naps in the afternoon there, but his morning walks through the neighborhood and our visit to a nearby museum were normal. One morning, Dick asked John to help him move a heavy wood-cutter next door.

"John couldn't lift his end of the wood-cutter," Kerry's mother said, sounding worried. "Of course, it *is* very heavy."

"I'm not surprised. He hasn't completed his treatments," I said, making light of her concern. "He told me he's in a weakened state until after the last treatment takes hold."

After his last infusion, as he had before, John walked home. That evening, sitting on the sofa with our ritual scotch, we toasted the end of Rituxan. I breathed a sigh of relief. Now, with John properly infused, we could get on with our life. Based on his predictions, it would be a few weeks before he was back to full strength. To help him recoup, I had given him a Christmas gift of six sessions with a personal trainer at our health club. I had no doubt that Rituxan together with a trainer would be a winning combo.

Over dinner, we discussed our recent nonstop travels and agreed that one foreign trip a year might be about right.

"Taking one trip out of the country a year will give us time to enjoy living in both Reston and Santa Fe." John refilled my wine glass.

"Yes." As much as I loved foreign travel, I also enjoyed nesting, savoring the moment in familiar territory. Having tasted Santa Fe, I longed for a bigger bite. At the same time, I took comfort in John's not pushing to root ourselves in one place, not yet. His "let's give ourselves four or five years to decide" echoed without rattling my brain.

My vision of our life together was one of creative endeavor punctuated by periods of travel. I believed in John's promise as a landscape photographer and mine as a nonfiction writer. I imagined our collaborating on beautiful books filled with his photography and my prose. I envisioned our traveling to places both familiar and exotic, including the landlocked state of Bhutan and remote parts of South Asia.

It was easy to envision such a future for us because John did not dwell on the Waldenstrom's. It was a fact of life he seemed to take in stride. He told me that shortly after being diagnosed, he had decided a positive attitude was all-important, and that's what he strived to maintain. No matter that he had dealt with a critical bout of spinal meningitis and, several years later, salmonella. He had pulled through. That was the important thing as far as he was concerned. Only much later did I realize that both infections must have preyed on his compromised immune system.

"How long were you out of commission?"

"About three months with the meningitis. One morning, I woke up paralyzed on my left side. They thought I'd had a stroke, but tests ruled it out. They asked permission to test me for AIDS. 'Go for it,' I told 'em. Finally, a doctor figured out it was spinal meningitis. I started physical therapy in the hospital, and when I came home, I was able to negotiate the stairs, using a walker. I started doing yoga and Pilates. By the time I got back to work, I was probably in the best shape I've ever been in."

"Three months is a long time. How did TRW treat you?"

"They kept paying me."

"Without missing a beat?"

"Yes. Before I could return to the office, I was able to work from home. I was on the A team, meaning I worked on special projects. I thought about making a move to another company once, but I didn't act on it. I never knew when I might be incapacitated. I figured if I switched jobs and became ill before the new employer knew my value, I might be out of a job.

"I never knew when I might be incapacitated." I jerked to attention hearing those words. Was John trying to clue me in to the likelihood of another infection?

The next time I saw Dick, I mentioned the meningitis and salmonella, looking for reassurance. "Oh, he has a medical file two inches thick at least," Dick said, as if I should know.

My shoulders tensed. I felt vulnerable and frightened. What lay ahead? But then I thought, Of course he had a thick medical file. He's been under a doctor's care for sixteen years, since the cancer diagnosis. His medical story struck me as being about something a long time ago. The salmonella episode had occurred at least five years before we met, about the time his mother died. I knew they had been close, and could imagine John's being emotionally and physically run down when he succumbed to the salmonella. The meningitis had happened even earlier, and he hadn't been ill since then that I knew of.

Following John's lead, I resolutely gave Waldenstrom's little thought. Shortly after we were married, he had said he needed to find an oncologist in Reston. I figured that someone with a cancer diagnosis needed an oncologist just as someone with a heart condition should have a cardiologist. I knew he had one in Santa Fe, but now that his home base was Reston, it made sense for him to have one there. After John found Heyer, he would see him monthly for blood tests. A week or so later, a lab tech would call him with his IgM protein number, which he would record in a leather-bound diary. It was filled with these numbers recorded over the years, along with phone numbers, birthdays, and addresses of friends and relatives. He knew the numbers' pattern: climbing first and then falling after an infusion. "When the number reaches a certain level, it's time for Rituxan, every nine months or so." I assumed he had undergone infusions in Santa Fe—nine months earlier would have been about the time we met. He never mentioned it; I never asked.

In mid-January, we returned to Santa Fe for two weeks with the goal of moving in. The shades for the windows had been installed and the bedroom closet redesigned. It took us a couple of days to grout, our aim being to complete the job before the movers arrived with

John's furniture from storage. But after rechecking the contents of the storage units, my uneasy feeling about moving most of the furniture into the condo was mounting. I had to speak up.

The night before the movers were scheduled to arrive, we were reading in bed at the Hotel Santa Fe. "Sweetheart," I said, "I think it's important to *really* like whatever we put in the condo, which I envision as a small gem. I've seen a bookcase arrangement with space for a TV and a small leather sofa and chair in a Crate & Barrel catalog that I can visualize on the lower level. How do you envision the photo studio looking?"

"You're not going to be happy with my stuff."

"Why is that?"

"Because nothing goes with anything." When he mentioned the floor printer in combination with the large, heavy oak desk, I had to agree. At the time, I had no idea that he had bought the desk just a few months earlier. He never told me. Months later, I stumbled across the receipt in a file.

"There's no point in having the movers come." John sounded resigned.

"Really?"

"Yes. There's not enough for them to move to make it worth their while."

Whew! Relief washed through me. I had made clear that I wasn't happy, and John wasn't angry. Or at least he didn't appear to be. The next morning, I managed to intercept the movers minutes before they were to leave Albuquerque for Santa Fe.

Later that morning, we drove to the air-conditioned storage unit to pick up John's laptop computer and returned to the hotel. Sitting on the bed, I read the paper while he searched websites.

"I think this could work." He moved the computer from his lap to mine, and showed me a picture of the furniture arrangement he had in mind.

"Yes. I like the look. Best of all, it would take up minimal floor space." Hugging two walls of the studio, the modular unit would give John enough counter space for computer monitors and a desktop laser printer, plus a work area. It would also allow space for us to work together and provide under-the-counter storage. After another trip to the condo with a tape measure, John placed his order. With the sudden demise of the oak forest in the photo studio, I was feeling jubilant.

The next day, after having a bed, mattress, and bedside tables delivered, we moved from the hotel into the condo. We were thrilled. After an exhaustive two-day search, we found a dining table and chairs to fit the small alcove. John shopped for replacement hardware for the bathroom, finding beautifully designed brushed steel towel racks and a tissue dispenser, which he promptly installed, using an electric drill. While he worked on the hardware, I installed shelf liner in the kitchen and pantry. I had bought the shelf paper in Reston and shipped it along with recently purchased linens. The unintended big project was assembling the wooden wine racks from Scandinavia. Stored in the garage for a few months, they had warped. Together we pushed and tugged the pieces as if we were playing with ill-fitting Tinkertoys, and after a few key adjustments by John, they fit the coat closet space exactly. Using a felt-tipped pen while referring to his computerized inventory, he coded the wine racks.

With the "cellar" in place, we drove to the air-conditioned storage unit to retrieve the cases of wine, only to discover our path to them blocked by the large, heavy furniture I had shunned, not to mention boxes of books, a lot of photography equipment, and a small mountain of outdoor gear—tents, sleeping bags, snowshoes, etc. At John's suggestion, we called Habitat for Humanity, which picked up most of the furniture. Once John had rearranged the book boxes, camera equipment, and all the rest, we could reach the wine.

"Let's keep everything else in storage until we have a place for it to go," he said. "I don't want to clutter up the condo with unopened boxes."

Our last night in Santa Fe, we celebrated at Maria's New Mexican Kitchen, eating tacos and sipping margaritas. "I want you to see my artwork and go through the china, maybe our next trip out." John was thinking ahead. "My hope is that once we get reasonably settled, we can fly to Santa Fe every six weeks. It's a good jumping-off point for traveling to the Grand Canyon and a lot of other places."

"Sounds good to me." Until I met John, I hardly knew the Southwest existed. Now that he had introduced me to New Mexico, however briefly, I wanted to see more. I was delighted that he was eager to show me some of his favorite sites. Relatively frequent trips to Santa Fe would also give him a chance to use his large-format printer since he didn't have one in Reston, and also to participate in local photography workshops.

"Once in a while," John said, "we can come here without telling anyone and just enjoy being together and go wherever we feel like going."

"I'm all for it." I knew he enjoyed seeing his friends, and so did I. On every trip out together, he had made a point of contacting them, arranging lunches and dinners. Had he done it more for me than for himself, wanting me to feel welcomed in new territory? It didn't matter. We were on the same wavelength. I looked forward to being in Santa Fe often enough to enjoy both company and time alone with John.

A Man of Contradictions

"I'M NOT READY."

"No?" I said, swallowing my frustration. "I'll cancel and you can reschedule." Calendar in hand, I turned to walk back to the office.

"No, don't do that. I'll keep the appointment." John, seated in the leather chair in front of the ficus, went back to the newspaper he'd been reading when I interrupted.

Had he sensed my dismay? I'd made an appointment for him with a personal trainer I knew. We'd been taking yoga classes at the athletic club, followed by workouts for me in the downstairs gym. I thought it was time for John to join me on the machines. But when I had given him the Christmas gift of a personal trainer, he told me he didn't want to start until the Rituxan treatments had kicked in. Now it was late January, four weeks since his last infusion. I assumed he was ready.

Later that week, John met with Liu in one part of the gym while I worked out in another. I was hoping he would like this tall Chinese woman, a one-time volleyball champ. After half an hour, I saw her approaching and put my ten-pound weights back in the rack. I couldn't read her face.

"How did it go?"

"John is one of the weakest people I've worked with."

My heart sank. I knew he was weak, but to hear Liu say he was one of the weakest confirmed a fear I had been holding at bay. When I met John, he seemed normal. I was expecting the Rituxan to work, and to work more quickly. I thought he would be back to his old self by now.

"But . . . I can help him." Had she read the concern in my face? Her voice was quiet, resolute.

"I was probably pushing too hard. He said he wasn't ready." Silently, I told myself to back off.

"How was it?" I asked when I met John in the lobby.

"All right. She's figuring out a program for me. I have another appointment next week." Not a word about his weakness.

I didn't want to push him, but it appeared that was what I had done. I wanted him to be well, to be strong. What Liu had said kept echoing. That afternoon, I emailed Kerry, confiding to her that John was very weak and that I was so afraid it meant he was also very ill.

"I wouldn't worry," she wrote. "I've seen John when he was really ill. I'm confident this is temporary and will pass."

My shoulders relaxed. I chided myself for overreacting. I should have discussed the whole matter with John in the first place and taken my lead from him.

A couple of weeks later, reassured by John's continuing workouts with Liu, I mentioned her earlier comment. I thought he might confirm her assessment, attributing it to Rituxan's delayed effect, and tell me how much stronger he was feeling. But he said nothing. The next day, he canceled his scheduled workout with Liu. Once again, I was exercising downstairs after yoga while he waited for me in the lobby.

We were at home, sharing a can of Progresso soup for lunch, when I put down my spoon and looked John in the eye. "When are you going to schedule more workouts? It's been nearly two weeks since you canceled your last appointment."

"I'm not going to schedule any more with the trainer you selected."

"Why not?"

"I think it was inappropriate for her to have told you what she did."

My jaw dropped. Who *was* this man? How could he allow a question of ethics to preclude his need to exercise? And why hadn't he said something earlier? Much later, I wondered whether John's anger at the trainer was based less on ethics than on his deep need to believe, and have me believe, that his health was not in jeopardy. I was flummoxed. But I was determined to see John get strong again, and I was not going to be put off by his passive-aggressive stance. I probably should have asked him what he wanted to do, but I didn't.

Two days later, working out after yoga, I spotted Liu. I explained the situation, blurting out my frustration. "I don't know what to do.

He's got to regain his strength, but he's not going to schedule more sessions with you. I'm sorry."

"Shirley, it's all right. I would recommend Bob Bernhards for John. He's a master trainer, and he's here today. Let me introduce you."

Like the other trainers, Bob was wearing black pants and a red T-shirt. A one-time champion weightlifter, he was narrow hipped and broad shouldered. Dark eyes behind rimless lenses gave him a quiet mien. Without visible reaction he listened as I told him a little about John, his recent treatment for cancer, and his preference for variety in any exercise regimen.

"John's upstairs right now. Would you be willing to go up to meet him?"

"Sure."

John was sitting in one of several low, brown leather chairs. As we approached, he stood up and took a step toward us.

"Shirley asked you to meet me, didn't she?" He was matter-of-fact, his eyes fixed on Bob.

"Yes. Hello. I'm Bob." They shook hands.

I went back downstairs, not knowing what would come of my actions. I never knew what they discussed, although John told me that someone close to Bob had had a cancer scare. From that day on, John was a regular at the club with the personal trainer, although I don't know if he actually got stronger.

* * *

A year after meeting John—our whirlwind courtship and wedding notwithstanding—I was still discovering who he was.

He had a strong sense of personal morality and held himself, more than others, accountable. Although he didn't confront people directly, anyone whose behavior he deemed inappropriate was cut off. So too were those who did not play by the rules of the game. I saw this trait in him with the trainer, and again later with a poker group.

A neighbor had introduced John to the poker group in our condo. Its other members older than he by ten to fifteen years, the group would play late into the night once a week downstairs in the social room.

I was in the living room reading when John walked in after his first session. "How was it?"

"All right." He joined me on the sofa.

"Did they play Texas hold 'em?" This was one of his favorite poker games.

"Yes. But they seem to play by their own rules rather than those of the game."

Uh oh, I thought. John seemed to know the rules for every game played, and I had to assume he knew them for poker. I sensed a red flag.

One night, he returned earlier than usual, foregoing the post-poker chitchat. "I'm not going to play with a group that has so little regard for the game. Someone said, 'I don't mean any offense, but I'd rather play by Pepper's rules [referring somewhat obliquely to long-time football coach Pepper Rodgers] than yours.' I told them they're not my rules."

John stopped playing with the group. I was sorry not only because I thought he enjoyed the male companionship but also because I knew he wanted to play poker. "The best way to perfect the game is to play at the table," he had said. Before moving to Reston, he had played on the internet every day for several months until dissipating the $2,000 he had set aside for the game. I was sympathetic with John's viewpoint. Why play if you're not playing by the rules, especially if you want to perfect your game?

He was rarely critical of other people's words or actions, including mine. "There's nothing you do that I don't like," he said when I asked. But he would not make allowances, even for me, if he thought something was morally wrong.

It was a Monday morning in February. We were sitting in the living room after doing the morning's crossword puzzles.

"I'm going to tackle our tax returns for the IRS and Virginia."

"Do you want to use my CPA?"

"No, I think I can do them on my own."

Impressed because I had never done my own taxes—even in my twenties with minimal income, I had sought the help of H&R Block—I compiled my 2006 donations. The list included a church donation with an asterisk noting that Joe had always used it even though we both knew it was fictitious. When John gave me the forms to sign, I asked, "Did you include the church donation?"

"No."

"Why not? I would have."

"I thought it was hypocritical."

Did he object to cheating the IRS or feel that taking a deduction for a church donation was not kosher for someone who neither professed a religious allegiance nor attended church? Whichever, I did not appreciate his moral rectitude. But, unwilling to argue, I let it go. Unlike John, Joe had harbored a touch of larceny and acted on it from time to time. John was unbending.

He was a man of contradictions. An independent thinker with a disregard of convention, he was conventional enough to care about the impression we made on other people. On the few occasions we invited guests over, I set the table and John did the cooking. What a treat! Married to Joe, I had been both cook *and* bottle washer.

"I love your dining area and your custom of eating salad after the main course." Marilyn, my condo neighbor, had come up for dinner.

"This is how we eat every night," John told her, surveying the candles fluttering in their crystal candlesticks and the white china on the glass table.

Later, he told me that when he and his ex-wife had belonged to a gourmet group, the other members had given them high marks for "understated classiness." "I like to think that's how *we* come across." I heard the pride in his voice.

He also cared very much about the impression he made on me. "I think you'll like the shirts I just ordered on the internet from Territory Ahead," he said one day. I did. And he hadn't hesitated to buy two expensive suits at Nordstrom before our wedding because he foresaw a need for them in Virginia. Yet he railed against buying good-looking Italian-made loafers, saying "Diane [his fiancée] made me get a pair, and I swore I would never get another" because they had fit so poorly. When, with notable reluctance, he agreed to go with me to Saks to buy a pair, I was chagrined to discover that his arch was too high for all but one pair he tried on.

He was caring and generous but not unmindful of money. He spent without complaint, yet when he asked me what I wanted for Christmas and I told him "a watch," he said, "Get whatever you want, but remember, it will diminish our funds for travel." A few months earlier, he had paid cash for a silver Infiniti SUV but not because I'd asked for a new car. "You need a winter-worthy car," was all he said before driving us to the dealer. I'd never thought about a car in terms of its being "winter-worthy," but I was touched by his caring and overwhelmed by his generosity.

Although John's bent was to act quickly and follow through, house maintenance was an exception.

We were in the living room reading one day when I noticed that a light was out in the overhead track.

"I'll take care of it." John got up, took his jacket from the coat rack, and was out the door. In minutes, he was back with not one replacement bulb but a half-dozen.

"Thank you." I greeted him with a kiss. I could hardly believe his quick response. And then I waited. I waited several days before getting out the ladder, setting it up under the track, and asking him to replace the bulb—which he finally did.

It was John who noticed that the kitchen faucet was leaking.

"I'll ask Mr. Lee to check it out," I said.

"Don't do that. I can pick up a faucet at Home Depot and install it for a lot less than paying the building maintenance man."

As in the case of the burned out bulb, John bought a new faucet that very day. But it took a few weeks before he installed it, nudged by my reminder of a family story from his sister-in-law of how his father once told his mother he would build a banister for the basement stairway. Years went by. Shortly after he died, John's mother had a banister installed. "But you hired the most expensive contractor to do the job!" a friend said. "What's important," she replied, "is that I finally have a banister!"

John's apparent contradictions were confounding, but they were a part of him that I found fascinating, a puzzle whose solution I could sense but never find.

Now that we were both retired, we had the time to do what we had always wanted. For me, that was writing. For John, of course, it was photography.

He devoted considerable time to his digital photography, thanks to the high-end Mac system and fine art table-top printer he had set up in the office. Shortly before our wedding, he had submitted his photographs to a juried art competition sponsored by the Fairfax County Arts Council. One of my favorites, *Glorieta Color*, had been displayed at the Greater Reston Arts Center (GRACE) the previous summer. John planned another submission for a juried competition before we left for France.

"Let's walk over to GRACE," he said one morning after putting our breakfast dishes in the dishwasher. "If Joanne is there, I want to talk with her about an idea I have for an exhibition."

"All right. Give me a couple minutes to put on my face." I was eager to hear John's proposal. The director liked him. I knew she would be interested in what he had to say.

Skirting the small park near the end of Market Street, we pushed open the clear glass door to the gallery. In the white-walled exhibit space, we reexamined paintings and sculptures we'd seen at an opening reception a few nights earlier. We were looking at an exhibit that included a tree—whose size we marveled over—lying across the wooden floor with small ferns growing from grooves along its trunk, when Joanne walked up.

"Hi." A slim blonde with soulful blue eyes, she listened attentively as John told her what he envisioned.

"It will be a floor and wall installation. Embedded in the floor and covered by a transparent surface that people can walk over will be a series of large photographs forming a question mark. I'll select these from a collection I'm working on called "Patterns." Framed photos, replicas of those in the floor, would be displayed on a wall. Playing in the background would be the Simon and Garfunkel song "Patterns.""

"I like it," Joanne said." We'd have to be sure there's not a copyright issue with the music."

"I think we can work that out."

"When could you have it ready?"

"It will take me a year and a half to complete."

I was struck by John's ambition and the scope of his vision. I knew about the photos in his "patterns" file, but this was the first I'd heard about how he planned to use them. He was not proposing a mere exhibition of photography but a provocative multisensory experience for the viewer. His confidence was stunning. Had he ever had any doubts about what he set out to do? A degree of long-range planning was intrinsic to his vision, whether it was a year and a half to complete the installation or four to five years to be a successful photographer and decide where in the country we would live full time. How many other ideas were percolating, I wondered on reflection, how many that I would never hear about?

I wondered whether we would be able to combine our interests and work together on joint projects. I hoped that we could, but I wasn't sure where my writing was going, and I assumed John could not be the editor I needed and had found in Joe.

For the first time in years, I was tranquil enough to read books and inspired enough to write. My work over the years had been intense. I had been intense. Joe had been intense. It was only after marrying John and retiring that I had started to feel relaxed, devoting more than an occasional morning to yoga. When I wasn't reading or plink-plonking on my piano, I was often at my computer, writing travel articles.

After completing a couple on our African experience, I found myself longing for Joe's capable editing. I remembered that John had once said he considered himself a good writer. I pondered briefly before walking from the office into the living room. He was sitting in the comfortable Brazilian leather chair, reading. "Sweetheart, would you take a look, with an editor's eye, at these pieces I've written?"

He glanced up from his reading and gave me a quizzical look.

"I'm serious. Every good writer needs an editor. I'd really like you to look at what I've written and make any changes you wish. Here's a pen." I handed him my pages.

"All right."

Since I'd never thought of John as a writer or editor, although he had written numerous scientific articles, I didn't know what to expect. An hour or so later, I picked up the sheaf of papers from the coffee table where John had placed them and started looking at his edits. There were not a lot, but the suggestions he had made were good ones. The idea of our working together now seemed feasible.

In March we offered a Show & Tell to our condo neighbors on our trip to Botswana, featuring the eighteen photos that John considered his best and my write-up, "A Day on Safari." Before our little production, I was nervous, not for me but for John, a self-described nontalker. I needn't have been. In front of our audience, he stood tall, a glass of South African wine in one hand, and spoke seamlessly. Without a note, he relayed highlights of our safari trip, including the fact that we had decided on the "honeymoon" trip before deciding to get married, which made everyone smile. That evening, for the first time, I could visualize presentations he must have made on aerospace projects and as a trainer for Northrop Grumman. After the last guest left, we turned to each other and simultaneously exclaimed, "You were wonderful!"

A few days later, we agreed to be on a fall program titled "Trip Tales" for "Learning in Retirement," sponsored by George Mason University. Initially, John said to me, "We need to find out more about what's expected before deciding. I can make a fool of myself anytime . . . . I'd rather not schedule it." After finding out more about the audience and ascertaining the availability of AV equipment, we confirmed our participation.

I was in the office, checking email when John walked in. "The co-ordinator for George Mason wants to send out an early promo on our presentation. We should probably spend some time today discussing the content so I can get back to him."

"How about this afternoon?"

After lunch, we huddled on the sofa while John, yellow tablet in hand, drew up a working outline. "I'll pull an aerial map from the internet to use as a backdrop to orient the audience to where we were, and we can use your point-and-shoot photos to illustrate the game camp experience."

"Really? You mean the nonphotographer's photos will have a place in the sun?" I laughed, remembering how I had struggled to photograph a leopard in late afternoon. Like the tree I had tried to capture in the restaurant with Oprah, I got zip, but others that I took in strong daylight had turned out pretty well.

"They're not bad, and we need them." John had taken nothing in the game camps. "Using them for illustration, we can each talk about different aspects of the trip.

"And conclude our presentation by showing your eighteen photos, the pièce de résistance."

"Yes. That should do it. I'll tell the fellow at George Mason what we've come up with."

Unlike me, John was not an enthusiast. He was matter-of-fact, which could sound a little dismissive. That he considered my photos "not bad" was high praise. I sometimes chided him for saying things were not bad when he thought they were good, even great. But that expression, along with the absence of adverbs in conversation, was a part of him.

Our planning session was over almost before it had started, thanks to John's ability to capture the essence of our two-hour presentation in a few minutes. Buoyed by his apparent return to good health, I now pictured our life together as one of tremendous promise. No longer was there a question of whether we could work together. I was hopeful about the future with this fascinating man, whose behavior at times befuddled me but whose love I never doubted. Our lives would be filled with creative endeavors, travel, and connections with friends old and new. I had some reservations about the frequent trips to Santa Fe that John envisioned, but I was sure the timing would resolve itself. After all, we were still a work in progress.

A French Anniversary

Tall candles on the glass-topped dining table were flickering, the air fragrant with the aroma of Indian spices flavoring yogurt and chicken. We were having dinner at home.

"I have an idea." John lifted his wine glass, fixing me with his gaze. "Let's go to Brittany in the spring."

"I'd love to!" I lifted my glass to meet his, my heart thumping in delight. "We could end up in Paris!"

"Yes. I'll show you Brittany, and we can celebrate our first anniversary in Paris."

"Shirley will travel anywhere," Joe used to say. He wasn't far wrong. I would never have thought of going to Brittany, but John was familiar with that part of France. The fiber optics company that he represented, Le Verre Fluoré, was based in Rennes. We would go in late April, driving from the airport outside Paris through Brittany and then back to the capital where John wanted us to celebrate at a Michelin-starred restaurant. Friends in Santa Fe recommended a small hotel in Paris near the Musée d'Orsay, while John's business colleague in Brittany suggested a hotel in Rennes and invited us to stay with him and his wife at their new home on the northwest coast. Apart from these reservations at the beginning and end of our trip, we would go wherever the spirit moved us.

A few weeks before leaving for France, I awoke late on my birthday to find an array of colorful gift bags lined up on the strip of hardwood floor between the rugs in the living room. John was standing behind them.

"Happy Birthday!"

"How exciting! Does it matter which I open first?"

"Yes. Sit down. I'll hand them to you."

I sat in the comfy leather chair. Opening one bag after another, I flushed red with surprise. Each contained a bit of erotica—from a skimpy leather lace-up outfit to leather cuffs for wrists and ankles. I had asked John about his sexual fantasies, but I did not remember his mentioning S&M. Who would have thought? Who *was* this man? Reaching into the last bag, I paused to look up. John was beaming. It was obvious that his experimental talent was not limited to classroom science competitions. But where was this going? The book I lifted from the bag made clear John's bent—on the cover, a pair of stiletto heels and the word "Dominatrix." Taking a deep breath, I read the copy on the jacket. I knew a few women I could picture in the role of dominatrix; I was not one of them. But my curiosity was piqued. If this new angle was important to John, I would give it a go. I placed the book on the coffee table and gazed up at John. "How did you know I'd be receptive?"

"I didn't. I figured if you weren't, I'd throw everything away and forget about it."

"Well, I'm game."

I sensed that John had at least skimmed the book before giving it to me. I mentioned something I had just opened to and he said, "I think you can find what you need in the kitchen."

"Have you done this before?" I asked.

"No."

Our forays into S&M lovemaking became an adventure for both of us, an adventure based on love and trust. In the role of dominatrix, I found myself challenged creatively in ways I had never imagined. I called the shots, but I took my cues from John, who trusted me implicitly. Not that our lovemaking became solely S&M, but, time and circumstance permitting, we ventured into that territory more than occasionally.

Packing for our trip to France, I tucked four long silk scarves—a robin's-egg blue, a white and black geometric, a green fleur-de-lis, and a red paisley—into my suitcase. These I would not be wearing around my neck. At the last minute, I grabbed a fifth silk scarf to be used as a blindfold.

*   *   *

Brittany was a bigger experience than I expected. At times, it was hard to believe I was in France. People seemed taller and more raw-boned than my memory of the Parisian French, and the food—robust soups and crepes with few sauces—smacked of Mediterranean fare. The landscape was strewn with rocks, from giant boulders along wind-stung coasts to low human-made rock fences separating small plots of land planted with green grasses or yellow blooming flowers. Then there was Mont Saint-Michel—and an unexpected encounter with a doctor in Quimper.

For starters, I thought I would be the one speaking French, only to discover that John had, on his own, mastered enough French to get by, and preferred to order from French-only menus. One waiter smiled after we asked for the menu in French, and said, "Oh, you want to work for it, do you?" John was also more than passingly familiar with Breton, the language of Brittany, saying it no longer sounded "like noise."

Unlike Joe, John seemed to make quick sense of maps. Driving from the airport to Rennes took far less time than expected, largely because he found a route that bypassed the worst of the traffic congestion. It was late afternoon when we arrived at our hotel, one night early.

"I am sorry, monsieur. We do not have a room for you tonight." The clerk shrugged. "There is no room for tonight in all of Rennes," a city of some seven hundred thousand people.

"What do we do now?" I asked.

"We have a map in the car. Let's look at it." Pushing dark aviator glasses to the top of his head, John pulled the map close to his face, then held it out for me to see. "Vitre looks large enough on the map to have accommodations, and it's close enough to Rennes that we could drive back for our early morning appointment with Gwenael." The president of Le Verre Fluoré would meet us at the optical fiber plant, which had relocated since John's last visit. More energized than perturbed by the logistical challenge, we set off. We were resilient, undeterred by seeming setbacks. We were in sync that way.

Buckled into the silver hatchback, John maneuvered through rush-hour traffic while I checked *Lonely Planet* for hotels in Vitre. Finding two listed, I opted for the Hôtel du Chateau, "next to a castle." It was still daylight when we drove up.

"This is great!" I was panting. We had just climbed three winding flights of narrow stairs to the one available room, on the top floor with a view of the castle. "Oh my god. How are we going to get our suitcases up these stairs?"

"Let's take out what we'll need for the night and leave the luggage in the car."

"Good idea." I was exhausted, having slept poorly on the flight, but John had done all the driving. I marveled at his stamina.

That evening, in a small creperie on a cobblestoned street not far from the hotel, I tasted my first galette complète—a crepe made of buckwheat flour filled with ham, egg and Emmental swiss cheese—and Breton cider. John had told me about galettes ("like crepes but more substantial, with all kinds of fillings") and the alcoholic cider. While waiting for our galettes, we listened to music playing in the background. It sounded familiar.

"It's Alan Stivell!" John's blue eyes sparkled.

"Oh, it is!" I had never heard of Alan Stivell before John retrieved the French harpist's Breton C.D.s from storage in Santa Fe. He'd played them before we left Reston.

Listening to Stivell while quaffing cider, I remembered John's cider venture.

"Tell me your cider story again, please. This time with details."

"I was in Brittany, checking out the optical fiber plant for a project at TRW when I discovered Breton cider. It goes well with galettes, and I was eating a lot of them."

"The cider's delicious," I said, interrupting. "I can taste the alcohol."

"Yes. The alcoholic content is low but enough to give the cider a singular taste. Before leaving Brittany, I started thinking about importing Breton cider to the states. Back in California, I talked with a few distributors who were interested."

"Did you know there were cider producers in Brittany who would be able to export?"

"No. I talked with Gwenael who referred me to his brother-in-law. He arranged for me to meet with several small cider producers who could produce enough to export."

"You came back to Brittany to meet them?"

"Yes, a couple of months later. After that trip, I firmed up distribution plans in the L.A. area, got the licenses I needed, and scheduled shipping with the Breton producers I'd met."

Right on schedule, the first shipments of cider arrived on the docks of Los Angeles. And that's where they remained, unclaimed. The day John was to take delivery of the cider, he was rushed to the hospital with what turned out to be spinal meningitis. He didn't return to work for three months.

"Did you think about trying to revive the business?"

"No. It was over."

John said nothing more. I didn't know why he dropped the cider importing idea, and I didn't press him to explain. Was his health a factor? Or maybe he had embarked on a new project. He was forward focused. It struck me that he did not spend time looking back with regret. If his life was one of broken dreams, he never acknowledged it, not to me. "Life interferes with plans, but it's important to have plans."

Early Sunday morning, John sat relaxed behind the wheel, driving us through small villages with stark, two-story, gray stone houses fronting the narrow road. Green pastures, some with a few cows or black-faced sheep, connected one village to another. There was little traffic in either direction.

"I feel as though we own the road." I glanced at John. "Do you suppose anyone else will be at Mont Saint-Michel this morning?"

"I don't know. On a Sunday, it could be crowded."

I could not have been happier. Unknown to John, I had long wanted to visit Mont Saint-Michel. Had he read my mind? Or did he just want to show me places that meant something to him?

In his aviator glasses, John looked as though he should be driving a sleek sports car. Instead he was folded into our small hatchback, with very little headroom to spare. Now and then, he would rest his hand on my jean-clad thigh but usually kept it loosely draped over the steering wheel or the stick shift. I would make occasional notes—scenic impressions or random thoughts on earlier experiences—in my small notebook.

We tended not to talk a lot while driving. This was different for me. When Joe and I had traveled together, we talked about any number of things—work-related issues or people we knew and their idiosyncrasies. John did not chitchat. He didn't verbally explore other people's psyches. Unlike Joe, a novelist who wanted to know what made people tick, John's focus was elsewhere and not readily shared.

"Did your parents love each other?" I once asked.

"Yes." He fixed me with a look of incredulity.

"You know," I said another time, "your brother might be jealous of you."

"I don't know why."

"Because of what you've accomplished. And because you're older, you may have gotten more attention from your parents."

"Dick was a National Merit Scholar; he was valedictorian of his class; he was always more social than I. I admire that about him." End of discussion.

John saw himself as being on the autistic spectrum. "If the spectrum is a hundred eighty degrees, I'm probably at the ninety-degree point. I couldn't convince my therapist of this, or anyone else I discussed it with, but that's how I see it."

Impressed by John's forthright self-assessment, I mulled it over. When he had something to talk about such as our African experience, he was eloquent. But I'd noticed that in a crowd of strangers, without a focused purpose other than to mix, he might stand alone. At monthly socials in our condo complex, if we were initially separated, John would soon find his way back to my side. I understood. I sometimes felt uncomfortable myself in the midst of strangers.

"I believe you may be," I told him, "but not as much as ninety degrees. I think a lot of people are on the spectrum. It doesn't seem to have hampered you professionally."

He laughed. "Over fifty-five years, I would hope, I learned a few things about what to say and what not to say. But I would have been more successful if I had been better able to pick up on social cues."

"Oh, look!" The abbey-fortress loomed off to my right. "It's almost ghostly." From a distance, through a haze of mist, the island seemed to rise out of the water like a gigantic, forbidding sea creature. Soon, feelings of wonder overcame that vision as "A Mighty Fortress Is Our God" flashed through my brain.

As we got nearer, we could see that the tide was out, revealing vast sand flats stretching far and wide around the island, providing a parking area filled—even at the relatively early hour of 10 a.m.—with hundreds of cars, RVs, cyclists, and people on foot.

Once inside, we joined throngs of visitors on the move in both directions. The majesty of the island all but disappeared.

John seemed to know where we were going. In front of one eatery along the cobblestoned street, he paused. "Wait for me a moment." He gave my hand a squeeze and disappeared into the restaurant while I watched the passing scene. "We'll come back here for lunch," he said when he returned, reaching for my hand.

Minutes later, we were climbing rocky steps spiraling skyward. At intervals, we paused in front of small cemeteries circled by wrought iron fences. From these mini-mesas, we gazed out between conical spires and took photos of the lush countryside beyond the tidal basin. Despite the cool weather, I was hot. The climb was steep. Here we were, two atheists on their way to the abbey. I chuckled over the irony.

Did John want to go inside? He hadn't mentioned wanting to. "I'm not a typical tourist," he'd said before we left home. "I don't have to see the must-sees on most people's lists." I shared his disposition. Ever since I endured a physically sapping first trip to New York with my mother and brother, I had vowed I would never play tourist that way again.

Nearing the top, John checked his watch. "We need to go back if we're going to keep our lunch reservation."

I was surprised. He hadn't mentioned a time constraint. I didn't like stopping short of attaining presumed goals. I had hoped to see the interior of the abbey, but I could tell by the crowd ahead of us that it could mean a long wait. I also sensed that lunch would be special, one that neither of us would want to miss.

"All right." Turning around, we retraced our steps back to the restaurant. After checking in with the hostess, we waited in the foyer. Through a large glass window, I could see white-aproned staff members hugging large copper bowls filled with eggs. With notable vigor, they beat the eggs by hand, then poured the airy mixture into skillets held over a wood-burning fire.

"What a production! I've never seen such large, puffy omelets."

"La Mère Poulard is known for them."

"Monsieur Bessey." A young blonde hostess pronounced John's name as if it were French, which it was. With the accent on the last syllable, it sounded much better than the American version. She led us into a sunlit room and seated us at a linen-covered table set for two with a small vase of yellow flowers. On the wall beside us was a large hand-drawn caricature of Leon Trotsky, who must have eaten there decades ago.

Hard to believe that the Russian revolutionary would have set foot in the abbey. But then, maybe he came for the omelet.

"This is fabulous."

"My parents ate here once, in the late '60s when my father was posted to the University of Utrecht on sabbatical."

"Really? Did they sit under Trotsky?"

"I don't know."

I wondered how many times John had been there, probably at least once with Margot, his ex-wife. "Judging by the menu and what I saw in the foyer, there's only one thing to order."

"Yes, the *Omelette Traditionnelle au Manual.* Let's start with champagne."

I delighted in how much John enjoyed food and drink. The French champagne was bubbly and frothy, and the inch-high omelet nearly filled the plate. Leaving Mont Saint-Michel, I felt immensely gratified by our day trip despite not setting foot inside the abbey itself.

* * *

It was windy and cold when we arrived at a house high above the wildly beautiful estuary of Aber Wrac'h, where tides move up and down rock-faced walls.

From Gwenael and Pierrette's front lawn, we stared down at the relatively still waters filled with something I couldn't identify. "What am I looking at?"

"Oyster beds," John said. Vast numbers of oyster beds set between low-lying crags extended far into the ocean. Off in the distance, a tall lighthouse dominated islands of rock scattered over a watery expanse.

"That is Ile Vierge, the tallest lighthouse in Europe." Gwenael, wearing a navy pullover against the cold, looked past the oyster beds toward the lighthouse. A head of curly gray hair combed back from a broad forehead framed his face, giving him the air of a scientist. I liked his warm brown eyes and easy smile.

After carrying our luggage into the guest quarters, we joined our hosts in their cozy great room in front of a warming fire. "I like blue," Pierrette said when I admired her chintz-covered furniture. She was wearing a sheer white linen blouse with a long crinkled turquoise skirt the color of her eyes. Her auburn hair fell just above her shoulders.

We were about to sit down when John presented Gwenael with a special bottle of wine. "This is for you and Pierrette. I found it at the wine shop you showed me." I remembered how happy John had been when finding the shop and purchasing the Grand Cru bordeaux.

"I know we will enjoy this because you select only the best wines. Shirley, the last time I met John in Rennes, he said that he wanted to visit a good wine shop. I took him to a very old wine shop where he found a big, thick, and expensive book about wine. I told him, 'It will be heavy to carry in your luggage.' 'It will not be a problem,' he said. 'I want this book; it will make my friends jealous.'"

After a restorative cup of hot tea, our hosts took us to nearby medieval castle ruins, the Castle of Tremazan, where they told us the blood-curdling Celtic legend of Tangi and Eodez. As we stood beneath the ruins, Breton horses, their short-legged, sturdy russet bodies topped with blond manes, galloped straight toward us across rain-soaked pastures, as if guarding the castle grounds. Unflinching, John held his camera steady, catching the mares running head-on in a remarkable shot.

Before returning to the house, we stopped at a local seafood market. I had never seen such an array of fresh shellfish.

"What do you like?" Pierrette asked. She was wearing a long ivory woolen cape over her blouse and skirt and, despite the cold, open-toed heels.

Scanning the day's catch, I was not sure I liked anything until I spotted a familiar shape. "Crab is one of my favorites."

"Very good. They will cook them here." While the crabs were steaming, Pierrette selected bagsful of other fish. That evening, joined by Gwenael's sister and her husband, who had spent time with John on a previous trip, we sat down to feast on platters heaped with oysters, clams, and giant steamed crabs.

"We drink to you and Shirley." Gwenael's red-cheeked brother-in-law, Erwan, held his champagne glass high, repeating his toast in French for the benefit of his wife.

"And to all of you," John responded. With these near strangers, I felt accepted and welcomed. Between my fractured French and body language, we were communicating. As I looked across the table at John, he looked the happiest and most relaxed I had ever seen him.

"They like you," John said when we were getting ready for bed.

I had been wondering what our hosts thought of me compared with Margot, whom they had met at least once.

"Margot didn't speak French," John said, as if reading my mind. "She couldn't communicate with them."

We were staying in an adjacent apartment built for our hosts' son, an artist living in Paris.

"This is some of his work." John pointed to prints and paintings hanging on the walls. "I have samples of his art."

"Oh? Why?"

"I offered to represent him in the U.S."

"Really? Did you?"

"I've made a few inquiries." I was surprised. I didn't see John as a marketer, but he had a great appreciation of art and an entrepreneurial spirit. If he said he was going to represent Gwenael and Pierrette's son,

I had no doubt that he would. I was learning that John would do whatever he could to help his friends.

After a breakfast of steaming cappuccino and toasted baguettes, Gwenael drove us to nearby villages to see castles and historic stone churches.

"*S'il vous plaît, non!* Do not move the bicycle!" John was speaking to a young man who had seen him photographing and thought his bicycle was in the way. In fact, his yellow bicycle was what John was photographing as it lay against the side of a mossy-stone chapel beneath a red door. Whew! That was a shot that nearly didn't happen. John would consider it one of his best photos, and sold at least one print.

That evening back at the house, the four of us sat down to supper. Pierrette had prepared a hearty fish soup and salad, accompanied by a sliced French baguette and wine.

"Please, Shirley, excuse our absence. I must take John away to discuss work." Gwenael and John went upstairs to Gwenael's office while Pierrette and I cleared the dining table and talked in the kitchen.

"Pierrette, do you understand Gwenael's optical fiber business?"

"No, I am not, how do I say, it is not so very interesting to me. It is the interest of Gwenael. I prefer the world of literature and my life in Aber Wrac'h. It is tranquil here, and I can work very well."

More than once, Gwenael had referred to their home in Aber Wrac'h as "Pierrette's house." He had an apartment in Rennes where he lived during the week. On weekends, he was in Aber Wrac'h.

I handed the dinner dishes to Pierrette, who rinsed them and placed them in a dishwasher. "I enjoyed reading your short story, 'The Purple Hat.'" Earlier, she had given me a copy of the literary journal she edited and published. Glancing through it, I had seen a number of stories in French and Breton. This one by Pierrette was in English.

"Thank you. My written English is better, I think, than what I can speak."

"Did you learn English in school?"

"Yes, English and French."

"French?"

"Yes. We spoke at home Breton, but in school, we must speak French. If we speak Breton, we are punished."

"Really? Punished how?"

"There was a medal, very heavy. When someone speaks Breton, he must to wear this heavy medal around the neck. But when he listens,

I mean when he hears some other speak Breton, that person must wear the medal. The government was, how you say, it wanted to kill the Breton language."

"It is ironic and wonderful that you now publish a journal in Breton."

"It is important for me. You said that you write. What do you write?"

"Now I write travel articles about my trips with John. One day, I would like to write a book about women between the ages of sixty and ninety who feel good and wise about life."

"Why do you want to write this?"

"It's my age plus I think there's a market for a book like this. People today, especially women, can expect to live longer and healthier lives than their parents. Some may need role models. I like reading about women who are thriving mentally, emotionally, and physically despite growing older. Of course, it would be important to find women whose backgrounds and passions differed from one another. And I would have to hone my interviewing skills and figure out what questions to ask. In a nutshell, I like the idea of doing something that is not only challenging and interesting but also worthwhile. And I wouldn't mind making a little money doing it."

"I would like to read such a book," Pierrette said. Having dispensed with the dinner dishes, we sat down at a narrow blue-and-white-tiled counter in the kitchen, sipping after-dinner wine.

"Do you sometimes travel to the United States with Gwenael?"

"No. I do not like to travel far because I like to work on my journal, but I would be interested to see New York City."

"New York is one of my favorite cities."

"Shirley, I have a confession. I like very much to watch on TV 'Sex and the City.' The women are, how do you say, glamorous, and the life in New York, very exciting, non?"

"Pierrette, I think you would love New York. You must come to the United States with Gwenael. John and I could meet you in New York. We would have a wonderful time together." I imagined the four of us eating at Tavern on the Green after traipsing up and down Fifth Avenue.

"Perhaps, one day."

* * *

We were packing to leave Aber Wrac'h when John looked up and caught my eye. "I think I'm getting a sinus infection."

"Oh, no. Do you have Cipro?"

"No. Before we left home, I called the doctor for a prescription. Whoever was covering for him didn't want to give me one. 'There can be any number of infections, and whatever I prescribe might not be the right antibiotic,' she said."

"I can't believe it. How could she not have given you something?" What I really couldn't believe was John's not *insisting* that she prescribe an antibiotic after what happened in Africa. Maybe he didn't feel vulnerable; after all, it had been just four months since the Rituxan infusions. Visions of his being flat-out flooded my brain. Without an antibiotic, he could be bedridden in a foreign country, and I wouldn't know what to do. Even at home, I wasn't a nurse, not by instinct. "I hope I'm never gravely unwell around you," Joe once said. "You don't even think to fluff a pillow for someone who's ill." He was right.

"What are we going to do?"

"I'll ask Pierrette if she knows a doctor who'll see me."

Pierrette gave John the name of an English-speaking physician in Quimper, where we were headed. John called him and made an appointment for later that morning.

Finding the doctor's office was easy. The building, white with blue trim around the windows, resembled a cottage. The front door was open; we walked in. Within seconds, a robust, good-looking man with salt-and-pepper hair filled the doorway to an adjacent room. As he strode toward us, I was reminded of Peter Ustinov. He was wearing khaki pants with a short-sleeved sports shirt.

"Good morning." He extended a hand to John and then to me before inviting us to sit down in two straight-backed chairs facing a large desk.

"What can I do for you?" He was looking at John.

"I need an antibiotic for a sinus infection." John paused. "I have Waldenstrom's macroglobulinemia."

The doctor tore a yellow sticky from a pad and handed it to John. "Please, write down the diagnosis you said."

Extracting a silver pen from his shirt pocket, John printed his diagnosis and handed the paper back. The doctor raised his eyes and looked straight at John.

"Welcome to the club. I have the same diagnosis, but nobody except my wife and the doctors treating me know. Here, the doctor is expected to be free of illness. If anyone knew of my diagnosis, I would lose my university position and my practice."

My mouth fell open. Imagine meeting someone else, a doctor no less, with the same diagnosis! It made John seem less alone. Here was a kindred spirit. It would be good for John and for me too to know someone with whom we could share our experiences and concerns.

"How old were you when you were diagnosed?" I had to know how long he had been living with it.

"Fifty-three. Ten years ago."

My shoulders relaxed, and I breathed a little more easily. I was heartened to meet someone who shared John's cancer and looked to me to be the picture of health.

John didn't say anything.

"Let's go into the next room. I want to listen to your lungs."

I followed them into the examining room and took a seat near the door.

Holding the stethoscope to John's chest and back, he listened as John breathed in and out. I thought I heard him say, "You may need a nurse." Did he mean now or in the future? Then he looked at me and said, "No, you don't need a nurse. You have a beautiful wife." He wrote a prescription for an antibiotic and gave it to John, who paid a nominal sum for the visit. We chatted about the coming national election before shaking hands goodbye.

"Have you ever met anyone else with Waldenstrom's?" We were back in the car, driving to the hotel. John's eyes were on the road.

"No, he's the first."

*   *   *

John said nothing more about the good doctor in Quimper. I have never forgotten him. Now and again, I wonder how he is doing. Is he still alive? Still living with his closely guarded secret?

As now, John never considered contacting the doctor again. He was not someone who sought support. He thought he could handle his disease himself with a positive attitude, and anything that might take away from that was not something he wanted to entertain. In some ways, I was not so different from John. I too believed in the importance of a positive attitude—lemonade out of lemons and all that. I too was reluctant to ask for help. I don't know where this terrible need to be self-reliant came from. But I had limits when it came to death. Without caring friends and eventually the help of a grief group and a wise therapist, I would not have been able to handle Joe's death. When John could no longer stave off the cancer, I was in desperate need of someone to talk with who knew what was going on, someone who could help me help myself and John too. His oncologist was not able to help me. But it didn't occur to me to contact the doctor in Quimper. I wish now I had talked with him. Perhaps he could have been a support for me. Perhaps if John had entertained the nearness of his death, he would have suggested we remain in touch with the doctor, not so much for himself as for me.

I didn't anticipate John's dying. He had lived with his cancer for nineteen years, a long time. I think he covered up a lot. It was his way of coping, by refusing to acknowledge even the most obvious signs. In Quimper, John did not apologize to me for becoming ill. In fact, he hardly acknowledged it. "I had thought we would spend a few days in Quimper," he said, putting a positive spin on his need to stay there and recover his strength. "Let's pace ourselves. We don't have to do and see everything at once."

We went to bed early and slept late. We explored on foot in Quimper's charming Old Town on the River Odet. Walking along the cobblestoned streets and noting the medieval half-timbered buildings, I was relieved to hear John say he was hungry.

"Let's go into this creperie. If it's the one I remember, it has good galettes."

After lunch, he suggested we stop at a wi-fi cafe. "We can rent computer time to check email."

"All right. I'm not expecting any earth-shaking messages, but one never knows."

At the computers, John looked up at me grinning: "I'm in!"

"What are you talking about?"

"The judge for the Fairfax County Arts Council selected one of my photos for the exhibition this summer."

"Oh, darling, that's wonderful! Which one?"

"I don't know. The details will be in a letter, so we won't know until we get home."

In fact, the judge had selected not one but two of John's four submissions. Learning that the judge's specialty was contemporary art, John had decided to "posterize" his dramatic panoramic photo of Comb Ridge, a forty-mile-long chain of mountains in southeastern Utah. The result had been a compelling abstract, hardly discernible as

Comb Ridge. The other selection was his striking photo of reflections on the Zambezi River taken from the *African Queen,* a boat we'd spent an afternoon on during our trip to Africa.

John seemed to be feeling better. One morning, we visited the Faïencerie Henriot-Quimper store not far from the hotel, where we bought hand-painted pottery for John's collection and a few Christmas gifts. Back at the hotel, I pulled the scarves from a dresser drawer. "Are you game?" I waved the colorful silks in front of John, who was admiring our purchases laid out on the generous bed.

"Yes." Giving me a wink and a smile, he quickly cleared everything away.

Although the bed was not a four-poster, the frame was accommodating. That afternoon, I felt that John would be okay. The fact that I could still sustain this intimate part of our life together gave me hope.

Sunday, May 6, was Election Day throughout France. By day's end, our Quimper doctor's fevered wish for a win by Nicolas Sarkozy would be granted. Early that morning, we packed the car and left Quimper.

John's obvious delight in showing me the Brittany that had captured his fancy on earlier visits—from galettes and cider to the windswept rocky coastline; from the perplexing megaliths and castles to wine country—touched my heart. Relatively laid back and comfortable with open-ended situations, he relished every part of the journey. I found our travel together an invigorating counter to my years of results-driven activity. Knowing that Paris was our target did not lessen the adventure and joy of driving through the country on little-trafficked roads, stopping in small villages, some not even on the map, for lunch or to spend the night.

We had been away from home seventeen days. Despite John's close call with a sinus infection, we'd had a great time in Brittany and now eagerly anticipated our stay in Paris.

It was mid-afternoon on a Friday when he drove us into Paris. John had looked at a map of the city earlier that morning. Without a hitch, he maneuvered the silver hatchback through city traffic, finding the Hotel Bersolys on a narrow one-way street in the district of Saint-Germain-des-Pres. The narrow gray building looked modern despite its seventeenth-century age. A small elevator, one person with one bag at a time, took us to our third-floor room.

"Darling, this is spacious! Who would have thought?" Even though the windows overlooked the street, John said as he opened them, "I think we're high enough we won't hear the noise."

As we looked out at the foot traffic below, it started to rain.

"Let's celebrate by opening a bottle of Sancerre. There are two Michelin-rated restaurants I want to check out. They're not far from the hotel." After studying the menus, John made a reservation at L'Atelier. The featured "Menu Découverte" (Discover Menu) was priced at 110 euros, about $150 per person. "It'll be a splurge," he said, "but worth it."

Filled with anticipation, we stepped out of the hotel. We had walked three blocks toward L'Atelier when the sky darkened and the downpour became torrential. With our umbrella back at the hotel and no taxi in sight, we did the only thing we could—run toward the restaurant, trying not to trip on the uneven sidewalk. Breathless and more than a little damp, we arrived at L'Atelier only to find the front door locked.

"Oh, no!" I looked at John who looked at his watch.

"We're fifteen minutes early, but I see staff inside." John knocked on the door, catching the eye of a white-aproned young man who pointed to a watch on his wrist, indicating the door would not open for fifteen minutes.

"We're going to be drenched!" I said. We tried with little success to flatten ourselves against the door under a narrow canopy.

When the door finally opened, we stepped into a room so dark I felt blind. I lifted a hand to my damp hair, fearing it was stick-straight. "It must look perfectly awful."

"You look wonderful!" John was exuberant. One shoulder of his jacket was sopping wet, but he gave it short shrift. "It'll dry."

Within seconds, we were transported from petty concerns to another world. A black-suited maitre d' led us to two seats fronting a wide counter of rich dark wood.

"If I'd been told we were going to be seated at a counter for dinner in Paris, I wouldn't have expected this. Talk about sleek, modern, posh. We could be in the heart of New York City at MoMA!"

Suddenly, a head and shoulders popped up above the counter wall.

"Bonsoir, monsieur, would you like the sommelier?"

"Yes."

From behind us appeared a woman dressed in black carrying a black, leather-bound book.

"What do you wish, monsieur?"

"We want to start with two Kir Royales, and I'd like to see the wine list. John scanned the pages until he found the reds. In short order, he selected a 2004 burgundy.

Within minutes, someone lifted two Kir Royales over the wall and set them down in front of us. Another set of arms delivered an *amuse-bouche* of tomato aspic topped with avocado cream in a short-stemmed glass, and a small plate of thinly sliced salami and prosciutto. Enchanted by the start of this new culinary experience, we lifted our Kir Royales.

"Here's to Raleigh," John said.

"Yes, to our magical encounter." I still marveled over our chance meeting, although John seemed to think it was providential. "Can you believe that despite our disparate lives, despite everything, we got together?"

"Maybe it's *because* of everything. I just wish we'd met earlier." Was John thinking of his foreshortened life? Was he anticipating the brevity of our life together?

"But I wouldn't have been ready for you," I said, oblivious to the possibility of a future cut short. Earlier, I might not have appreciated this reserved but loving mental giant who had such difficulty discussing feelings. Earlier, my head had been turned by the chiseled good looks and strong personality of Nikos, the Greek. With Joe, another strong personality, I had grown and flourished. Now with John, whose quiet strength allowed me to breathe, I could discover new pleasures and the simple joy of being alive. Older now but still healthy, I was free to experience life with a man who seemed to thrive on the adventure of travel as much as I did, while sharing my creative bent.

We had sipped the last of our Kir Royales when the sommelier appeared with the burgundy, which she not only opened but also, much to our surprise, tasted!

After giving it her approval, she poured a glass for each of us and walked away. Rolling his eyes, John tasted the wine and nodded *his* approval. Holding each other's gaze, we raised our glasses in a toast, this time "to us, to our first anniversary."

Our first year had been crammed with traveling and learning how to live with each other. Trying to get a fix on who John was—his thoughts and feelings—I had pummeled him with questions. "Shirley can be counted on to ask the embarrassing question," he'd said to friends. And yet I felt there was much more to know about this man who had captured my heart. Given enough time, I was sure I would come to know John deeply. From the start, we had been on the move—small trips between Reston and Santa Fe and big ones to Africa and now France. In fact, we had shared a lot with each other in a year—

our friends, our dreams, insecurities, passions. Overarching all, we continued to celebrate being together.

"Oh, I almost forgot my camera in the bottom of my purse. Do you think we could ask someone to take our photo?"

"Absolutely." John asked one of the head-and-shoulders waiters to do the deed. The photo turned out blurry but we look happy, and we were.

When we emerged from L'Atelier, the rain had stopped. Holding hands, we strolled ever so slowly back to our hotel. I would long remember our Michelin-starred anniversary dinner. How would we top this? That night, I thought we had years of anniversaries ahead of us.

Making Up for Lost Time

IT WAS MID-MORNING. I HAD JUST PUT AWAY GROCERIES AFTER A quick trip to Whole Foods when John walked into the kitchen. "Come with me." Reaching for my hand, he led me to a rattan chair in the living room, next to the glass-topped coffee table. "I want you to sit here and close your eyes."

I couldn't imagine! Without a murmur, I sat down and closed my eyes. A few noiseless seconds passed.

"Okay, you can open your eyes now."

My jaw dropped. "What is *this?*" A profusion of dark red roses erupted from a long-necked clear vase, their solid green stems pressed against the sides. Next to the vase, beneath the roses, was a Nordstrom bag.

"Happy anniversary!"

I was dumbfounded. By now, it was a few days after our official anniversary. "Darling, I thought we celebrated in Paris."

"We did." He was grinning, his eyes fixed on mine. "I wanted you to have these."

My heart was doing flip-flops. I reached for the bag and placed it on my lap.

"Oh my god." I lifted out a large white box with black lettering: Coco Chanel. "You remembered!" When we were with Gwenael and Pierrette, I had told John I wanted to find out what kind of perfume Pierrette was wearing because she smelled soooooo good. He had asked and . . . he remembered. John once told me he had never been good at finding gifts for other people, but that morning, complete with red roses, he'd hit the jackpot.

"Oh, there's more," I said, peering into the bag.

"Yes."

In the bottom of the bag was a book. I pulled it closer to read the title: *Sensuous Magic, A Guide to S/M for Adventurous Couples,* by Patrick Califia.

* * *

A few weeks later, John flew to Santa Fe for a photo workshop. I took advantage of his being away to spend time with friends in New York and see *The Year of Magical Thinking,* the play starring Vanessa Redgrave as Joan Didion. I had bought Didion's book when it came out, two years after Joe's death. But after reading the jacket blurbs—a "penetrating account of personal terror and bereavement" that lets the reader "watch her mind as it becomes clouded with grief"—I had placed the book on a shelf in my library, unread. It hit too close to home. Didion's husband, John Gregory Dunne, had been a writer. So too had Joe. Her husband had died unexpectedly. So too had Joe, two months after Dunne. I wasn't ready to be reminded of any of it. But a year later, I wanted to see the play. Redgrave, reportedly a good friend of Didion's, had received rave reviews. I called Gay in New York.

"I'd like to see the Didion play. Will you go with me?"

"Yes." Gay, widowed many years earlier, may have had reservations about it, but if so, she held them in check.

Seeing the play would be a test of sorts. Since falling in love with John, I felt stronger, less vulnerable to immobilizing bouts of grief. I had not forgotten, but I had moved on, opening my heart to love another.

Mesmerized by Redgrave's portrayal, I found myself focusing on the character without identifying with her. She was consumed by the thought that her husband would return, whereas when Joe died, my mind never entertained the possibility. I knew he was gone forever; it was a stark truth which, coupled with his sudden absence, was almost unbearable. Only after I sold the house and the new owners called to report the mysterious periodic opening of the garage door did I begin to wonder. I had scattered Joe's ashes under a large oak tree near the garage. Had his spirit entered the house that he loved so much via an open garage door? Didion and her husband were "unusually depend-ent" on one another, in her words. Joe and I were dependent on each other, but I did not consider that in any sense unusual. My grief over his death had been deranging but less, I felt, than Didion's. Was her shock greater than mine? Her loss greater? Did she feel more than I?

The day I returned to Reston, I received an email from John:

Darling, I am delighted that you had such a good trip and visit with everyone and that you are home in good order. Melinda and Gary send a big hug to you. We had a good time—I think this was the first time we had been together since February. Dinner at Kasasoba (sp?) was great. They do small Japanese dishes, sort of like tapas or dim sum that you order and share.

We talked about the four of us going there when you and I are back here in late July. Will tell you more about the visit when we talk. I am off to do more unpacking (storage) and work on the valance. Will call you sometime late afternoon or early evening your time. Hope your day goes well.

P.S. I can't stand being away from you this long, especially knowing you are home. I long to be with you and can't wait to see you again. All my love, J

Reunited in Reston, we attended the reception for the juried exhibition at GRACE. Walking into the gallery, I squeezed John's hand and took a deep breath. "Let's find your photographs before we get wine." I was trying to scan the walls, but my view was blocked by a crowd of bodies and heads.

"I see one of them." John, taller than most everyone else in the gallery, led the way.

"Oh, it looks fabulous." Mounted against the white wall under a spotlight, his image looked more like an abstract painting of rippling blues and grays than a photograph. My eyes moved to the descriptive plaque: *Zambezi Reflections* Digital Photograph by John Bessey. I could feel myself glowing. "I feel so proud, you'd think I was the photographer."

John laughed. "You're closely related."

"I see it! I see *Comb Ridge Afternoon.*" Grabbing hold of John's hand, I led him through the crowd to his posterized print of the Utah mountain formation. Lights were twinkling in my brain. "It's wonderful seeing your work on display."

"Yes. This is a beginning. One day, I'll have my own show."

I did not doubt that he would. Outside validation was key. That was what these shows were all about as far as John was concerned. He had submitted the images that were chosen not because he considered them his best work but because he thought they might appeal to the judge, a contemporary art expert. He had judged correctly. To have his creative work validated by a third party meant that John's belief in his talent— or in this case, his judgment—was not misplaced. Nor was mine.

* * *

In mid-June, he kept a regularly scheduled appointment with Heyer, who joked about how we seemed to squeeze appointments with him between trips he wished he were taking. Together, he and John reviewed blood counts and decided to schedule another round of Rituxan for mid-August, with a pretreatment appointment a week or so prior, after our return from the Pacific Northwest. That would be about nine months after his last round. It was the pattern John had mentioned: Rituxan every nine months or so. I filed "Rituxan in August" away in my mental calendar without another thought.

Back in Santa Fe in July, we packed up the Nissan Xterra, loading it with a case of New Mexico wine for hosts along the way and a couple of bottles of scotch for ourselves, and headed north. We would spend three weeks showing each other our childhood haunts and homes.

It was late afternoon when we arrived at the Manitou Lodge, a B&B deep in a coastal rain forest in Washington state. Ours was the only car in the parking area.

"It looks deserted. And there's a For Sale sign out front."

"Let's take a look inside," John said.

Before making our reservations, he'd shown me pictures of the lodge on the internet. "What do you think?"

"It looks appealing, lots of wood and a great stone fireplace. Where is it?"

"A place called Forks, on the southwestern side of the Olympic Peninsula. It's in the woods but near the coast and not too far from Olympia." Olympia would be our next stop.

"Looks like a great place to recoup." We would be staying with relatives and friends, mostly mine, at the beginning of the trip. Now and then, we would be on our own. John preferred to travel unencumbered by reservations, but the Olympic Peninsula was an exception. With camera at the ready, he wanted to explore Ruby and Rialto beaches near Forks, where accommodations were scarce.

Carrying our luggage, we checked in with the concierge and climbed the wide wooden stairs to our spacious room. Against one wall was a king-sized bed with a headboard of wood crafted to resemble antlers.

"Oh, look, there's a balcony." Pushing open a screen door, I walked out onto a sizable plank-wood balcony with a couple of weather-beaten lounge chairs. The air was humid, redolent of mossy oak and other trees beyond a small grass-covered clearing. "It's hard to believe we're close to any beach," I said. Since driving onto the peninsula, we had traveled through woods alongside vast Lake Crescent into the rainforest.

"We'll see beach country tomorrow. Let's have scotch out here before we find dinner." John dragged one chair next to the other and went back to the room for glasses and our bottle of single-malt.

"To us." Looking at me, he raised his glass.

"Yes, and to our free day." Our glasses clinked. "I'm sooooo ready!" As much as I enjoyed seeing my relatives and friends, I needed some quiet time to recharge.

The next morning, still in bed and only half awake, I started caressing John's face, my fingers running down one cheek, up the other, and across his forehead. "What's *this?*"

"What are you talking about?"

"There's a bump the size of a quail egg in the middle of your forehead, just under the hairline." The flesh-colored bump was under the shock of hair that fell forward.

John lifted a hand to his forehead. "Oh, I think I remember hitting my head when I got up too quickly after rearranging computer cords under the desk at Zócalo."

"That must have been quite a hit!"

"It doesn't hurt."

The fact that the bump wasn't black and blue registered, but I gave it short shrift. John's explanation sounded plausible. Was I willfully blind?

Now, it is clear that this was the beginning of the end, but I was still focused on beginnings, not endings. I thought we had years left together.

Leaving Washington, John and I drove to Mist, Oregon, my father's birthplace and the site of many summer visits when I was a child. I needed to see it again, this place whose very name conjured visions of early morning mist hovering over my grandparents' farm along the Nehalem River.

"Mist was magical."

"Magical?" John was at the wheel, taking in the poverty as we neared the rural community—houses shuttered or in disrepair, a gas station closed. Except for the occasional pickup, the two-lane road was deserted.

"It's not the way it was." I was taken aback as much by what I saw as what I didn't see. The whole area seemed to have fallen to ruin. The old general store, where my brother Al and I would stock up on licorice, was gone, having recently burned to the ground. Built in the 1870s, it had been the oldest continuously operating business in the state. "There used to be a huge sawmill on the river here. Whenever we'd drive by, I'd pinch my nose to block the stench of the pulpy wood fumes. I don't see or smell it. Maybe it's gone too."

What I saw now gave the lie to my memories of hot summer days when Al and I would ride on hay wagons from the field to the barn, play hide and seek among the hay bales, collect warm eggs from under chickens, pick wild blackberries, and set off fireworks in front of the farmhouse. I wanted to share the magic of that time with John, to give him a bit more of me and my roots, so different from his.

And I had some unfinished business as well.

"Tell me where you want to stop."

"First, the cemetery, then the farm. My cousin isn't expecting us until later." Peering ahead, I spotted a small white church. "There it is."

John pulled off the road, parking outside a chain-link fence that wrapped around the steepled church with its faded green trim. When I was a child, there had been no fence. No cemetery either, or not one I was aware of. I remembered potluck picnics after Sunday school under the trees next to the church. It wasn't until many years later, after my grandparents had died, that I visited the cemetery.

"I remember when my father contributed $500 toward the fence, just a few years ago. I don't like it, but I suppose it's one way of keeping out vandals."

"The gate appears to be open," John said.

From the back seat, I lifted two dozen long-stemmed red roses. Walking ahead of John, I paused in front of the church. A construction permit was tacked to the wooden door: Renovation underway. As I walked toward the cemetery, my heart started racing. I had never been there without my father leading the way. And when I found what I was seeking, how would I feel? I stopped to catch my breath. The grounds looked manicured, the grass around the headstones recently cut. Looking toward the far end of the enclosure, I spotted the familiar red granite headstone of my grandparents, and next to it, another. I took a deep breath and started toward them.

My parents' ashes had been buried beneath a headstone I ordered three years earlier but had never seen. I had asked for red granite, as much like my grandparents' as possible. Standing in front of the new headstone, I admired the engraving and read the text, relieved to find no misspellings or incorrect dates. It was simple:

Alphons Richard Melis
June 10, 1915–March 17, 2004
Arvella Kubin Melis
November 16, 1914–January 20, 2001

Names and dates. No other verbiage and no quotation. I laid the roses—my father's favorite flower and my mother's middle name—at the base of their headstone. John stood behind me off to the side. Stepping back, I sighed. I had carried out my father's last wish, and now I was standing at the gravesite. The air was warm and still. Wasn't there something more I needed to do? For the last few years of their lives, they had taken so much of my attention and concern. And now all of that was over. My eyes were moist as I pictured my parents in California, in the backyard playing croquet and Ping-Pong. Those were the good years—at least that's how I remembered them.

It felt strange to be paying tribute to the memory of my parents accompanied by a man who had never met them. And yet being there with John made me feel whole. In a way, he was meeting my parents for the first time. I sensed their approval. I had not shared with him the bitterness of their life together. Joe had known and understood it all too well. John, who was incredulous when I asked if his parents had loved each other, might have found it mystifying. I reached for his hand. "Thank you for bringing me here. Thank you for being here with me."

"I'm glad I'm here with you."

"I have a funny story to tell." We were facing the headstone.

"I'm listening."

"My father told me—in fact, he gave me a sketch of the family plot—that his ashes were to be placed right here between my mother and his. When I asked him why, he said, 'Because your mother and mine did not get along. My being between them will keep the peace.'"

John smiled in amusement.

Feeling complete, I wandered through the cemetery, laying roses at my grandparents' headstone and at the graves of other relatives. "Let's go to the farm."

John drove slowly, giving me a chance to observe the passing scene. The farm was about a mile from where the Mist store once stood.

"Oh, no."

"What?" John asked.

"The giant fir tree in the front yard is gone." Planted by my father when he was a boy, it had been cut down. Without the shielding tree, the two-story white clapboard house with its wide front porch that nobody ever sat on looked naked and stark. So too did the large front yard where my father had played many a croquet match, usually besting anyone who challenged him. "Apparently, my cousin doesn't spend a lot of time mowing the lawn." The grass, more brown than green, looked like fine stubble. During the Depression, the land, dubbed "Sunnybrook Farm" by my grandmother, had been a haven for the children of my father's older siblings. "There's a creek that runs through the farm on the other side of the cow pastures, or what used to be cow pastures. My brother and I would catch crayfish there. Did you ever spend time on a farm?"

"No, although my great-grandfather was a farmer before he became a botanist.

"Is that your cousin?"

Verne, trim and slightly balding, with a meaningless Cheshire cat grin, was standing outside the kitchen door. For as long as I could remember, the kitchen door had been the point of entry for both family and guests. No one ever used the front door with the leaded glass window. No one ever entered the foyer with the organ, which no one ever played.

After retiring from Boeing, my cousin had bought the homestead and was restoring the barn, where he boarded horses, and some of the other buildings.

"I've been concentrating on the outbuildings. The house needs a lot of work, still."

"Can we go upstairs?"

"Sure. Watch your step."

Upstairs, I opened the door to the bedroom above the kitchen. Work boots and cardboard boxes covered much of the floor. There was no bed, no bedside table with a reading lamp and a book of billy goat stories.

"This was my room when I visited. This is where I wrote my infamous letter."

John gave me a quizzical look.

"Did you ever feel abandoned by your parents?"

"No." John stared at me. He was not smiling.

"Well, I did, once. I was eight years old. It was summer. My parents left me in Mist while my mother attended summer school and my father was working in California. I don't know where my brother was, probably with my other grandparents. I was lonely and very unhappy. I remember lying on this very floor with lined paper and a pencil, writing a long letter to my parents, enumerating my complaints, most of them having to do with my grandmother who did not know how to French braid my hair, and made me polish the banister and memorize parts of the Bible for Sunday school. When I didn't know how to spell a word, I would call down through this register in the floor, asking my grandmother how to spell words like "French braid" and "banister." I don't think she ever mailed my letter, which I sealed in an envelope and asked her to address and mail. Many years later, my father's older sister gave it to me, saying she had thought it "so very sweet.""

"What do you remember about your grandparents?" I asked, driving out of Mist.

"Not much. When Dick and I were about seven and eight years old, our parents drove us out from Laramie to Michigan to visit my father's parents. They lived in a large house on a hill near the university. The house was very quiet. I remember mowing the lawn. It was a hill, a steep one. Dick and I used a hand mower, and it took us a long time."

"What about your grandparents as people? What do you remember?"

"The only thing, and I mean the only thing, I remember is that my grandfather liked his toast burnt."

From Oregon, we continued southeast to Laramie, John's home town. "I want to show you the Snowy Range," he said, driving into town.

Looking west, I was struck by a seeming fortress of snowless mountains with a jagged ridge line. "I see it." The Snowy Range looked more enticing than the flat city of Laramie.

"Yes, but there's more than you can see from here." John had told me about the "rock crack" climbing, the skiing, and the fishing. "I'll take you there tomorrow."

The next day, we were munching on chips and sandwiches at a picnic table in a meadow decorated with purple, pink, and yellow wild-flowers. "Darling, this is wildly beautiful." In the near distance, two climbers were ascending cracks that slashed the mountainside. "This is what you and Dick did?"

"Yes."

"It looks treacherous."

"We liked it."

Back in the car, John drove us to another part of the Snowy Range and got out. I followed him up a slight incline to the bank of a wide, gurgling stream. The fast-running water looked cold and so clear I could see rocks on the bottom.

"This is where Kerry caught a fish."

"Really? I have a hard time picturing Kerry fishing."

John laughed. "Yes, but I'm pretty sure she did. She would have come here with my father. He spent a lot of time here fishing."

I looked around. From the great barren height of the mountains, the land sloped down into densely forested hills punctuated by lakes and flower-filled meadows. The scent of pine wafted through the cool air.

John turned away from the stream and walked toward a grove of trees. He stopped walking and stood still, hands on hips. "This is where Dick and I scattered our parents' ashes, on the other side of these trees."

"Oh." I gasped. John had not mentioned *his* parents' ashes. And now, without warning, here they were: Wynn and Bob. Unlike my parents' ashes, confined in an underground chamber in a family plot, theirs were scattered and free. John reached for my hand; we stood in silence.

Would they have liked me? How would I have stacked up next to Margot? John's mother had been crazy about Margot. At least that's what Kerry's mother thought. Whether she would have been crazy about her after the divorce was another question. John had told me that Margot was upset because she was not mentioned in his mother's will. What did she expect?

That afternoon, we drove to the University of Wyoming, where John had studied astronomy before transferring to the University of Arizona to study physics. We were walking across a campus dotted with beige buildings.

"I'd like to see your father's office."

"We can't get in." It was a Sunday in summer. Few people were on campus.

"Even a glimpse from the outside would do."

"All right."

From the ground-floor windows, I could see very little, and could discern next to nothing about the office.

"Did your mother ever attend your father's classes?"

"I think she attended his Physics for the Non-Physics Major."

"That sounds like one I would have liked."

"It was one of Dad's favorite classes. It was always oversubscribed, but he never turned anyone away. To get the class down to a manageable size, he would move the 10 a.m. start time to 9:30, then to 9 and earlier—I think 7 a.m. was typical—until enough students who didn't want to get up that early dropped out."

"Clever." I wished I'd been able to meet John's dad. I had heard so much about him from Kerry and from Alan, a good friend of John's whom we had just visited. "I wrote to Bob," Alan said, "never having met the man, and told him I thought I wanted to study physics but didn't know where to start or even whether I could. He wrote back a wonderful letter, recommending books and articles I should read. Because of him, I went to the University of Wyoming and majored in physics. We became great friends."

One afternoon, after an early morning drive to the Snowy Range, John parked on a residential street in front of an unusual-looking house. Part of it was red brick, part stucco.

"This is it. You said you wanted to see where we lived. Here we are." John's tone was matter-of-fact.

From the car, I could see that the house and yard sat on a corner lot, fronted by large cottonwood trees. "Look, there's someone in the driveway in front of the garage. Maybe they'd let us in."

"My mother sold the house to an older woman. I don't know who these people are."

"It can't hurt to ask."

"All right."

When John told the new owners that he had lived there as a boy, they invited us in. They were renovating and hadn't yet moved in. The basement, which had been John's room, was still pretty much as he remembered it.

"This is where Dick and I were smoking pot with our dates, with the door closed, when our parents came home a day early from some trip."

"What did they say?"

"They came in and said, 'Hi, we're back early. Just wanted to say Hi and let you know we're home.'"

"That was it?"

"Yes. We knew they had to have smelled the pot, but they never said a word to us about it."

I laughed. How many parents would have shown such restraint? I knew of some who went ballistic at the mere mention of pot. Maybe they considered it a plus that the boys were smoking at home. They had taught John and his brother how to drink wine with dinner at home. John's father had taught each of the boys to drive when they were only twelve years old. His parents struck me as smart, open-minded, and not easily rattled.

"So they didn't really discipline you per se?"

"No. They told us we were intelligent and that they expected us to use good judgment."

Climbing the stairs from the basement, I noticed the wooden handrail that John's mother had installed after Bob died, and smiled to myself. Unescorted, we went up to the attic, which had been Dick's room. One of the sloping walls was covered with maps.

"These maps of Utrecht were Dick's! And over there are the plank and brick bookcases he built!" John sounded stupefied. It had been a full fifteen years since their widowed mother had sold their home.

When we left the house, John was quiet. He had said very little in response to the changes the owners pointed out. Did he regret seeing what his boyhood home was now? Had he revisited the house only because I was insistent? He told me that once his mother sold the house, she didn't care what happened to it. "I'm like that too," he said. "The past is the past." I wasn't so sure. When he told Dick about his return to the house, he reported enthusiastically on his findings in the attic, and added that "the changes to the kitchen were a great improvement."

In Laramie, we spent early mornings and evenings with our hostess, a friend of John's mother who shared stories about her. "I didn't know John's father well, but I knew Wynn. She had a wicked sense of humor coupled with an underlying kindness."

"Tell me more." I wanted a sense of who John's mother was.

"I remember the time my son, who loved chocolate, offered Wynn the last piece of chocolate in a box. Despite knowing he was a chocoholic, she took the piece and ate it without a word. Two weeks later, my son received a box of premium chocolates in the mail."

John shared the story of a faculty picnic he and Dick had attended with their parents when they were fairly young. "Dick and I found a snake nest in a rock cave filled with squirming snakes. Taking one in each hand, we proudly showed them to our mother, saying, 'Look what we found!' A friend of hers was horrified and started shrieking at us. All my mother said was, 'Boys, that's very nice. And now I think you'd better put them back where you found them.'"

When we arrived back in Santa Fe in late July, we had been in six states, visited with twenty-six relatives and friends, eaten pounds of salmon—each prepared differently, each delicious—and covered five thousand miles over the course of three weeks. John had done the driving from start to finish. He had been a good sport. Not once did he complain. In fact, he said he enjoyed the encounters. "This is the sort of thing we might do once in a lifetime."

Looking back, our trip was about much more than covering five thousand miles of road. We had shown each other our childhood places, our families, and our friends, some of whom we hadn't seen in years. John had stayed up all night talking with his friend Alan—"catching up on our lives," he said the next day. In a sense, we were catching up too. That's what Mist and Laramie were about, entrusting each other with the children we were and with precious memories. We had taken each other home to meet our parents, and sensed their blessing. By stepping into our pasts, we had revealed parts of ourselves easily forgotten in the hurly-burly of the present. With every shared stop and memory, we had fleshed out our sense of one another.

That night, buoyed by the accomplishment but starved for intimacy—all but two nights we had stayed with friends, often in twin beds—we made up for lost time. We didn't even think of scarves in our hunger for each other.

A Sudden Reversal

"Aren't you going to ask Dr. Heyer about the bump on your forehead?"

"Oh, yes." John lifted his hair to reveal the bump.

"It's been there for at least a couple of weeks," I said.

Heyer peered at the bump. "I can't tell what it is. You should probably have it x-rayed. Staff at the front desk can schedule an appointment."

A couple of days after his first Rituxan treatment, John's forehead was x-rayed. When he arrived for his second treatment, Heyer was on vacation, but his nurse, Melanie, said he wanted John to have a C.T. scan, "because the x-ray didn't really show anything."

A couple of days later, we returned to the Fair Oaks Imaging Center outside Reston for the scan. We had planned to meet that morning with our financial adviser, who was driving down from Doylestown, Pennsylvania, but I felt apprehensive and rescheduled. John was napping in the afternoon with increasing frequency. I reminded myself that he had napped before treatments the previous December but then stopped a few weeks afterward. What did this bump on his forehead mean?

"Maybe some of your brain power is leaking out," I said, trying to cover my unease.

John laughed. "Now that I'm retired, maybe I don't need it anymore." He didn't seem concerned.

The following week, when I left John at the oncologist's for his third infusion, we agreed that when it was over, he would call me and

I'd meet him in the cubicle where he was treated. Since Heyer was still on vacation, Melanie would tell us the C.T. results.

It was late afternoon when the phone rang. "The infusion is over."

"Good. Have you seen Melanie?"

"No."

When I arrived at the cubicle, John was sitting upright in the gray leather EZ-chair. He was wearing his shoes, which he would take off before the hours-long infusion and then stretch out, fully clothed, with his feet elevated. His arms were resting on the wide leather armrests, the sleeve of his orange linen shirt still rolled up a little higher on his left arm, through which the drug dripped into his bloodstream. The needle had been removed. The metal scaffolding that had held the liquid Rituxan aloft was gone.

"Hi, sweetheart." I gave John a soft kiss and sat down in a straight-backed chair beside him. Silent minutes ticked by.

"Does Melanie know your infusion is over?"

"Yes. I've seen Melanie."

"Really! What did she say?"

"I think she wants to tell you herself. She came in after you called."

Melanie, wearing a white lab coat and dark-rimmed glasses, came into the cubicle holding a printout in one hand. Without saying hello or making eye contact, she sat down on a low stool opposite us and began reading, her face partly hidden by curly dark hair that had fallen forward. "The computed tomography of the head was performed with contrast on . . . ," she read, her voice a monotone. She did not sound like the usual upbeat and cheerful Melanie. I leaned forward, trying to decipher the medical terminology: ". . . shows three masses on the cranium, one measuring . . . and located on the frontal . . . ." I stopped breathing. Melanie kept reading. I stopped listening. I was on my feet, throwing my arms around John, who was standing. When had he stood? Why? Was it seconds before "three masses on the cranium," knowing I would jump up distraught? Or had he read my body language and reacted to comfort me?

"No! Oh no! No! No! There are so many things we want to do together!" Sobbing, I pressed my face into John's chest.

"We have time," he said, holding me close. But I knew that time was the one thing we did not have. It was shocking that the news had come from a nurse rather than the doctor himself, but I assumed it was so that John would know as soon as possible.

When Melanie was finished, John and I walked, mute and will-less, past the front desk and out to the car where I handed him the key. We drove home without a word. Retreating to our office, I sat in front of my desk, staring at the blank, dark computer screen. Our life was over—plans and dreams dashed without so much as a by-your-leave. That night, John called Dick, who drove down from New York the next day to spend the night.

"I put our names on the list for dinner at Clyde's," John told him.

"Sounds good."

The three of us walked through Town Center past the outdoor concert venue and into the restaurant.

I liked the dark wood interior and the model aircraft hanging from the ceiling. It was here that I had told John about Joe's death. I'd wept, and he had reached across the table to clasp my hand. I didn't want to cry again, not tonight, not ever. We sat in a dark leather booth. I sat beside John, feeling the warmth of his body.

Dick picked up the wine list. "How about a bottle of good cabernet?"

"Yes." John, like Dick, preferred red to white wine.

I nodded. I didn't care what we drank or ate. John and I had not discussed the results of the scan. He must have told Dick on the phone, but none of us mentioned it that night at dinner.

"I showed Shirley the Snowy Range."

"What did you think?" Dick asked.

"It was beautiful. Actually, more breathtaking than beautiful. We saw a few people climbing cracks in the rocks."

"That's what we used to do, John more than I."

"John told you about the house and finding your maps of Utrecht still in the attic?"

"Yes, why they're still there I'll never know. I guess the woman who bought the house never went up there."

"Or maybe she was a fan of Utrecht." I managed a rueful chuckle, relieved we were talking about safe subjects, distracting ourselves from the elephant in the room. "Why Utrecht?" I asked, looking at Dick.

"Dad was on sabbatical at the university there. They brought those prints home with them, and they got moved up to my bedroom—I was at C.U. [the University of Colorado]—when the walls in the rest of the house filled up with other stuff."

Leaving the restaurant, John led the way. I hung back to walk with Dick.

"Did John discuss the C.T. scan with you?"

"Yes."

"Three tumors. It's devastating."

"I know it's hard, but I think you should try not to jump to the worst conclusion. Have you talked with the oncologist?"

"No, he's still on vacation." Dick had a point; we hadn't talked with Heyer. And John had once mentioned a backup treatment. Skipping ahead to walk with him, I breathed a little easier, letting myself feel hopeful.

That Saturday, Kim Beach, who had married us little more than a year and a half earlier, was throwing a surprise birthday party for his wife at their farm. It was a long drive, which we had planned to do on our own. Now I asked John if he would like Pat and Philip to drive us, and to my surprise he said yes.

"I'm going to tell them about the C.T. scan," John said minutes before they were to pick us up.

"All right." I was glad John felt he could share the awful news with two of my closest friends. Maybe we would both feel less alone.

We were nearing the farm when John broached the subject. "You know that I have Waldenstrom's macroglubulinemia. I wanted you to know that I recently had a C.T. scan. It showed three tumors on my skull bone. We see the oncologist next week to discuss the results and what to do." He was matter-of-fact, calm.

I reached for John's hand and squeezed it, feeling the smoothness of his long, slender fingers wrapped around mine. Philip, in the passenger's seat, didn't say a word. Pat, eyes on the road ahead, broke the silence. "I'm very sorry to hear this, John. I hope the oncologist has encouraging news." Her tone, like John's, was calm.

I wanted to scream, "I'm so frightened, so afraid John's going to die!" I felt that his unruffled delivery had camouflaged how dire the diagnosis was. His dispassionate tone had not let anyone react. I would talk with Pat as soon as we were alone. Remembering Dick's cautionary words, I tried to deepen my breathing.

It was late afternoon when we drove by Kim's fledgling vineyards and parked near the house. Our hosts offered us a tour of their upstairs renovations. John declined, saying he would wait for us out on the patio. After the tour, Pat and I, with cameras in hand, walked to the edge of a tree-shaded pond.

"Pat, John's been living with Waldenstrom's for eighteen years. These brain tumors are foreign to anything he's ever experienced, and

I'm so afraid. There's a backup treatment, but I don't know whether it's for tumors. I'm not sure John knows either."

"Shirley, I'm so sorry." She put her hand lightly on my arm.

"I know I'm jumping to conclusions and I shouldn't, not before we've talked with Dr. Heyer."

"Why don't I take some photos of you and John before we change clothes for dinner?" We were both in jeans and cotton tops.

"Thank you. That's a wonderful offer."

Turning away from the pond, we walked up a grassy hill and into the house. Through a window, I spotted John sitting alone on a low stone wall of the patio, a glass of wine in one hand, his other petting a long-haired orange cat. As Pat and I approached, I could hear the cat purring. John was looking at the cat and seemed to be smiling. Was he thinking about his Maine coon cats, Ventana and Chablis, both beautiful and longhaired? They had been alive when he dealt with his meningitis and later salmonella. We both knew from experience how comforting cats could be. Watching John, I wished we had a cat, for both our sakes.

"Hi, sweetheart."

"Hi." John looked up and smiled ear-to-ear.

My heart skipped a beat. He looked good and sounded good. Maybe I *am* overreacting, I thought. "Pat's offered to take some shots of us before she and I change for dinner. Are you game?"

"Yes."

Within minutes, Pat had taken a number of unposed photos, one of which we would select for our Christmas card. In it, John is wearing dark glasses, his hair falling over his forehead. He has on gray flannel slacks and a light blue shirt with sleeves rolled up above the wrists. One of his arms is stretched toward the cat, the other is pulling me close. My shirt appears to be the same sky blue as John's. We look happy.

He had his fourth infusion of Rituxan the following Tuesday, and on Thursday, he went in to have blood drawn. We were told that Heyer wanted to talk with us early the next week. The appointment was set for Tuesday, three days before our scheduled departure for Santa Fe and Houston, plans we'd made weeks earlier before the scan. We would be in Santa Fe just long enough to move cases of wine and boxes of books from storage into the condo before flying to Houston to see my brother and nephews.

As we waited for Heyer, sitting in straight-backed chairs in the examining room, John was holding the leather-bound Day-Timer with all the IgM numbers in one hand. His eyes did not meet mine. Since the C.T. scan and Dick's cautionary words, I had tried to steady my nerves by breathing deeply and focusing on our trip to Houston. Now, in the white-walled silence, I wondered what Heyer would have to say.

"Apparently, the Rituxan is not working, not the way it once did," he told us. John, who had opened his Day-Timer to look at the figures, nodded in agreement.

"The IgM didn't decrease as markedly after my December infusions as it did after earlier treatments."

John had never mentioned this to me. Perhaps he had not seen it as a red flag. Maybe he considered it an anomaly; after all, he perceived patterns, and one-time events did not a pattern make. Or maybe he was determined not to look for negative omens.

My brain was on fire while John and Heyer—voices calm, comments reasoned—talked as though they were analyzing a lab report on some alien.

"I want to begin a regimen of Fludarabine the day after you return from Houston." Heyer's tone was commanding, confident. Fludarabine, a chemotherapy, was the backup treatment John had mentioned when we took our first walk together through the streets of Raleigh. "It will involve an infusion once a day for five days once a month—one week on, three weeks off. You won't lose your hair." Great, I thought, reassured by Heyer's confident manner, a perk we can embrace. John and I exchanged smiles.

"Meanwhile, I want you to have an MRI of your brain and spine before you leave for Santa Fe to be sure there's nothing new that could affect the proposed regimen."

Thursday at 11 p.m., John completed the MRI of his spine, a day after the imaging of his brain.

"When will we know the results?" I asked the receptionist.

"They'll be sent to Dr. Heyer in a few days."

The next morning, after claiming our luggage at the Albuquerque airport, we made our way to the waiting area for the shuttle to Santa Fe. Exhausted by the late-night MRI and our inability to sleep on the plane, we dropped into side-by-side wooden chairs cushioned in hard leather. We were alone. The shuttle wouldn't leave for forty-five minutes.

John unzipped a pocket of his blue windbreaker and took out his cell phone. "I'm going to check messages on our home phone."

"All right." I closed my eyes, wondering why he would care about messages when we had hardly been away.

"There's a message from Dr. Heyer asking me to call him."

"Oh no." I held my breath. John pulled the small notebook in which he recorded details of photos he took out of his jacket pocket and set it on his jean-clad thigh, then took a pen from his shirt pocket. Once Heyer was on the line, I watched the pen move across and down the lined page. I could not decipher what John was writing.

"I want to discuss this with Shirley. I'll call you on Monday to tell you where we are." John's voice rang with unusual authority, as though he were speaking to an underling. He put the phone back, zipping his pocket shut. Looking at the notebook in his left hand, he started talking, his tone softer now, more matter-of-fact.

"The MRI shows two masses on the spine and the likelihood of a tumor *in* the brain, not just in the bone. Dr. Heyer wants us to return immediately for follow-up."

"Oh, my darling."

Ignoring the wooden armrest between us, we turned and wrapped our arms around each other. Tears spilled down both our cheeks. I had not seen John in tears since we said goodbye to Sami. His arms were still holding me when he spoke quietly into my ear.

"We have to go to Santa Fe. We have to see Gary and Melinda. If something happens to me, you'll need all the help you can get with the condo." Gary had sold John the condo, and John considered him and his wife good friends.

"But we have to go back. We don't need to see anybody."

"Yes, but we can't go back now. We're too tired."

The next day was Saturday. John arranged for us to fly back Monday morning. He called Gary and Melinda and made a date for lunch on Sunday but didn't say anything about the cancer. I assumed he was waiting to tell them in person.

I called my brother and nephews in Houston.

"We won't be coming after all, not this time. John is seriously ill." My voice was tremulous.

"Aunt Shir, I'm sorry," my nephew Sean said. "We were looking forward to seeing you and meeting John."

I started to cry and hung up.

In Santa Fe, we drove over to see the new owner of the house John had sold on Tano Road. She had mail for him that arrived after the postal service's forwarding time expired. Curly-haired, effervescent Anne and her white woolly dog met us at the front door. Smiling, she handed John a nearly empty cardboard box. On previous visits, we had chatted over a glass or two of wine. Not today. "We'll just drop by to pick up mail," John had told her over the phone.

The three of us were standing in the foyer. I thought we were leaving when John started to tell Anne about his diagnosis, the MRI, and our aborted stay in Santa Fe. I was surprised. She was not a close friend. His voice was calm, without a hint of self-pity.

Anne's brow furrowed; her smile was gone. "John, I'm so sorry. You know Mark survived late-stage cancer of the lung following drastic surgery. Doctors didn't expect him to make it, but he did."

This was unexpected good news. I had met her husband Mark, a good-looking blond from Minnesota who was still working there but joined Anne in Santa Fe during the winter. "I'm crazy about the radiant heat in these floors," he'd said once, greeting us at the front door in his stocking feet. Hearing about Mark gave me hope. If Mark had survived life-threatening cancer, why not John? It could happen to him too. I didn't realize that the miracle had already happened for John: He had lived eighteen years past his diagnosis.

Sunday morning, after breakfast, we lingered at the dining table, coffee cups in hand.

"I think I have a pretty bad sinus infection that hit me during the night." John, ever matter-of-fact, sounded tired.

"Oh no. Why don't you call the oncologist's office and ask him to call in a prescription to a pharmacy in Santa Fe? I'll get the phone number for CVS."

John reached an oncologist covering for Heyer and then called Gary to cancel lunch, saying we would be back out in November. He did not mention the cancer. It was as though by saying we'd be back, we would be.

On a previous visit to Santa Fe, I had insisted that John let me drive the stick-shift Xterra so I would know how to handle it. To me, it seemed silly for him to have to do all the driving. Now I was glad I had learned. I grabbed the keys to pick up the prescription. But that morning, I struggled to put the car in reverse. With my left foot depressing the clutch, I grasped the gear knob with my right hand and slid it to the right and down. Easing up on the clutch, I felt the car inch forward. Damn! It was in fourth gear, not reverse. Again I tried, and failed. I would *never* get out of the garage! I checked the diagram of the gears. I was moving the knob in the right direction, but it wouldn't go in the slot. Beads of perspiration dampened my face. I started to panic. Why couldn't I do it? I didn't recall John ever having this problem. I had to do it! Again and again, I tried, and when I had all but given up, I felt the gear slip into reverse. I sighed, wiping the sweat from my face with the sleeve of my shirt.

At the time, I didn't equate my struggle with our sudden reversal of roles. Until then, John had been in the driver's seat. Now I was the driver. But putting that car in reverse signified more than changing roles. After months of leaning into the wind, going forward without a backward glance, we had come to an abrupt standstill. From now on, we would go backward. Exiting the garage, I drove to the pharmacy and hurried back with the antibiotic. It was lunchtime.

"Would you like a little soup?"

I opened a can of Progresso, filled two glasses with water and carried them to the table along with napkins and a couple of soup spoons. John was already seated, his back to the wall, leaving the seat at the end closest to the stairway for me.

"Do you want some crackers?" I asked, placing a bowl of steaming soup in front of John.

"No. The soup is enough."

A C.D. was playing softly in the background. "Is it Monty Alexander?" He had become one of my favorite jazz musicians after John introduced me to his music.

"Yes."

We were finishing the soup when John put his spoon down and looked at me.

"I have something important to tell you."

"Yes?"

"I want to tell you . . . ." He paused.

John's eyes looked extra blue because of the blue shirt he was wearing.

"Yes, I'm listening, sweetheart."

"I want to tell you . . . ." He paused again. "I want to tell you . . . . I want to tell you . . . ." like an L.P. stuck in a groove.

Oh my god, what was going on? My eyes locked on his. He was frowning in frustration.

"I'm experiencing brain fade."

I had never heard that expression before. "Darling, why don't you try to take a nap?"

"Good idea." John got up from the table and walked into the bedroom. Fully dressed, he lay down on top of the beige duvet and closed his eyes.

I shut the door to the bedroom. After the MRI that went so late and the news from Heyer, he must be exhausted, and the infection wasn't helping. A nap might give the antibiotics a chance to kick in. Mindful of Pat and Philip's impending arrival for a week's stay, I started cleaning the condo. They didn't know the latest, the likelihood of a tumor *in* the brain and others on John's spine. I shuddered.

After a couple of hours, I went in to check on John. He opened his eyes and smiled.

"I think I've finally figured out what I was trying to tell you."

"I can't wait to hear." The nap seemed to have been just the ticket. I sat on the bed and smiled hopefully.

"I want you to know . . . . I want you . . . ." John stopped trying. I would never know what he was trying to tell me.

I touched his forehead with the back of my hand. It was warm. His face felt damp. Not unusual for Waldenstrom's. Days before his Rituxan treatments; John had perspired through many pillowcases. With the treatments no longer working, I surmised that the Waldenstrom's was out of control. We had to get home; we had to get back to Heyer before it was too late. And we would need help.

"Darling, I'm going to request wheelchair service for the flight home. Is that all right with you?"

"Yes."

While John remained in the bedroom, I called American Airlines and upgraded him to the last available first-class seat for our flights the next morning and requested wheelchair assistance in Albuquerque, Dallas, and at Dulles. When I told John what I'd done, he said, "Good."

When he got up to use the bathroom, he looked unsteady. Alarmed, I rang the doorbell of my neighbor, whose husband had died of cancer. "Renate, John is having trouble thinking, talking, and walking. Do you think these are symptoms of his cancer?"

"Shirley, I'm sorry. I don't know. I can take him to an emergency room here in Santa Fe."

"Thank you, but I don't want to do that." The prospect of taking John to an E.R. in Santa Fe where no one knew his condition was out of the question. I didn't think of trying to contact John's former oncologist in Santa Fe, since John had given him up after moving to Reston and finding Heyer. To my mind, Heyer was the one person who knew what was going on. He alone held the key to John's survival. He had asked us to return "immediately." John was the one who had balked, postponing our return by three days. I imagined the cancer invading John's spine and brain, pressing on nerves affecting his mobility and speech. Feverishly, I packed our bags, took them to the front door, and placed my cell phone on a charger in the kitchen.

During the night, John had diarrhea. The next morning, I told the oncologist covering for Heyer and said we had a flight home in a few hours. She said it was up to me whether we came back or sought medical attention in Santa Fe. I didn't ask what was wrong with him. I thought I knew.

After I hung up, I asked John whether he thought he could travel to Reston. "I want to try," he said. As he lay on the bed, I dressed him, in double layers from the waist down, and tied his shoes. "We haven't called a taxi to take us to the shuttle." He was right. I'd forgotten to do that. John took several halting steps into the living room and sat down in the leather chair. After ordering the cab, I called Renate and asked if she had anything John could take to counteract his diarrhea. She brought a cup with a powder she had mixed with water. He took two sips and set it down. I rolled our luggage outside to the curb, and when the taxi arrived, the driver loaded it. John held onto the walls for support and, leaning heavily on the driver, slowly made his way to the cab.

When we arrived at the Hotel Santa Fe to get the shuttle, it was already loaded and ready to leave for the airport in Albuquerque. I asked the driver if he could arrange for John to take the front passenger seat, and the occupant graciously moved into the back of the van. I tipped the driver and settled into a seat behind John.

An hour later, the shuttle pulled up at American Airlines. I was breathing rapidly, my brain ablaze with the jumble of hurdles between there and Dulles. If we were flying United, we'd be on a nonstop, but John preferred American and didn't mind changing planes in Dallas. "The arrival times are better than United's," he said, "and with American, we get priority seating." Peering through the shuttle window, I could see a small crowd in front of the curbside check-in. No wheelchair in sight.

"Please get our luggage and help my husband," I said to the driver before rushing through the crowd to the agent. "I requested wheelchair assistance for my husband."

"We'll page for the chair. It should be here momentarily."

Momentarily? How about immediately?! I glanced over my shoulder, relieved to see John standing behind me, our luggage beside him.

Suddenly, I felt a great weight on my back. It was John, falling forward.

"Help! Somebody help me! My husband is falling!"

Three men nearby kept him from hitting the ground. Just then, someone arrived with a wheelchair, and the good Samaritans sat John down in it. I stared in amazement. He was alert! I thought John had passed out, but his legs must have given way.

"You're all right?"

"Yes."

The young man who arrived with the wheelchair wheeled him into the terminal, where we proceeded to check in.

At our departure gate, knowing time was short, I called Heyer's office. Someone answered just as a flight attendant wheeled John into the jetway.

"Please tell Dr. Heyer that John and I are on our way to Reston. I'll call him back when we land in Dallas. I must speak to him."

On the plane, John was able to stand and, with help, maneuver into a window seat in first class. I had settled into an aisle seat in economy when a flight attendant told me the seat next to him had ended up being vacant, and offered it to me.

"We're coming in from an unusual direction," John said as we made our approach into Dallas.

"Really?" I had no idea. All I could think about was reaching Heyer, and getting us from Dallas to Dulles.

After landing, we waited while the other passengers disembarked. I was grateful to have been able to sit with John and sorry I couldn't upgrade to first class myself for the final leg home, since no other first class seats were available.

I was in the gate area on hold, waiting for Heyer to pick up, when a flight attendant wheeled John into the jetway.

"Shirley, this is Dr. Heyer."

"Dr. Heyer, yesterday John had a problem articulating his thoughts; last night, he experienced diarrhea, and this morning, he had difficulty walking."

"He needs immediate medical attention."

"But they've already wheeled him onto the plane, and we both want to be in Reston."

"In that case, as soon as you land at Dulles, go directly to the emergency room and ask the E.R. doctor to call me."

Whew! I hung up, relieved to have reached the doctor, and entered the jetway, thinking I might be the last to board. We were almost home! Rounding the galley corner, I looked down the aisle expecting to see seats filled with impatient-looking people. My jaw dropped. The plane was empty except for John, who was seated in a narrow wheelchair in the aisle, with two small men hovering nearby. As I tried to figure out what was happening, I saw that they were struggling to lift John from the wheelchair up over the armrest into his first class seat. Their faces were wet with perspiration. I could feel their frustration.

Behind me, a loud, strident voice barked, "Lady, I've got to load this plane, and as long as your husband is in the aisle, I can't!"

"Can you stand?" I asked John.

He shook his head no.

I looked at the two men. "Let's try to stand him up, then slide him into the seat." I counted aloud—One, Two, Three—and with our concerted effort, John was moved into the aisle seat. The seeming victory, however, was short-lived. I felt I had to tell the head flight attendant that if someone sat in the window seat, John would not be able to stand up to let the person out or back in.

"Lady, I suggest you and your husband take the next flight." His exasperation was undisguised.

"No! We have to go to Dulles. We're not getting off this plane!" I looked at the two men who had helped me move John and said, "We have to move him into the window seat." Because the armrest between seats was not retractable, the challenge was obvious. The three of us— one man leaning over the back of the seat to lift John under his arms from behind, and the other and I lifting his legs—got him over the armrest and into the window seat. Clearing the aisle, I left John and went to my seat.

Midway through the flight, I walked up to first class and made eye contact with John, who looked at me and smiled. He was holding a plastic cup of water. Great! He was alert. My shoulders relaxed. I returned to my seat. We were almost home! We would take a cab from the airport to the hospital. Our condo was along the way; I could ask the driver to stop to drop off our luggage.

"In preparation for landing, put your tray tables up and return your seat backs to their upright and locked position." The flight attendant made a final sweep down the aisle, picking up newspapers and plastic cups.

I sat upright, my body tense in anticipation of the landing. When we touched down, I felt a wave of relief. Despite countless obstacles, we had made it. We were home.

Emergency

THE PLANE WAS NEARLY EMPTY WHEN I LEFT MY SEAT TO WAIT with John for the wheelchair. He looked different. He was not wearing his glasses.

"Where are your glasses, sweetheart?"

My question didn't seem to register.

"I don't know where my husband's glasses are," I told a flight attendant.

"I don't remember seeing him with glasses."

"He was wearing glasses when we boarded." I checked the floor near his seat, and there they were. I put them in my purse.

"With any luck at all, our bags will be in baggage claim by the time we get there," I said to the wheelchair attendant on our shuttle ride to the main terminal. A large man, he had lifted John into the narrow aisle wheelchair alone and transferred him to a regular wheelchair before entering the jetway.

We were home, but we had to keep moving. John had not said a word since leaving the plane.

"Wait here while I get our bags." I left the attendant with John in the open corridor a few feet from the baggage carousel. Snaking through the waiting throng, I planted myself next to the still-quiet carousel, ready to spring. Within minutes of starting up, it disgorged both of our bags. Whew! "If we hurry, we can get to a taxi ahead of the crowd."

"We'll follow you," the attendant said.

Rolling the bags behind me, I hurried down the familiar ramp to the taxi waiting area. The glass door was open. No one was waiting. I smiled, relieved to see a dispatcher in his red jacket walking toward me.

"Where to?"

"Reston. My husband's behind me in the wheelchair."

"Here's your cab." He motioned toward a gray sedan idling at the curb and handed me the usual brochure about Dulles taxi service.

"Thank you." What luck! We got our bags straightaway and now a cab. We were almost to Reston! While the driver lifted our bags into the trunk, I stepped aside and waited, expecting him to help John into the back seat.

"Lady, I can't take your husband anywhere." The cabbie's voice was gruff, his manner threatening.

"What do you mean?" I stared at his stubble-bearded face. How could he not take us?

"Your husband can't stand up, he can't walk—you need an ambulance."

"Ambulance? We need an ambulance? No, just take us to Reston!"

"Lady, I told you. I'm not taking you anywhere." In two swift movements, the cabbie lifted our bags from his trunk and dropped them on the curb.

It was dark. I couldn't see John's face. I didn't know what to do. Angry and confused, I blinked back tears of frustration.

"Miss, let me call Airport Fire and Rescue." The voice was kind.

"All right. Thank you."

I stood as if in a trance. I didn't know who had offered to make the call—maybe the taxi dispatcher—but I knew Airport Fire and Rescue was a good thing. These were the people with all the gear who showed up at middle school career fairs. They were the most popular, telling kids about the job of a fireman or an emergency medical technician, and letting the students try on their heavy boots. Firefighters saved people's lives.

A distant siren jolted me to attention. It got louder and louder. I looked to my left, blinded by bright lights approaching fast. Sound filled the air. An ambulance pulled to a stop in front of me and the siren cut off, the sudden silence deafening.

Transfixed, I watched three men and a woman jump from the back. Without missing a beat, they lifted John out of the wheelchair onto a portable bed and wheeled him toward the back of the ambulance. They were running.

"Get in the front, Miss, and wait there for me." The man who spoke was wearing a dark blue uniform. He held open the door of the ambulance cab.

"All right." I climbed up onto the high seat. I heard the door close. I turned, trying to see what was going on behind me, but the back window was too small. I couldn't see John. I could only glimpse parts of people moving and standing, presumably over him.

The door on the driver's side opened. The man in blue got in and closed the door. He turned toward me.

"What happened?" His voice registered concern.

"I'm not sure. Since yesterday afternoon, my husband's had difficulty talking and walking. He has cancer, and I think it's out of control. His doctor, when I talked with him from Dallas, said to go directly from here to E.R. in Reston."

"Your husband is very dehydrated; we've got him on an IV. We want to stabilize him for a few minutes before we take him to E.R. Once he gets some fluids in him, he should be feeling a whole lot better. Every airport has fire and rescue teams. They could have helped you in Dallas."

And then it hit me. The taxi driver had been right. John needed an ambulance. And I had imagined stopping at the condo with our luggage. What had I been thinking? I hoped John would feel better, but I was doubtful. My sense that his cancer was exploding out of control overrode every other feeling I had about his condition. Nonetheless, I was grateful to this man and his crew for trying to help John, for coming to our rescue. He made me feel proud of having been associated with the Airports Authority.

"I used to work for the Airports Authority."

"Oh, what's your name?"

"Shirley Nagelschmidt."

"Really? I know who you are! You were a very important person at the Authority. We all used to get emails from you when you were recruiting volunteers for the schools."

I was flattered that he remembered me. My life with the Airports Authority seemed a very long time ago. And yet it was less than a year since I had retired.

"I'm going to check on things in back, and then we'll leave."

I waited a long time before the ambulance pulled away from the terminal. Siren blaring, it speeded toward Reston, passed our condo, and screeched into the E.R. entrance.

John was wheeled straight into the treatment area, no questions asked. I hurried after him.

"Can you please call Dr. Heyer?" I asked a dark-haired woman at the nurses' station.

"Yes, I can."

"Do you have his number?"

"Yes, I have it right here."

"Please tell him that John Bessey is in E.R. He asked to be called the minute we arrived."

I turned toward the room where John had been taken. The striped curtain over the entrance was pulled open. I couldn't see him. I stepped in, threading my way through the crowd in white coats, and stood against the far wall. Nurses hovered over John, taking vital signs. One of them withdrew blood from his arm and hurried off. John looked pale. His eyes were closed. I couldn't tell if he was conscious or unconscious.

"Is your husband allergic to any medications?" a nurse asked.

"Yes, there's one—but I don't know what it is, and I can't describe his reaction." John hadn't told me, and I'd never seen what happened. Why hadn't he prepared me for this so I could have been some help?

The crowd of bodies kept moving around John's bed. Monitors sounded; machines blinked green. The room felt too small. Maybe I shouldn't be there. I'd stay out of the way, but I didn't want to be too far away. What if someone needed me? What if John needed me? Wondering who was in charge, I felt a hand on my arm and looked up into the face of a dark-haired, dark-eyed man. He was not wearing a lab coat, but the nameplate on his white shirt read: Emergency Room Physician. With a firm hold on my arm, he ushered me into an empty curtained area.

"Does your husband have DNR?"

I blinked, trying to comprehend. "What is DNR?" I thought he was asking about a disease. I'd heard the acronym many times and knew what it meant, but that night, I could not relate it to John.

"Do Not Resuscitate."

Fireworks exploded in my brain. "Why are you asking me this!"

"Your husband is very ill with a rampant infection. His heart rate is 178. If we can't get it down, he may not survive the night." The doctor's voice was calm.

"You've got to help him; you've got to save him!" Staring at these dark eyes staring back, I could hear myself screaming.

"Then you want us to do everything we can to keep him alive?"

"Yes!" In my head, I was still screaming. Oh my god, it's *not* the cancer! I was wrong, so terribly wrong! *John won't die of cancer. He'll die of infection.* That's what the wife of John's best friend had said to me. She, who knew John for years, had given his cancer short shrift, which I found reassuring. But I hadn't given her other words much, if any, thought. Now they came roaring back at me.

The doctor disappeared, leaving me aghast. Frantic, I groped for the phone and book of numbers in the bottom of my purse. I looked at my watch: 10 p.m. It was late, but I had to make the call. Trembling, I punched in the New York number. Gay had worked closely with doctors as an administrator at UCLA Medical Center and Cedars-Sinai in Los Angeles. She was wise, and I trusted her judgment. She was the closest thing I had to a mother.

"Gay, I apologize for calling so late. I'm at Reston Hospital. John's in the emergency room. He has a raging infection. The E.R. doctor just told me he could die if they can't get his heart rate down!" Gripping the phone like a lifeline, I stopped talking.

"Sweetheart, I'm so sorry."

Her tone was soothing. I stopped trembling. "I don't know what to do. I'm so scared. I thought it was the cancer."

"You need to talk with a doctor you trust, and listen well."

"That would be Dr. Heyer."

"Whoever it is, you've got to talk with him right away."

Minutes later, Heyer walked in. I rushed to greet him. "Thank you for coming."

"Shirley, I need to see what the tests show."

For several minutes, he stood at the nurses' station looking at printouts of blood tests. This was the man we had come all the way from Santa Fe for—the doctor John liked, the doctor I trusted. "You see why I like him," John had said the first time I accompanied him to an appointment. He and Heyer had bantered back and forth about the University of Michigan football team, talking little about John's condition except to predict his need for Rituxan based on the increasing IgM protein numbers. They seemed to be on the same wavelength. "John is the first rocket scientist I've ever met," Heyer had said to me, beaming. It was a relationship based on mutual admiration.

With printouts still in hand, Heyer walked toward me. He was frowning. Thick, short, salt-and-pepper hair framed his youthful face.

"I'd planned to have a serious talk with you and John after you came back from Santa Fe, because the treatment ahead for John, in view of the masses, would be fairly formidable to endure."

Why was he talking about the cancer treatment? Was he trying to cushion the blow of the infection? "The E.R. doctor told me it's an infection, not the cancer."

"Yes, and that's what they're treating. If he survives the infection, then we'll deal with the cancer. Are we in agreement that the infection should be treated to the hilt?"

"Absolutely."

"I'll talk with the E.R. doctor. For the moment, John's cancer is on a back burner." Heyer walked toward John's room.

I was still standing at the nurses' station when the E.R. doctor approached.

"We're calling in a pulmonologist. Where will you be?"

"Here. I'll be here, in the waiting area."

I was sitting alone in the dimly lit waiting room when the pulmonologist walked in from E.R.. He was slender and dark-haired. Beady brown eyes punctuated his long narrow face. Without introducing himself, he started speaking. "Mrs. Bessey, your husband is in septic shock. His white blood count is twenty-one thousand when normal is seven thousand. The infection could be from the brain. I don't think it's from the lungs. He doesn't appear to have pneumonia. We're giving him everything we can, but your husband's heart rate is still too high. I would say his chances are fifty-fifty. He should have been treated in Santa Fe or Dallas."

My mouth was dry. I started to speak, but no words came out. I nodded my understanding. The doctor turned and disappeared through the double doors. His matter-of-fact words had laid the blame squarely on me. John's life was hanging in the balance because *I* said no to Renate, because *I* thought it was the cancer and we had to get back to Heyer. We could have returned on Saturday. Why had John ignored Heyer's advice? Was it during our tearful embrace at the airport? Had he shifted his focus from himself to me as his survivor and decided he needed to do whatever he could to help me? Is that what the dying do? Choose to look after their loved ones more than themselves? And why did I allow it? Why didn't I insist we leave? If we had returned Saturday, would it have made a difference? Would John have lived longer?

Could we have kept the dam from breaking?

"We're moving your husband upstairs to the Intensive Care Unit," the nurse said. "You should go home and try to get some sleep." It was close to midnight.

Sleep? What if John dies? Shouldn't I be here? She was telling me no, that it would be better to be at home. I should go there. But where was our luggage?

Back at the E.R., it was semi-dark and quiet, the crowd in white coats nowhere to be seen. The earlier drama seemed never to have happened. Our two bags were standing against a wall in the empty curtained room. The fire and rescue crew must have brought them in. In the silence I heard footsteps approaching.

"We just brought in another patient and wanted to check on John. How's he doing?" It was the woman from the rescue crew.

"They've taken him to ICU. He has a raging infection. The doctor told me his chances of surviving are fifty-fifty."

"I'm sorry. Is there anything we can do for *you?*" She placed a hand on my shoulder.

"Could you give me a ride home?"

"Sure."

It was nearly 1 a.m. when the ambulance, its siren now silent, delivered me to the building. I was home. I was home without John.

Walking into the condo, I flicked on the lights. It looked unchanged. I was surprised. I felt I had been gone for weeks, not a mere four days. I would call Dick in the morning. I had to get some sleep. The phone could not ring! If it rang, it would be the hospital, and I was not prepared for that.

The phone did not ring.

The next day, Dick drove up from Raleigh, arriving late.

The following afternoon, John, though heavily sedated, was able to answer Dick's questions by nodding yes and no.

"Did you grow up in Laramie?"

Yes.

"Did you go to graduate school in California?"

No.

"Is George Bush president of the United States?"

Yes.

"Are you married to Shirley?"

Yes.

I started feeling hopeful.

After Dick left, I sent a long email to friends. It helped me in some way make sense of the continuing drama which had caught me so shockingly unaware and unprepared.

> John is critical but stable with signs of gradual improvement. It'll be 2–3 days before we know which direction this is going, but the signs are encouraging. His heart rate is down to 70, and his breathing is assisted with some but not a lot of oxygen. He responds by nodding his head yes or no. Dick asked him some fairly complicated questions, and his responses were appropriate, so we know he's mentally right in there.

> When we mentioned Bush and Cheney his BP went up, so we decided to curb talk of politics. Under heavy sedation, he opened his eyes halfway and recognized each of us last night and this a.m. . . . John's ability to fight infection is impaired by the Waldenstrom's, which suppresses his immune system. Also not helping is the absence of his spleen, which was removed 18 years ago. Doctors expect John to be in the hospital for another 10 days. No one, apart from immediate family, is allowed to see him. . . . I'm utterly shattered. At the same time, I'm hopeful, in large part because John looks so much better even with all the tubes and because the medical staff—from doctors to ICU RNs— seem to be on top of the situation. . . . I'm so thankful we made it back to Reston, not only because we're close to A-one medical care but also, and perhaps especially, because we have wonderful, supportive friends nearby.

A week after John's admission to the ICU, I stepped into his room to find him sitting up in bed. The large ventilator tube that had carried oxygen down his throat into his lungs was gone; he was breathing on his own.

"Oh my darling!" Gasping, I walked to the foot of the bed and sat down. After catching my breath, I stood up and sat down again beside John. Leaning over, I kissed him lightly on the lips and sat back, my eyes locked on his.

"Have I ever told you how beautiful you are? You're a joy to look at." John could speak—although he sounded an octave or two lower than usual. He had never said those words to me before.

"You made it, darling. You survived!"

"I did it for you, because of you, for us."

My eyes welled up. "Thank you" tears of relief and joy spilled down my cheeks. "How do you feel?"

"My throat feels raw." He kept looking at me with those blue eyes I so loved and had not seen in such a long time. "I probably need a haircut." He did. In fact, he'd needed one before we went to Santa Fe. The nurses had combed his hair straight back.

"You have a new do, and it's not at all bad."

"Dr. Heyer stopped by."

"Oh?" I hadn't seen him since that night in the E.R.

"He said it's going to be a long haul."

"Well, I think we're both up for it." After surviving the infection, surely John could survive anything. "How much do you remember, sweetheart? *What* do you remember?"

"I remember getting on the plane in Albuquerque and the plane's unusual approach into Dallas. I have no memory of anything else after that up until a couple of days ago."

"Do you remember seeing Dick and me standing over you?"

"No, but I was aware of your presence."

"There seem to be fewer pieces of equipment around your bed than there were yesterday. Maybe it's just the absence of the ventilator."

"I don't know. They told me I'm off the BP meds." He'd been started on the three meds to keep his blood pressure up when he was taken to the ICU.

When I took my eyes off John's face, I noticed his hands and arms. They looked like balloons filled to bursting.

"They're swollen because of the IV infusions," the nurse said when I asked. "The swelling will diminish as fluids are reabsorbed by his body."

Before I arrived the next day, John was given a swallowing test, which he failed. He would have to settle for an occasional ice chip in lieu of water and continue to be tube-fed through a nostril. Although the tube was slender, I thought it must be annoying. John didn't complain. It must have been far easier to tolerate than the ventilator, which he had tried to remove, even under heavy sedation, before the nurses restrained his hands.

The day John failed the swallowing test, he got out of bed and stood up with the help of a physical therapist who advised him to start bending his knees, fingers, and arms in bed to exercise his joints. Once, when I thought he wanted to hold my hand, he didn't. He was simply intent on doing the exercises.

The next day, a speech therapist stopped by but decided to postpone a lengthy visit. John was quieter than the previous day and appeared tired. He was still on a lot of antibiotics to fight the pneumococcus bacteria rampaging through his body. The doctors were still debating the source of the infection: The infectious disease specialists thought it was the sinuses; the pulmonologists now thought the lungs.

Two days after saying goodbye to the ventilator, John was transferred to a private room on another floor. The walls were painted off-white and decorated with large pastel prints. A large window was next to the bed—not much of a view but a lot of natural light. On one wall was a TV controlled by a patient-held remote. It was quiet in the room.

I sat in a comfortable chair beside the bed. "Darling, isn't it wonderful to be out of ICU and in your own private room?"

John smiled ruefully. He was looking at the wall calendar. "I've been in bed for more than a week, and I'm utterly exhausted."

That afternoon, Dick returned for a quick visit. At John's bedside, Heyer showed the three of us the MRIs of John's brain, pointing out the large mass and a couple of smaller lesions.

"I would recommend a biopsy of the obvious tumor as soon as possible," he said. "We need to find out exactly what it is to determine treatment options." Heyer looked at John, who didn't hesitate: "Do it."

Returning alone that evening, I pulled a chair up to the bed.

"I'm in a real fight." John paused for a moment. "I might conquer this thing after all."

"I feel confident you will, darling." Hearing his optimism, I believed he could and would prevail. He had faced terrible odds in the past and survived. Why not again? Still elated by how he had beaten the infection, I could hardly process the fact that the battle against the cancer had not yet begun. Heyer had said the treatment would be "fairly formidable to endure," but John was a survivor. He had proven it time and again. I was determined that he would make it. He simply had to. I could not imagine living without him.

Another MRI of his skull was taken for the neurosurgeon who would perform the biopsy.

"How did it go?" the nurse asked when John was returned to his room.

"There was nothing there," he said, winking at me.

Four days after John left the ICU, I emailed an update to friends:

> The antibiotics continue. And although he's still being tube-fed, John is hoping to pass the swallowing test today so that, at long last, he can drink water and begin to experience the texture and taste of real food. Physical and occupational therapists are teaching John and me a variety of movements to strengthen his arms, hands, and legs. He's pushing himself to do it all and today managed to stand up and walk a few steps, aided by a walker, to a chair where he succeeded in sitting for 30 minutes. His speech, affected by the ventilator tube in his throat, improves each day, thanks to oral exercises recommended by the speech therapist, which I lead John through at least twice a day.
>
> John is tremendously strong-willed. He is a big-picture kind of guy who, at the same time, is well aware of the trees in any forest. When I first met John, he told me that shortly after he was diagnosed with Waldenstrom's, he made a conscious decision to be positive. He felt strongly that this attitude had played a role in his ability to work effectively at TRW and Northrop Grumman where he was highly regarded, despite some very real medical hurdles. I feel compelled to take a page from John's book and think we must hope for the best, taking each day as it comes and making the most of it.

Now that the worst was over, I developed a routine. I would arrive at the hospital in the morning, hoping not to miss the doctors on their rounds. Late in the afternoon, I'd return home to check phone messages and grab a bite to eat before returning to the hospital in the evening. Old friends who lived in my condo building would leave simple messages under my door: "If you'd like some wine and dinner, just come on down." And more often than not, I would get on the elevator and make my way to their condo. It was wonderful not to have to drive anywhere for the solace of company with sympathetic friends.

When John complained of being "bored," I tried to relieve the feeling, as well as my anxiety, by doing crossword puzzles together. I would give him the clues, and he would give me the answers. When he lost interest in that, I started reading snippets of news aloud from the *Washington Post* and *New York Times*. More often than not, John would offer an insightful one- or two-word commentary that made me laugh, especially on political topics.

Even though John was out of the ICU, I was in a state of unrelieved agitation. No matter what time I went to bed, I slept fitfully. Exhausted by fear and hope, I was still reverberating from the shock of John's near-death and my feelings of guilt. After hearing the pulmonologist say he should have received medical attention in Santa Fe or Dallas, I wasn't sure I could have lived with myself if he had died.

Now, although he was still on intravenous antibiotics twenty-four hours a day, treatment of the cancer was taking center stage. Before a biopsy could be taken, John's system had to be free of infection. The clock was ticking. I had seen the big tumor and other lesions in the MRIs of his brain. The sooner treatment could start, the better. But would John be able to withstand it? He was still very weak.

The only appointments I didn't cancel were the weekly sessions with my therapist, Barbara. While we had once discussed my reactions to John's analytical take on life—at times jarringly different from mine—I no longer cared about petty relationship issues. The stakes had changed. It was a whole new conversation.

"John has to have a biopsy that can't happen until he's off the antibiotics. The waiting is excruciating. I feel as though I'm just holding my breath."

"Has anyone suggested how much longer it might be?"

"No. I don't think anyone knows. He's so weak. He needs real food to build his strength, but he hasn't passed the swallowing test. He's still got that damned feeding tube. And despite it all, he's cheerful. I can barely keep it together, and he's saying witty things that make me laugh. I do the speech exercises with him three or four times a day, but that doesn't seem to help the swallowing."

"Are you sleeping?"

"Not well. And even when I do, I wake up feeling agitated and exhausted. I'm trying to be upbeat for John but feel I'm barely holding on."

"Would you consider taking something to help you sleep?"

"I've never liked the idea of taking meds."

"It's important you get a good night's sleep. I'm sure Dr. Hong would prescribe something to help you sleep if you asked. Maybe a little Ambien."

"All right. I'll call him today." Chun Hong was my internist. His office was in a building across from Barbara's.

"I still can't bear the sound of a ringing phone, and I don't want to talk with anyone unless it's face-to-face. That's why I'm emailing updates, hoping no one will call. When Joe died, the phone rang incessantly, even the messages beeped until I thought I would go out of my mind."

"Does emailing help you?"

"I think so. It gives me a chance to focus. I like receiving responses. They're comforting, and some I can share with John."

The only new appointments I made were with a massage therapist. Soon after John was out of the ICU, I scheduled an hour and a half hot stones massage at the spa. I told the massage therapist how fractured I was feeling, and what he did I will long remember. As I lay on my back, he placed a small flat hot stone on my forehead and left it there. The sensation of heat radiating across my forehead and scalp was at once relaxing and calming. That night, for the first time in many days, I slept soundly.

On Friday morning, four days after John's move to a private room, Dr. Mudit Sharma, the neurosurgeon, called me at home.

"I talked with John a few minutes ago and wanted to talk with you. Two of the lesions in John's brain are on the skull bone, but the third, the large one, is growing in the brain and must be removed."

"This will be the biopsy?"

"Yes. I'll make a two-inch incision across John's scalp and … of course, it's brain surgery and there are always risks, such as stroke."

"When will you perform the surgery?"

"Next week when I believe the pneumococcus will be out of John's system and his strength sufficient to withstand sedation and another intubation."

Another intubation? My heart sank. "How long will the surgery last?"

"Two hours."

"Will he be back in ICU?"

"Yes, at least overnight."

A pulmonologist who had not seen John since he was "critical" stopped by and told him how much better he looked than when she first saw him. She said the pneumococcus had come from outside the body, and can take hold in a receptive host within twenty-four hours of exposure. I remembered being airborne on that Friday en route to Albuquerque with a man seated two rows behind us sneezing repeatedly and openly; by early Sunday morning, John was going downhill.

The following Wednesday, two weeks and two days after he was rushed to the E.R., the antibiotics were stopped and both the feeding tube and the Foley catheter were removed. The day before, the feeding tube in John's nostril had come out prematurely. To reinsert it, the nurse directed John to swallow repeatedly until the tube reached his stomach. It was an action that helped strengthen his throat muscles and ready him for real food. John said that even puréed bananas—his likely first meal—sounded good.

Friends were sending email messages, stories, and jokes that I would print out and read to John. A couple of people sent sudoku books to augment his crossword puzzles. At first, John thought the sudoku would be too difficult for him now, but he sailed through a couple of them one afternoon, which made him feel good. One baffling message arrived with a lovely floral arrangement delivered to John's room: "John, we need help with binary logistic regression. Get well soon. Hadley"

"Do you have any idea what this means?" I asked.

"Yes, I specialized in it." John winked.

I suspected we could have been married thirty years without my ever knowing John was a binary logistic regression specialist. It was a type of statistical analysis, he told me. With John, one had to ask the right question.

A couple of days later, Hadley forwarded a real problem from another colleague in a two-page email asking John for help. I printed it out and gave it to him

"I think someone is making this much more complicated than it needs to be," he said after a quick read. "I'll dictate a response for you to email back to Hadley." He ended it with, "Shame on you, taking advantage of some poor sod in the hospital. Where's my contract you promised me? (wink, wink)"

"I agree with your reasoning and the Poisson distribution and have forwarded it to the stakeholder," Hadley responded. "Thank you."

I didn't have the remotest idea what Hadley and John were discussing, but I was thrilled to see John mentally engaged.

The neurosurgeon scheduled surgery for Friday of that third week of John's hospitalization, and said he expected John to be in the hospital another week afterward. Heyer said he would have to see the pathology report, which would probably take a week after the surgery to prepare, before he could discuss treatment options.

John, who had been stoical throughout his ordeal, commented on how patient the nurses and technicians were with him. "After I get back home, I want to present the hospital staff with one of my photo prints."

"That's a lovely idea, sweetheart." I wondered which one he'd select.

A couple of days before his surgery, I asked him how he felt about it.

"I have some feeling of trepidation." John's voice was his usual calm.

"Could you be more explicit?"

"It's not rocket science. It's brain surgery, and I'm scared shitless!"

Treatment

TALKING WITH MY FRIEND KATHY IN THE HOSPITAL WAITING room, I stopped in mid-sentence. "It's Dr. Sharma." Still in green scrubs, he was walking toward me, his head and shoulders leading. He was an imposing man, tall and on the husky side, with straight black eyebrows above almond-shaped brown eyes. *He and his colleague are meticulous, and that's what you want in a neurosurgeon.* Heyer's words flashed through my mind.

I stood up, trying to read his face. He was not smiling.

"It went well. The tumor was pushing against the membrane covering the brain, but it had not penetrated the dura into the brain, and we were able to remove it. All of it."

"Thank God."

"Because the bone over the tumor was diseased, I removed it too and replaced it with a titanium plate covered by something flesh-colored."

"Does it resemble the top of your head?"

"Yes but not as pretty." He grinned. Sharma's well-shaped head was bald.

It was a while before I learned that the "flesh-colored" covering was *under* the scalp and that John would not be bald.

"The lesions in the skull bone will be treated with radiation. John has been taken to ICU. I would come back in a few hours."

That evening, I took the elevator down to Kathy and Jack's where the three of us drank a celebratory toast to John before dinner. Later, I drove back to the hospital, hoping he would be awake.

John was sitting up in bed in a red gown, his head above the hairline wrapped in white. No ventilator!

I kissed him softly on the lips. "Darling, you look good, rather regal. How do you feel?"

"All right except for a headache across my forehead. Whatever they gave me for it isn't working."

I stepped away to tell a nurse, then shared Sharma's report and told him I had celebrated the good news with Kathy and Jack.

When I said goodnight, John looked at me and smiled. "The headache is almost gone. Say hi to Jack and Kathy for me, and thank Kathy for waiting with you during the surgery."

Driving home that night, I felt more hopeful than I had in a long time. John was alert, upbeat. He had prevailed over the infection, and now in the battle against the cancer, the most threatening brain tumor was history. With so much behind him, he simply had to make it. With all my heart, I wanted him to live.

John was back in a regular hospital room when Sharma appeared again. Wearing a dark blue suit, gold cuff links, and Italian-made loafers, he looked as though he had stepped from the pages of *GQ* magazine. Standing at the bedside, he leaned toward John.

"How are you feeling?"

"Good."

"Dr. Sharma, would it be possible for me to see the incision?" I asked.

"Yes, of course." With notable care, his long, tapered fingers unwrapped the gauze bandage from around John's head.

"Oh my." The incision, as predicted, followed John's hairline, but was far more than two inches long; it appeared to be closer to eight. John's beautiful head of hair was still intact except for a one-inch band along the hairline, which had been shaved down to his scalp.

That afternoon, John's college roommate Ron called from California. "What am I doing?" John laughed after I gave him the phone. "I have an oxygen tank here, a small tank with about two hundred PSI pressure. I'm using the hospital's white board and a felt-tipped pen to figure out the number of oxygen molecules in the tank. I want to determine whether there are enough molecules there to cover the entire globe one molecule deep."

The week after the craniotomy brought confusing highs and lows. Early in the week, John was deemed an ideal candidate for intensive P.T. at a major inpatient rehab center in Arlington, Virginia. Wonderful, I thought. This meant he could regain his strength before coming home. But no sooner had the hospital social worker gotten the needed approvals for his discharge to Arlington than John developed an on-again, off-again fever that put everything on hold. Ruling out infection as the source, doctors concluded that John might have what is known as "tumor fever."

About the same time, Heyer received the pathology report. I was sitting at John's bedside, in front of the window, when he walked in. Standing on the other side of the bed, he glanced at the report and looked at John. "The pathology identifies the malignancy as a low-grade lymphoma. This is consistent with Waldenstrom's and far better than a high-grade lymphoma, which by definition is an aggressive cancer." He paused. "What I want to do is start radiation therapy right away, here at Reston Hospital."

"Does this mean John won't be going to Arlington for physical therapy?"

"Yes. Radiation will be daily Monday through Friday for five weeks. It will target the other tumors that were left after Dr. Sharma got the big one, and the two lesions on the spine. At the conclusion, an MRI will show us to what extent the tumors have shrunk. Shrinkage is the goal. After the radiation treatment, chemotherapy will follow, but the recipe and delivery—drip or injection into the spinal fluid—we've yet to determine."

Heyer walked over to my side of the bed where I was now standing and looked me in the eye. "We don't want to delay and then later regret that we didn't start earlier." His voice was quiet. I didn't think John heard him.

I nodded my understanding. While disappointed that John could not start the intensive physical therapy now, I was as eager as Heyer to begin the assault against the remaining tumors.

When I returned that evening, John spoke before I could sit down. "I now realize that the halcyon days of Rituxan are over, and what lies ahead are many bridges to cross." He looked wistful.

Pulling up a chair, I reached for his hand. "Thank goodness, the cancer is not aggressive."

"Yes." He squeezed my fingers.

The goal now, as it had been since he was first diagnosed with cancer, was to contain the growth and spread of malignant cells so he could enjoy life as long as possible. With the successful removal of the large brain tumor and the pathologist's defining John's cancer as nonaggressive, I, at least, was hopeful.

The next morning before I arrived, a mold was made of John's face.

"Why?" I asked him.

"It's part of the prep for radiation." He had spent more than an hour with an oncology radiologist. "She told me it was a privilege to meet a patient who understood the statistical basis for what was being done." John didn't tell me the nitty-gritty, that he would wear the mold during the radiation treatments to assure that his head was in the same position each time. He also did not tell me that the radiologist had ordered more MRIs to assure precise targeting.

"Did she mention any side effects?"

"Yes. Nausea, although she said it's usually controllable."

"That's it?"

"I'll lose my hair." John was not bothered by this at all. "I told the doctor I'd already started growing a mustache and goatee. I'll wear a bandana over my head and impersonate Lyle Alzado."

"*Who* is Lyle Alzado?"

"A defensive tackle for the Oakland Raiders in the mid-'70s who developed cancer in his forties. He claimed it was because of all the steroids he'd been on to build up his body. Of course, Lyle was a big guy. I'll be Lyle as a ninety-nine-pound weakling!"

John was in high spirits; in fact, the nurses on the floor commented on his "good attitude."

The oncology radiologist inquired whether radiation centers elsewhere had experience treating a patient with Waldenstrom's. A radiologist in San Francisco, ninety-two and still practicing, told her he'd treated a woman who had Waldenstrom's years earlier with protocols he developed using half the usual radiation dosage and half the usual number of days, and that "the tumors melted away." The patient, treated six years ago, was now ninety years old. After reading his response, the doctor altered the protocol for treating John.

Little more than a week after the craniotomy and still on IVs, John began radiation therapy. The next morning, he greeted me with an ear-to-ear smile.

"Hi, sweetheart." I kissed him and pulled up a chair.

"We should check out trips to the Galapagos. I figure by October, about a year from now, I should be recovered from all the treatments."

My jaw dropped. A trip to the Galapagos was one of my dreams. We had planned—before the bump—to go together in the spring of 2009. It was now October 2007. "Darling, what a great idea!" I sputtered after catching my breath. "I'm pretty sure I have an Abercrombie & Kent brochure on the Galapagos at home. I'll find it and bring it in." John's optimism was contagious. My spirits soared.

The next morning, we were reviewing the A&K Galapagos trip when Heyer arrived.

"How are you feeling, John?"

"We're talking about going to the Galapagos next October."

Heyer's eyes opened wide. "Usually, patients ask me what kind of pain to expect, and here you're asking me about going to the Galapagos!" He looked thoughtful. "If I were you, I'd go ahead and make the reservations but not pay the whole tariff without the possibility of a refund. We don't know yet whether you've hit a bump in the road or a Mack truck."

"Let's call A&K," I said after Heyer left. If John was testing my faith in his recovery, I was determined to pass.

"Yes."

I pulled the phone from my purse and dialed. Waiting for someone to pick up, I looked at him.

"Reserve the deluxe suite." His eyes were sparkling.

With John as my witness, I booked the deluxe suite on a small ship to the Galapagos, departing October 30, 2008.

"It's good to have a target," he said after I hung up. Soon he started reminding me how many days until our departure.

That week, Heyer and other members of John's medical team discussed his case in a day-long conference.

"I told the group about the positive attitude of the patient and his wife who had asked my permission to book a trip to the Galapagos." Heyer laughed. "I should tell you the consensus of the conference attendees was that John's current and planned treatment made sense."

After I was told that the hospital social worker wanted to see me, I went to her office on the same floor as John's room. She was wearing a white lab coat. Curly gray hair framed her pale, bespectacled face. I had not talked with her since the abortive arrangements for John's transfer to Arlington.

"Your husband is probably going to be discharged at the end of the week." She was matter-of-fact.

I felt my stomach start to churn. "He's still very weak."

"He's getting physical therapy, and once he's off the IVs, there will be no medical reason for him to be here."

"I have to tell you, I can't care for John at home, not until he's stronger. I don't know how to take care of someone who's ill. I hope he can be discharged to a skilled-care facility where he can receive physical therapy and be cared for by people who know what they're doing."

"I understand. I have a list here of insurance-approved skilled-care facilities."

Whew! I sensed we were on the same wavelength.

"There's one in Reston. It sometimes helps the admissions there if a family member visits to pave the way."

My shoulders tensed. I knew the one she was talking about. It was where Joe had died. Although he had been discharged to it after surgery to replace his aortic valve, I had not visited to pave the way. "That's where my first husband died. I hate to go back there."

"It's up to you. If that's where you want John to be, I would advise you to meet with the director."

I walked back to John's room and told him about the likelihood of his being discharged in a few days. "Darling, I don't think I can take care of you at home, not yet."

John agreed. "I want to be stronger than I am now before I go home."

"I'll check out the skilled-care facility here in Reston. It's across the street, very convenient for your radiation appointments." I would just have to steel myself against the memories of Joe.

That afternoon, I dropped by the Reston facility, but the director was out. Early the next morning, she told me there would be no "male beds" for at least two weeks. The social worker gave me a list of facilities outside Reston and encouraged me to check them out.

The unexpected developments over the past few days, coupled with the new pressure of finding a place for John, were taking a toll. I was increasingly tired. I had stopped taking Ambien because, although it did help me sleep, I felt drugged when I woke up. Knowing I had to keep going, I set out to visit the next-nearest facility, a forty-five-minute drive away. Although it was nicely appointed, I had misgivings when I detected an odor of urine in the oncology area where John's room might be.

On Wednesday, an oncology colleague of Heyer's stopped to see John and told us he understood that John would be discharged "when a bed can be found." He also said John might need a transfusion because his red blood count might be too low for the radiation to be effective. "This is not unusual in view of John's having been so profoundly ill," he added.

The next morning, John said he felt better than he had in days. He walked three hundred feet with a walker, showered—sitting on a bench—and dressed with no assistance. I was holding my breath when he emerged fully dressed. He had not been out of bed like this since arriving at the E.R. It took him close to an hour to shower and dress, but he did it.

That afternoon, I set out again, targeting the next-closest facility, which was fairly far from Reston. I had difficulty finding it, and decided it was too far away, with too much traffic. Returning to the facility whose odor had concerned me, I met again with the admissions director, who showed me a new wing where "younger patients" stayed for orthopedic rehab and suggested this for John. The downside was that there were two patients in each room. I returned to the hospital to discuss the options with John.

"I prefer being in a private room. The odor is not important."

"All right."

"I'm glad you've settled on a place," the social worker said when I told her. "I'll arrange for John's transfer Saturday morning, and I'll have a physical therapist show you how to help him get in and out of your car, since he's not a candidate for transportation by ambulance."

Relieved to have found a place for John, I breathed a little easier.

When I arrived at his room mid-morning on Friday, he looked thoughtful.

"How are you feeling, sweetheart?"

"Lethargic. Probably because of everything I did yesterday. Heyer stopped by. He said I'll be getting a transfusion before being discharged tomorrow."

"Really? I wonder how long it will take."

"I don't know."

"About eight hours," the nurse said when I asked. "The blood has to be irradiated first, so we might not start until late in the day, after John's afternoon radiation therapy.

Everything was happening at the last minute. I looked at John, wishing he felt better, and remembered that no one had shown me how to help him get in and out of the car. Oh, well, I guessed tomorrow morning would be soon enough.

I was on my way out of the hospital when the social worker stopped me.

"Shirley, you should go down to radiation therapy to schedule John's remaining appointments as an outpatient."

"Now?"

"Yes. It shouldn't take long. Just tell them what you want."

Heeding her advice, I went downstairs to radiology. But I did not know what I wanted. I took a chair in the small waiting room and waited to talk with the scheduler. In a few minutes, a young woman in a white jacket walked over and handed me a printed schedule. "These are the appointments for your husband."

I scanned the sheet. Every appointment was at 5:15 p.m. I knew this was what I did *not* want. "Could we possibly make these earlier in the day, before rush-hour traffic?"

"I'm sorry. Your husband's treatment is somewhat complicated, and for that reason, the department prefers to handle him at the end of the day."

So much for telling them what I wanted. Obviously, the difficulty of my getting John to his appointments was of no concern to the radiology folks.

Walking into Barbara's office, I dropped my purse on the sofa and sat down in the straight-backed chair. She waited for me to speak, her brown-eyed gaze direct and unwavering.

"John's being discharged from the hospital tomorrow. He seems to be making progress, but I'm not sure. Yesterday he walked three hundred feet with a walker and managed to shower and dress himself. But this morning when I saw him, he was so tired he could hardly lift his arm off the bed. We both know I can't take care of him at home. I wouldn't know how. I've spent nearly every day this week trying to find a place for him where he can regain his strength, if that's possible, while he completes his radiation therapy. Fortunately, I found a skilled-care facility where he'll get physical therapy, but it's not in Reston. There was no bed for him at the facility here. And now I've been told that his radiation therapy has to be at the end of the day, the absolute worst time of day in terms of traffic. I'm going to be on the road for hours. The appointments last an hour and a half or two because they're radiating two separate areas."

Barbara listened. "Can't you hire someone to pick him up, wait for him, and take him back?"

"Oh my god. I hadn't thought of that. I could, couldn't I?" I took a deep breath. "I remember meeting someone at a Reston Chamber of Commerce meeting, a small business owner who provided services for people who were handicapped. Transportation might have been one of them. I'll look for her card when I get home."

That afternoon, I was sifting through a stack of business cards at the kitchen table when the phone rang.

"Shirley, the skilled-care facility called." It was the hospital social worker. She was speaking quickly. "The insurer has denied coverage of John because he walked with P.T. more than a hundred feet today and yesterday."

"What?" I stopped breathing.

"I should have looked at the P.T. reports, but I didn't."

"How can this be? John is highly motivated to get well, but after any exertion, he's spent. His stamina is uneven, and so is his balance. He's having a transfusion tonight. I don't know what shape he'll be in tomorrow. He should probably be monitored by a nurse." This was the first I had heard that insurance coverage in a skilled-care facility depended on how much, or little, a patient walked while hospitalized. "What does this mean?"

"You'll have to come up with another plan for him."

"Come up with another plan? How?"

"Since it's so late in the day, the hospital's not likely to insist that John leave in the morning, which will give you the weekend to come up with a plan."

I looked at my watch. It was 4 o'clock. I could feel my face flush with anger. I had spent days finding a place for John, and this woman had told me she was making all the arrangements. Now, because *she* didn't check the P.T. reports, *I* had to come up with a plan! What kind of a plan could I possibly come up with now? "What if we pay privately?"

"You'd have to talk with the facility to find out if they have any private-pay beds available. It would be upwards of three hundred fifty dollars a day." She paused. "I'll see you on Monday. I'm off for the weekend." Her tone was nonchalant, without an iota of empathy or remorse.

Well, la-de-freakin-da! See me on Monday? Not on your life! Putting the phone in its cradle, I sat back down at the kitchen table and tried to quiet my brain. There had to be a place for John. And then it hit me. What about an assisted-care facility? It would probably be less expensive than skilled care. I knew of one in Reston. Thumbing through the phone book, I found Sunrise Assisted Care and dialed the number.

"Yes, we take residents for short-term stays, but we don't have an available room now and don't anticipate any for some time."

"Oh no. I don't know what to do. My husband could be discharged as early as tomorrow, Monday for sure."

"You might try Sunrise at Countryside in Sterling, Virginia." Sterling was ten miles from Reston.

I dialed, hoping I could speak to someone despite the late hour on a Friday.

"Yes, we have room. Can you drop by tomorrow morning to see our facility and talk with our intake representative?"

"Yes."

The next morning at 9, I was at Sunrise. The intake representative, Marci, greeted me with a warm hello. Tall, with brown hair pulled back from a triangular face, she was wearing a loose white top over a long cotton skirt.

"Let me show you the assisted-care building." Walking through the dining area, I saw several residents, all much older than John, in wheelchairs. "Here's a room where he could stay."

We stepped inside. Natural light through one small window did not dispel the dismal gray of the unadorned walls. I swallowed. I would have to bring in flowers, something to brighten the room.

"John's medications would be managed by the on-duty nurse, and he could receive physical and occupational therapy here."

"Would I have to make arrangements for his therapy?"

"No. Therapy would be ordered in his hospital discharge papers, and once he's admitted, we'd arrange for the therapists to come here."

Whew! One less thing to figure out. "Marci, how long do you think it would take to drive to Reston Hospital from here during rush hour?"

"It's a relatively straight shot. I'd say about twenty-five minutes."

We walked back to her office and sat down.

"What do you think? Would this meet your needs?"

"Yes. I'm very grateful that you can accommodate John. I'd like him to be here until he completes his radiation therapy in about two weeks. By then, he should be stronger and able to come home."

"All right. Let's do the paperwork."

I liked this woman's energy, her can-do attitude. But I had to tell her, "There is one thing."

"Yes?"

"I hope I don't have to talk with the hospital social worker."

"Don't worry. I'll communicate with Reston Hospital to get the information I need for John's admission on Monday. We'll be ready for him whenever he's discharged."

That afternoon, I found the card I was looking for and made the call. "This is Sharon of Senior Services."

"Could you provide transportation to medical appointments for my husband who'll need to be driven from Sterling to Reston Hospital for a 5:15 p.m. radiation therapy appointment Monday through Friday for two weeks?"

"Yes, I have a list of licensed drivers. I'd have to make some calls to find one for you."

"The driver would need to wait for my husband while he's undergoing radiation and then drive him back. It might be three hours, start to finish."

"I understand. I'll call you before Monday with the driver's name."

"Thank you."

Things seemed to be falling into place. With the transportation solved, I could relax, or at least try to.

Late Monday morning, after a stay of one month and four days, John was discharged from Reston Hospital to Sunrise at Countryside. The hospital nurse who wheeled him to the car gave me a walker and discharge papers for Sunrise.

Using the new walker, John made his way from the car to Marci's office. His pace was slow but steady.

"Hi, how are you feeling?"

"Good." John smiled and shook Marci's hand. His eyes were clear.

After we were seated, I handed Marci the discharge papers. "This is odd," she said. "The nurse wrote in the discharge papers that John has graduated from physical therapy."

"What?" I closed my eyes. Another snafu. How many more lay ahead? How could anyone get through a serious illness without someone watching out for him? The medical care systems were riddled with potential pitfalls.

"Don't worry, I'll call Dr. Heyer. He'll order physical and occupational therapy for John." Marci looked up. "You know, John, I wonder if you might prefer staying in an independent apartment rather than the assisted-care building?"

John looked at me.

"I didn't know you had independent apartments," I said.

"We have one that's available. Do you want to take a look?"

"Sure."

Bright, with an expanse of windows in the living room and bedroom, the furnished apartment was one floor above the dining room.

"What do you think, sweetheart? Would you like to be here?"

"Yes."

After putting away John's few pieces of clothing, we took the elevator down to the dining room for lunch. I recognized the other resident at the table we were led to. I had seen him when I met with Marci on Saturday. A nice-looking man, tall with gray hair, he had appeared in her doorway while I was signing papers for John's admission. She seemed to know what he wanted, answering his question before he asked. "He has aphasia," she said after he walked away. I must have looked puzzled. "It's loss of the ability, because of brain damage, to speak the way the rest of us understand it." Lunch conversation, after polite greetings, was minimal.

That afternoon, I was sitting with John on a bench in front of Sunrise when a small dusty gray sedan pulled up. Was this John's ride to the hospital? The car looked as though it had been tattooed, full of "Veterans Against the War" slogans and other similar ones. Sharon had told me the driver was a Vietnam veteran. The exhaust pipe, tied to the car with wire, rested on the driveway. A white-haired, grizzle-bearded driver got out and walked over to John. He was wearing faded blue jeans and a knit shirt over his protruding belly. "I'm Dave. Are you the fellow who's going to Reston Hospital?"

"Yes."

"Well, get in." Dave opened the door on the passenger side, revealing stained upholstery. The padding in the door seemed to be missing. "I'll put the walker in the trunk. Don't have room for it in the back seat."

Through the back window, I could see stacks of FOR SALE real estate signs and political campaign posters.

"Do you have a contract for me to sign?" I asked.

"Yes. Here it is. Sharon said you could mail it to her."

"You're going to wait for John and bring him back here?"

"Yes."

"And pick him up tomorrow at the same time?"

"That's what Sharon told me."

Holding onto the door, John lowered himself into the low seat and lifted his long legs into the car. His knees were chest high.

What had I gotten him into? Dave and his rattletrap were not what I had envisioned. That evening, I talked with John by phone. "How was the driver?"

"All right. He had a lot to say about politics. Sounded like a right-winger."

"I'm sorry, sweetheart. I didn't know about the driver or the car."

"It's not important."

"How was your dinner?"

"Not bad. I sat with the aphasic."

"Oh?"

"Yes. We had a rather lengthy conversation."

"How was that possible?"

"By listening to him speak, I figured out the patterns of his speech and what they meant, and then it was easy."

"Amazing."

The next day, I was out front with John waiting for Dave. When he did not show up at 4:30, I called Sharon.

"Dave hasn't picked up John for his 5:15 p.m. appointment at Reston Hospital."

"I'll try to find him and call you back."

Five minutes later, my phone rang.

"Shirley, I can't find Dave. I'm really sorry."

"I'd better drive John myself. He can't miss this appointment."

I was waiting for John in the radiology department when Dave walked in.

"Dave, what happened?"

"Something came up. Sorry. I'll wait for John and take him back to Sunrise."

"All right." How could I rest easy if I couldn't count on this man to show up? Back home, I found a batch of brochures I'd picked up at the hospital. One of them, Touching Hearts at Home, a locally owned franchise, listed transportation among its many services. Why hadn't I thought to look at these before?

"Yes, I can provide transportation for your husband. I can pick him up today." The male voice on the phone was reassuring.

"Wonderful. I'll be waiting with my husband out front at 4:30."

"By the way, my name is Cliff. I'll be in a black sedan."

I called Sharon to cancel my contract. She apologized and said she understood. That afternoon at 4:25, a sedan pulled up in front of Sunrise.

"John, look! It's a Mercedes. A beautiful black Mercedes. No slogans, no dents!"

The driver got out and walked over to us. Clean-shaven, he was wearing dark slacks and a crisp-looking sports shirt.

"Hi, I'm Cliff." He shook hands with us. "I'll wait for John and bring him back when he's through. Don't worry. I'll be back tomorrow, same time."

"Thank you." Whew! Another snafu overcome.

The denial of coverage at the skilled-care facility kept nagging at me. When I called the insurer just to understand the rationale, a case manager said there was no record of a denial. She offered to review John's case, but it was too late. His next move, we both hoped, would be to come home.

Despite John's mental acuity, he was weak. While occupational and physical therapy seemed to be helping his walking and balance, radiation was beginning to sap what little strength he had. I met him for lunch every day at the care center. Then we would take a nap together, although I never slept. While John was asleep, I would prepare a snack for both of us but mostly for him, which we would eat in the kitchen. When Cliff picked him up, I would drive home.

The food at Sunrise left a lot to be desired. A day or two after John's arrival, the Sunrise menu became more limited. I started bringing in bottles of the nutritional supplement Ensure along with cheese and crackers and anything else I thought John might eat to put flesh on his bones.

We allowed few visitors to preserve John's limited energy. Early in his stay, our hairdresser and friend Pia dropped by at my request to trim his hair. John was seated in a large comfortable chair, his back to the door, when she arrived. He did not stand. "Hi, Pia. Thank you for coming."

She draped a towel over John's shoulders before trimming his hair, mustache, and goatee. He was quiet.

"I'm leaving this electric razor for you, John, in case you can use it."

"Thank you."

"If you need me, Shirley, call any time." Pia gave me a warm hug before leaving. I sensed that she had been disturbed by John's appearance—the scar from the craniotomy incision and his thin neck.

Toward the end of his second week at Sunrise, I had showerheads with flexible hoses installed in both bathrooms at the condo, since I didn't know which John would use. Use of a shower bench or chair would depend on what the occupational therapist advised. Both therapists, whom John liked, would work with him at home. I replaced our faux Eames chair, which was too low, with a large Scandinavian leather chair with good support and an ottoman.

"I can't wait for you to see this chair, darling. It's made for someone tall, and should be super-comfortable."

"From what you say, I think I'm going to have to fight you for the chair." He laughed.

Looking ahead to the chemo regimen, John asked the hairdresser at Sunrise to shave his head. Because of the revised radiation treatment, he had not lost his hair. With winter fast approaching, I found a knit hat at Eddie Bauer for John's now-shaved head.

At Radiation Oncology, they presented John with a diploma, mortarboard, and candle on completion of his last radiation treatment. I didn't know whether this was usual or reflected the two oncology radiologists' appreciation of John's understanding of the treatment. Whatever their motivation, he was visibly moved. "You can take these home for me," he said the next day when I arrived for lunch. His eyes were moist.

That night I sent an email update:

> Yesterday John completed the last of his radiation therapy. And now, after two weeks of "independent living" at Sunrise, he will be coming home on Monday—a move we've both been anticipating. The good thing about the last two weeks is that despite the enervating effects of radiation, John has been gaining strength day by day, thanks to the visits of physical and occupational therapists, and I'm feeling that I've regained a degree of equilibrium that was notably absent upon John's discharge from the hospital. The therapists will follow John home. At this point, he's walking with a walker, and sometimes without, and gradually rebuilding muscles. We know he's lost a lot of weight.

After a diet of green, brown, and white purée at the hospital followed by "real food" of varying quality and appeal, meals at home are going to seem superlative! This morning, I took delivery of a "transportation chair," similar to a wheelchair but with four small wheels, easier to maneuver. We're renting this to use, for example, if we venture into Barnes & Noble and John needs a sit-down break.

At one time, we had planned to spend this fall exploring Virginia so that John could get a feel for "photographing Virginia," so different from western landscapes. We're now talking about day or half-day trips, as John feels up to it, using my point-and-shoot to reference areas John would like to photograph when he's stronger. With the newly arrived transportation chair and an Eddie Bauer knit hat covering his now-shaved head—yes, he's into the Lyle Alzado look—we're ready!

Earlier that week, we had kept an appointment with Heyer, who smiled when he saw John.

"It's good to see you up and walking. You've got some big admirers in the radiology department. Both oncology radiologists told me they wished they could go out for a beer or a glass of wine with you and talk." He paused. "We need to talk about the next phase of treatment. This next phase will focus on the malignancies in the spinal fluid. We'll begin the regimen on November 12, after you've been home for a week. You'll spend four to five hours here in the office, lying on your side while undergoing a spinal tap and an injection of chemo into your spinal fluid. The number of procedures is indeterminate. The side effects will be minimal. In about a month, after the internal fireworks have ceased, I'll order an MRI to determine the degree of tumor shrinkage resulting from radiation and chemo."

Listening to Heyer, it was clear that John's case was, as he said, "beyond the boundaries of knowledge." For some people, this would have been unsettling, but for John, it was invigorating.

Walking out of Heyer's office, he stopped and turned to me. "I'm going to make it!"

And that day, I thought he would.

A New Normal

IT WAS EARLY NOVEMBER WHEN I DROVE JOHN HOME FROM SUN-rise, a little more than six weeks since his near death. It felt like months, not weeks, since he had been home. So much had happened. How would it be now? How would our life be? I had no idea. I knew only that we would have one week together without his undergoing medical treatment of any kind—one week's reprieve before the start of chemo.

Turning my key in the lock, I took a deep breath. With one major exception, everything was pretty much as we had left it when we flew to Santa Fe. Pushing the door open, I turned to look at John. "Welcome home, darling." He crossed the threshold into the foyer and paused. Early afternoon light through the curving wall of bay windows filled the living room. The baby grand gleamed, its cherry red finish lustrous. Arching toward the piano, delicate branches of a potted ficus filled the space with light-filtered leafy green. On the coffee table, John's favorite purple irises erupted from a turquoise crystal vase.

Walking past him into the living room, I extended an arm toward the new chair. *"The pièce de résistance."*

John made his way to the chair, where he abandoned his walker and sat down. After lifting his feet onto the ottoman, he looked up at me and smiled. "Thank you."

"Would you like a PBJ?" Peanut butter and jam sandwiches were one of John's favorite quick lunches.

"Yes."

"The chair came with a tray that attaches on the side. You could eat in your chair."

"No. I prefer to eat in the kitchen."

Sitting at the kitchen table, eating PBJs, I had a sense of déjà vu. When we used to have lunch at home, before the bump, we would sit in the kitchen, sharing a can of soup or a couple of sandwiches. Could the new normal be just like the old?

"Do you want to take a nap?"

"Yes. I'll lie down in the bedroom."

Later in the afternoon, John got up and returned to the new chair to read the *Economist.*

"Are you up for a finger of scotch before dinner?" I was standing next to the bar.

"You have the scotch. I'll have a glass of water."

"For dinner, we're having chicken baked in a little sherry, French green beans, rice, and a green salad. I hope you're hungry."

"Yes. Sounds good."

After a late dinner complete with candles and softly playing jazz, John returned to his chair. I cleared the table and finished up in the kitchen. It was comforting to look across the counter and see him engrossed in his magazine. Apart from my preparing a complete dinner—before the bump, my only contribution to dinner had been salad—John's being home was feeling surprisingly normal. Sitting down on the ivory sofa across from him, I picked up the *Times* and for the first time in days read more than just headlines. "Sweetheart, do you want to watch a little TV?"

"No." John leaned forward and dropped his magazine on the coffee table. "I'm ready to go to bed."

"The lights are on. I'll be in as soon as I turn off the music." I watched him push himself up from the chair and disappear with the walker through the doorway to the master suite.

After completing my nightly ablutions, I walked into the dimly lit bedroom. John was standing naked on the other side of the bed, his back to me. In all the time I had known him, he never wore pajamas. Adjusting to the light, I gazed at him for a long moment and inwardly gasped. I had seen him every day for the past six weeks, but never undressed. Suddenly the horror of his recent ordeal came home to me. He was so thin—his once-muscular buttocks and thighs were withered—and with his head shaved, he resembled pictures I had seen of Holocaust victims. My eyes welled up with silent tears. He had been through hell and survived . . . and the battle was not over. He *had* to gain weight.

"We have a starting point," John said the next morning, sitting down to a breakfast of scrambled eggs and bacon.

"Oh?"

"I weighed myself before dressing."

"And?"

"I weigh a hundred fifty pounds."

"That must be an all-time low." I thought of how the bones stood out now on his six-foot-four frame.

"Yes. I'm down twenty-five pounds."

"Sweetheart, I'm going to start plying you with things you can't resist." I smiled, thinking of the eggs, bacon, cheeses, meats, and bottles of Ensure already in the fridge.

A couple of days later, I came home from Whole Foods to find John sitting in the new chair, his feet in white athletic socks resting on the ottoman. He was reading the *Times*.

"Hi."

"Hi." He put down the paper. "I don't want to appear like an old man shuffling about, but I'd like a pair of comfortable slippers that give me some support." His tone was almost playful.

"After lunch, I'll drive to Tysons Corner to see what I can find."

Most of the slippers I saw at the mall there were backless leather slip-ons that looked as though they would slide right off the foot. I bought a couple of pairs on approval. "Where can I find a slipper that has a back?" I asked the shoe salesman at Nordstrom.

"Isotoners have backs, and they're very comfortable. You can probably find them at Target."

That afternoon, I presented my slipper findings to John, who rejected the leather slip-ons in favor of the Isotoners made of navy microsuede fabric with a non-skid sole. "These are good. They're easy to get in and out of, and they might keep my feet warm."

I was out when the occupational therapist visited John.

"How did it go?"

"She said I could improve my strength, balance, and agility if I followed you around when you dust, perhaps sharing the task." He started chuckling. "It was all I could do to keep from laughing out loud."

I was laughing too. "I hate to be thrust into the role of thwarting your recovery, but there must be something else you can do." It was not that I never dusted, but it was so rare an event that John had never seen me do it. That was why we had a cleaner.

By the end of the week, John was walking without his walker in the condo, in the corridors, and downstairs in the lobby area. He was picking up the mail and stopping to talk with the receptionists at the front desk. He was showering in the master bathroom where he refused to use the shower bench advised by the occupational therapist. "If I need support, I can always lean against a wall."

His main complaint was a feeling of fatigue which, after being off radiation therapy for a week, he attributed to the antiseizure medication Keppra which he had been on since the craniotomy. Searching the internet, we found that "somnolence" was listed as its first major side effect. He called Sharma.

"I'm sorry but I cannot let you stop taking Keppra. You'll need to see a neurologist." The specialist, Sharma explained, would test John to determine whether he was experiencing internal seizure activity that might not be visible. If not, he could stop taking Keppra. The first available appointment was not for three weeks.

Sunday night, with candles still flickering on the dining room table, I placed a bowl of chocolate ice cream in front of John.

Spoon in hand, he looked at me. "I'm dreading the chemo." He looked away quickly.

"Sweetheart?" This was the first time he had voiced concern about any aspect of his medical treatment since the craniotomy. Chemo was scheduled for Tuesday.

"I've never been in such a debilitated physical condition before any treatment. I'm afraid of the side effects."

"I thought Dr. Heyer said the side effects would be minimal."

"Yes, but he can't be sure. Chemo is powerful."

I didn't know what to say. Back then, I had no idea how powerful it could be. John had been treated with chemo before the Rituxan but had never told me details, and I didn't press him. I did not want to know. He had feared the craniotomy and come through unscathed. He had endured the radiation. He *had* to be able to withstand the chemo. It was that or die.

Looking back, I see that my hope for John's survival was tied to the treatment proposed by Heyer, whom I perceived as his savior. I was blind to the possibility that none of it would make a difference. But John was less blind. Given his weakened condition, he knew he was starting from behind the curve. While I was still hanging onto his *"I'm going to make it!"* uttered two weeks earlier, he knew better. He had survived the infection, he said, because of me. Had he entered the cancer arena in his battle-weary state because of me, because of my blind hope? If he had been alone, what would he have done?

"I can't slow my brain activity," John said Monday morning at breakfast. "Thoughts, ideas race so quickly through my mind that I can't concentrate the way I want to."

"Sweetheart, I'm sorry. Maybe once the chemo takes effect, you'll be better able to concentrate." I didn't know what I was talking about. But ever hopeful, I was putting a positive spin on anything that smacked of a negative.

Later that morning, we were standing in the kitchen when the phone rang. It was Heyer's office calling to say he had a "personal emergency" that would mean postponing John's treatment for nine days until the twenty-first, the day before Thanksgiving.

Hanging up, John relayed the message and turned to give me a big hug. "This is not bad news."

"It's great news! A real reprieve. A gift of nine days to eat and grow stronger." I didn't contemplate the likelihood that the cancer too would be growing.

John was spending less and less time in his chair. One afternoon, after a visit by one of his two therapists, he left the condo. "I climbed the stairs to the fourteenth floor and back," he said when he came back with the mail.

Another day, I was in the office when I heard the front door open and close. "Darling?" I called out.

John appeared in the office doorway. "I took the elevator down and walked up." The pride in his voice was unmistakable. After little more than two weeks at home, his stamina was on the upswing and he had gained five pounds. His mood was upbeat.

The day before Thanksgiving, we were ushered into Heyer's office for John's first spinal tap and an injection of the chemo drug Methotrexate. Removing his shirt, John lay down on the examining table on his left side, his elbow bent to support his head. Heyer, large syringe in hand, sat down on a stool and rolled toward John's exposed back. I couldn't see what he was doing. A few seconds later, he rolled backward and stood up. Setting the syringe down on a metal tray atop a small table, he picked up another and sat back down on the stool.

Both procedures—the extraction and the injection—took less than fifteen minutes, a far cry from the predicted four-to-five hours. John did not complain of any pain.

A week later, we returned for the second treatment. John sat down on the examining table; I took a seat in a nearby chair. After a few minutes, Heyer walked in holding a manila folder, John's medical file.

"This appears to be a bump in the road, not a Mack truck." He looked at John and smiled.

John said nothing.

My heart was doing somersaults.

"The spinal tap showed malignancy." Heyer's voice was matter-of-fact.

My heart stopped tumbling. Did this mean the radiation had done nothing?

"There's another chemo, Depo. It would mean less frequent dosings, but the side effects would require taking heavy-duty steroids to reduce their effect, and the risk of inflaming the meninges, the membranes enclosing the brain and spinal chord, would still be relatively high."

John shook his head: no Depo for him.

"If we're not doing Depo, we're looking at a regimen of chemo twice a week for a month, then once a week for a month. The tricky part will be knowing when to stop the chemo." Heyer looked at John, who nodded his understanding. "With these more-frequent dosings, we'll alternate between two chemos, Methotrexate and Ara-C."

I was anticipating John's lying down on his side for another injection when Heyer's voice brought me up short.

"I want to change the site of the infusion. It will no longer be the spine. Instead, you'll have an Ommaya reservoir implanted in your brain for the infusions." He was calm, matter-of-fact, as though this change of venue were an everyday occurrence.

Transfixed, I listened. Heyer paused to pull a pen from his shirt pocket. He turned the medical folder over and sketched the Ommaya reservoir; it resembled a small martini glass with a long stem. "The top of this relatively long implant will be slightly visible under the scalp and allow easy access for injections of chemo, assuring that the chemo bathes the fluid surrounding the brain as well as the spinal area."

"Would Dr. Sharma implant the reservoir?" I asked.

"Yes. I've talked with him. He can see you tomorrow to schedule surgery."

Back home after the appointment, I stood in the kitchen fixing a
PBJ for John as he rested in the leather chair. "Darling, Dr. Heyer said
it appears to be a bump in the road. This should be cause to celebrate."

"But no one has said how big the bump is." John's tone, like
Heyer's, was matter-of-fact but rueful.

I chided myself. Of course it was too soon to know anything. The
spinal tap had shown malignancy, and the proposed treatment had
taken a dramatic turn. So I was puzzled. What had prompted Heyer's
comment? I never found out. Had he wanted to soften the impact of
negative news? If so, I took the bait.

Late the next day, I sent an email update to friends.

> We saw the neurosurgeon this morning. He plans to im-
> plant the Ommaya reservoir next week. Although the pro-
> cedure takes only thirty to forty minutes, John will have to
> spend the night in ICU. "After all, it's still brain surgery,"
> Dr. Sharma said. This particular area of the brain, he said,
> is considered the "silent region," meaning that motor and
> other nerves are not nearby. Late next week, John is sched-
> uled for two MRIs to determine the shrinkage of tumors as
> a result of radiation therapy, which concluded about a
> month ago.

> Meanwhile, tomorrow he will be fitted with electrodes for
> a seventy-two-hour ambulatory EEG. How he sleeps with
> that we have no idea. The results of this, together with the
> MRIs, will determine whether he can stop taking the sleep-
> inducing antiseizure medication Keppra.

> Apart from all of this, we're staying up late enough to watch
> pro basketball, hoping the Washington Wizards can pull
> off more wins than losses despite the absence of Gilbert Are-
> nas. John is back to his avid reading of the *Economist, New
> Yorker,* and the daily *NYT* and *W. Post.* We're enjoying oc-
> casional visitors, and this caregiver, at loose ends at times,
> is hanging in.

> We know now that we will be home for the holidays. We
> will miss sharing these with John's brother Dick and fam-

ily. But we are fully appreciative of being able to celebrate being alive!

Now that we're in a less dramatic phase, updates will probably be less frequent. Just know that we really enjoy hearing from you and what you're up to.

How could I have said "less dramatic" when brain surgery was in the offing? I must have equated drama with the excruciating tension surrounding the infection and the craniotomy. With John's having survived both, coupled with his recent weight gain and improving stamina, I was more than hopeful that he would prevail over the cancer. I was sure he would.

It was early evening when the neurology technician attached numerous tiny electrodes to John's shaved head. The long, very fine wires, covered in a variety of colors, cascaded like dreadlocks down his back into a receptor.

The next day, we drove to Arlington to have dinner with a good friend, Naomi, and her husband, Tom, who greeted John's new look with surprise.

"John, I almost didn't recognize you." Naomi had visited him at Sunrise. "Even with the new do, you look so much better than when we saw you a few weeks ago."

"I feel better."

Knowing that pecan pie was John's favorite, she had made one just for him, and insisted he take home what we didn't eat.

"Do you have Naomi's email address?" John asked the next morning. "I want to thank her for the pie."

At the eleventh hour, someone realized the Ommaya reservoir contained metal, which is incompatible with an MRI. Sharma postponed surgery until after the MRIs that Heyer needed to measure the effectiveness of the radiation so he could fine-tune the chemo regimen. A close call. Thank God someone was paying attention. I assumed it was Heyer who had prevented the snafu. He was calling the shots.

With imaging completed, John underwent his second cranial surgery. Because Sharma used the original craniotomy incision, John's appearance was virtually unaltered. The "lip of the martini glass," as Heyer had predicted, was barely visible under his scalp. I assumed that once he completed chemotherapy, the implant would be removed.

Three days after the surgery, we were back in Heyer's office. Sitting in a blue, straight-backed chair, I faced John as he reclined on the examining table a few feet away. My shoulders were relaxed. I was curious about this new procedure and grateful to be allowed in the office, which Heyer didn't usually permit during a treatment.

"Good morning. How are you feeling, John?" Heyer, wearing a blue shirt with the sleeves rolled up over his wrists, walked in smiling. He was carrying a tray with two syringes, which he placed on top of a small table.

"Good."

"First we'll extract fluid, and after that, I'll infuse the chemo." He stood over John, a syringe in his right hand. Again, his body blocked my view. I sat back and waited. I wasn't sure I wanted to see what the doctor was about to do. The extraction seemed to be taking a long time.

"I'm not getting anything." Heyer said it as if he couldn't believe it.

Startled, I sat up. What did he mean "not getting anything"? It *had* to work. The clock was ticking!

Again and again, he tried to withdraw cerebrospinal fluid from the implant but couldn't. The Ommaya reservoir was not working. Had the meticulous neurosurgeon made a mistake? Or was the device faulty? I never knew.

That afternoon, we drove to the hospital E.R. for an unscheduled visit with Sharma. We had been waiting nearly an hour when he appeared in the waiting area.

"Hello. Let's go into the back to talk." Decked out in a double-vented light gray suit and long-toed black leather loafers, he led us through the double doors to a cubicle in the E.R. treatment area. Standing, he leaned against the handrails of a narrow bed and crossed his ankles. John and I sat on a couple of black-cushioned metal chairs facing him. He bent toward us, his face close to ours. "We need to schedule another surgery." It was cut and dried. He didn't say a word about the failure of the first.

"How soon?" I asked.

"Right away. I'll remove the reservoir from the right hemisphere and implant another in the left." He paused. "This is not the silent region. It will be very close to the communications nerve center."

My shoulders tensed. I looked at Sharma's smooth olive skin. His expression was inscrutable. Although he had not spelled it out, I knew the proximity of the communications nerve center to the proposed site of the new implant carried a risk that John's ability to speak could be impaired. But there was no turning back. The cancer had to be confronted with chemo before it was too late. I didn't consider the possibility that it was already too late. John and I had a future together: a trip to the Galapagos and others to Burgundy, the Atlas Mountains, and Bhutan; innumerable projects and shared photographer-writer dreams. All we had to do was get that chemo where it was needed, and everything would be all right. That was my belief.

Between Christmas and New Year's, John underwent a third brain surgery at Reston Hospital. Again, my neighbor Kathy met me in the surgical waiting room to await the post-surgery report. She, who had spent many hours in hospitals after two of her three children were diagnosed with a terminal neurological disease, understood my anxiety. She arrived with two Starbucks cappuccinos in hand. Putting aside a *Times* crossword puzzle, I listened while she talked about her daughter Johanna's life in Salt Lake City; she had a great new job and was in love with a painter, a Utah native who painted cows for a living! Crossing and uncrossing my legs, I tried not to feel or think about what I couldn't see.

After three hours, Sharma, in the now-familiar green scrubs, found me. Again, he deemed the surgery a success, but this time, I wondered.

That night, I returned to the ICU, unable to take a deep breath.

"John Bessey?" I asked a white-clad nurse.

"He's in that room." She pointed toward an open doorway.

I walked into the darkened room to find John sitting up in bed, his head wrapped in a white turban. He greeted me with a smile.

I bent over to give him a soft kiss. "How are you feeling, sweetheart?"

"Not bad. No headache this time."

"Good." Hearing him speak, I breathed more easily. His ability to communicate had not been affected by the implant. But would this one work better than the first?

On January 2, we returned to Heyer's office where once again John assumed a semi-reclining position on the examining table. I sat on the edge of my chair, hands clasped between my thighs. Heyer stood in front of him, his arm raised over John's head, his thumb and two fingers controlling the movement of the plunger in the large syringe.

A deafening silence filled the white room. I held my breath.

"It's working." Heyer was jubilant.

"Oh thank God." Tears of relief stung my eyes.

The new chemo procedure, including prep time, took less than an hour. John would be in the doctor's office for chemo twice a week through the end of January. If the MRIs showed shrinkage of the tumors and the chemo killed off the remaining malignant cells, he would be home free. Those were big ifs, but that day, with the implant working, I was confident.

Later in the week, we learned that the seventy-two-hour EEG had shown evidence of seizure activity. John would have to remain on Keppra. I was despondent. I had been so sure he would ace that test. It was shocking that he was having seizures, invisible seizures. And I hated his having to be on the medication that made him so sleepy. Would he have to be on it for the rest of his life?

It seemed to me that the craniotomy had triggered the seizures. No one had mentioned them as a possible side effect. At the time, the craniotomy was deemed necessary to save John's life. That's what we thought. That's what the doctors advised. Looking back, I wish we could have foreseen the futility of it all at the outset—possibly avoiding the needless treatments and surgeries, the wrenching ups and downs.

On January 7, we returned to Heyer's office for the second treatment using the implant, and we learned the results of the MRIs.

"One tumor on your spine shrank. This is good news because it had appeared to be pressing on the spine." Heyer paused. "The other lesions in the spine and brain, however, were not affected by the radiation." He did not elaborate.

My heart sank. Would more radiation therapy have made a difference?

Driving home, John and I said little. The reports were worsening by the day. First the seizure activity and now the ineffectiveness of the radiation. If this was a bump in the road, what was a Mack truck? I was beginning to lose my sense that we could weather the storm.

Without warning, my former employer had just switched insurance carriers, and I worried about interrupted coverage of the many drugs John was now taking. Normally, this would not have been a big deal, but now, it was one more critical thing to coordinate. I felt like a juggler with too many balls in the air, not one of which I could let drop. The feeling of losing control, of not being able to hold it together, was beginning to crescendo. And on top of everything, I could not let John know my anguish. Maybe he sensed it. I hoped not. He deserved better than to see and hear how scared *I* was.

Back at the condo, I grabbed my cell phone and keys and headed toward the door. "I'm going for a walk," I said. In the parking area out back, I called Gay. "Thank God I reached you. We've just seen Dr. Heyer who gave us the MRI results on the radiation. Only one tumor shrank. The others were unaffected. This means chemo is our only hope."

"Sweetheart, I'm very sorry."

"There's been so much bad news. I'm so distressed. I don't know what to do or if there's anything I can do. And I can't let him know how down I feel."

"Sweetheart, why don't you call Dr. Heyer. Perhaps he could order nursing or other care for John."

I looked at my watch. "If I call right now, maybe I can catch him." Hanging up with Gay, I dialed Heyer's office. "This is Shirley, John Bessey's wife. May I speak to Dr. Heyer?"

"Yes, he's right here."

"Dr. Heyer, this is Shirley. The radiation therapy really didn't do much, did it?"

"It was not a dramatic win." He paused. "It did not produce the hoped-for results."

"I'm feeling at such a loss to know what to do. Is there nursing or some other care for John that you would recommend?"

"No, not now, Shirley."

I couldn't read his voice. What did he mean? Did he mean wait until he gets worse? John was his patient, and he was trying to keep him alive. I was hurting but I was not his patient, and he was at a loss to help me. What I needed was someone from Heyer's office like a social worker or patient liaison—someone familiar with John's case who could empathize, help put reports in perspective, and advise me on what lay ahead. But there was no such person. I felt I was losing my grip.

When I checked for mail at the condo building, I ran into my neighbor Helen in the lobby.

"How are things going, Shirley?" Her voice registered concern. She and her husband Stanley had been delivering delicious quiches and thin-sliced salami—food they thought John would like, food to help him gain weight. Their kindness had been unflagging.

I burst into tears. "I just want our life back!" But I knew there was nothing anyone could do to make that happen—not any more. Sobbing, I ran into the elevator and hit the close button. Back at our condo, I retreated to the office to dry my tears and try to calm myself.

I couldn't let John see me like that. He wasn't falling apart. He did not invite people to be emotional over his condition or share their emotions with him. That was how he controlled his disease. It was how he had exerted control over it for eighteen years.

That night, Dick phoned—Gay must have told him about my call—and offered to drive down to give me a breather. John and I accepted. He didn't mention the radiation report to Dick during the call. He didn't seem upset. Was I overreacting? I had to calm down. I started thinking about what I could do for myself during Dick's visit. That evening, feeling somewhat calmer, I welcomed John's turning on the TV to watch a Wizards game. Before going to bed, I sent an update to friends, filling them in on what had transpired since shortly before Thanksgiving.

> Meanwhile, John during his two months at home has maintained his initial weight gain of five pounds and may have gained more (he plans to weigh tomorrow a.m., too late for this message). His wonderfully dry sense of humor shines through, and his positive attitude continues, although he says he is struggling to regain the tremendous powers of concentration that once allowed him to spend great chunks of time at the computer working on his photography.

> On occasion, we venture out for lunch or dinner. Tomorrow John's brother Dick is coming down from NYC for three days to spend time with us and to give me a bit of a breather.

> We've been enjoying sundry gifts, including "Journey of Man," very interesting DVD from my brother and his wife, and the movie "Dr. Strangelove," gift from yours truly. We're still rooting for the Washington Wizards and reading with fascination the tales of political maelstroms here and elsewhere.

> Please keep us posted on what you're up to.

The day after Dick arrived, John had an appointment to have blood drawn by Heyer's associate.

"I'd be glad to go with John," Dick said.

"All right. Thank you. While you do that, I think I'll go shoe shopping, something I haven't done in a long time."

Dick laughed. "Retail therapy, that's what Jacqueline calls it." Jacqueline was Dick's teen-aged daughter. Just eight months earlier, we had attended her high school graduation in New York.

Returning from my mini-shopping spree, I showed off my newly acquired black boots.

"Those ought to be a big hit at First Friday," the condo building's once-a-month social, John said, his wry humor intact.

"Did you drive John to Heyer's office?" I asked Dick that evening.

"No, John wanted to drive. He insisted on driving."

"Really?" I shook my head in disbelief. He had not driven since he was hospitalized. They had gone in the stick shift Infiniti sports car John drove cross-country shortly before our wedding. He loved that car. Was he, despite my anxiety, getting better?

A couple of days after Dick left, I opened an email from a former colleague of John's at Northrop Grumman. "Honey, look at this!" I printed it out and dashed from the office to show John. I waited till he got down to the salient bit.

> Anything you could do for the company would be greatly appreciated. We have requisitioned a secure computer for your use, which will be sent as soon as you give the word.

Northrop Grumman was offering him a consulting contract. My angst evaporated. I forgot about the cancer and everything else that had gone wrong. Trembling with excitement, I looked at John's face while he read it.

He looked up. "This is something I would like to have been offered when I first retired."

"Darling, it sounds like a flexible arrangement." I could see him sitting at the computer, digesting problems and coming up with solutions that he would relay to the West Coast.

"I know what's entailed in getting set up to do the work, and I simply don't have the energy to do it."

"Couldn't I help you get set up?" I was pleading. If John could do this, he could get well.

"No." He stood up and walked into the office. Within minutes, he had sent an email back expressing his appreciation for the offer and his regret that he couldn't accept it. And that was the end of that.

In a split second, my hopes had soared, only to be dashed. I had clung to the unexpected offer as a life preserver in a turbulent sea. With one word, "no," John had let me drown. He knew what I did not. He knew that he was drowning, and could not save himself, let alone me.

On Monday, January 14, we were lingering at the dining room table after dinner when everything changed.

"Would you please get the walker?" John's voice was calm. "I feel too weak to stand up from the table on my own."

Alarms going off in my brain, I hurried to get the walker from the closet. Leaning on it, he pushed himself up from the table, went slowly over to his chair, and lowered himself into it. Extending an arm toward the coffee table, he picked up the remote and turned on the TV. In a few minutes, one of our favorite teams, the Boston Celtics, would be playing a key game that we had planned to watch.

Cleaning up in the kitchen, I glanced at John watching the pregame program. He looked all right. "Do you want something to drink, sweetheart?"

"No."

After turning on the dishwasher, I joined him in the living room. When the first half ended, John stood up. "I'm going to bed early."

"Really? Are you all right?"

"Yes. You can tell me about the game in the morning."

He must be really tired to be missing the game, I thought. Maybe he overdid physical therapy. During time-outs, I checked on him in the bedroom. He seemed to be sleeping. When the game was over, I slipped into bed. About midnight, I was awakened by John's voice.

"I think you'd better call 911."

I sat up and leaned toward him. "What's wrong?!"

"I feel very weak." He had once told me that when he was first diagnosed with Waldenstrom's, he felt acutely weak. "At the time, I was sure I would die at night."

Now wide awake, I reached for the phone and pushed 911.

"What's the problem?"

"My husband feels very weak." I wondered whether they would come, but I couldn't think to say more.

"Is he conscious?"

"Yes. Please come quickly." I hung up the phone.

"They're coming, sweetheart. Oh my god. There's no concierge downstairs. I'll have to let them in." Dashing into the closet, I put on jeans and was pulling on a shirt when the bell rang. I opened the door to a wall of dark blue pants and shirts, three men and a woman. How did they get in? They must have had a master key.

"You called 911?" The man asking the question strode across the threshold into the foyer.

"Yes. It's my husband. He's in the bedroom. Follow me."

John was sitting on the side of the bed. He had pulled on a pair of sweatpants and pushed his arms into a long-sleeved shirt he'd left by the bed.

"Hi. How do you feel?" the man asked.

"I'm almost overcome by a debilitating feeling of weakness."

"Let's check your vital signs." He placed a black bag on the bed and sat down beside John. The others stood at the foot of the bed while the man checked John's pulse and blood pressure and listened to his heart and lungs.

I sat on the other side of the bed, watching and waiting. It seemed to take a long time.

"Everything checks out." He kept looking at John.

Oh no, I thought. They're not going to take him to the E.R. They think he's okay. But something was wrong. John would not have asked me to call 911 without reason.

"We're taking you to the emergency room at Reston Hospital." The man stood up. One of the others disappeared and returned with a wheelchair.

Grabbing my purse and John's wallet with his ID and insurance card, I followed them all out the door and into the elevator.

"I'll see you at the hospital, sweetheart." I gave John a quick kiss before someone pushed his chair out of the elevator into the lobby and I continued down to the garage.

Driving behind the emergency vehicle to the hospital, I parked near the E.R. entrance. After completing the admissions paperwork, I joined John in an E.R. cubicle. He was sitting up in bed.

"Sweetheart, has anyone seen you?"

"Yes. Someone took blood."

A nurse in white whom I remembered from the last time was seated at the nursing station. "We're waiting for a particular E.R. doctor to see your husband. It might be a while."

It was quiet, and the lighting was bright. I lay down beside John in the narrow hospital bed. At around 4, a white-jacketed E.R. doctor appeared. I pulled up a chair. Holding a manila folder in one hand, he sat down on a stool a few feet from the bed. A thatch of curly salt-and-pepper hair fell over his forehead. After talking with John at length, he confessed that he was puzzled by the weakness.

"Here's what I think. I think you might have spinal meningitis. I'm going to admit you to the hospital."

After John was transferred to a private room, I drove home and wrote Heyer a long letter (thinking an email would be less likely to get to him personally) asking whether the E.R. doctor's hypothesis sounded plausible. I drove to his office and left it there before returning home to sleep. Heyer never responded. Looking back, it's clear that he did not want to discuss what had happened with me.

John was hospitalized for four days during which Heyer and Sharma determined that he had a "brain irritation." For whatever reason, neither of us asked what a "brain irritation" meant. I assumed the brain tissue was sensitive to the chemo and needed a rest. Later, I wondered whether this was the inflamed meninges associated with the stronger chemo that John had not agreed to.

While he was hospitalized, Gay called, urging me to get help at home. She had suggested this before John came home from Sunrise, but neither he nor I could visualize what kind of help that might be. Arely, who had been my cleaner in the house Joe and I built, came in every two weeks to clean the condo, which seemed often enough. But because Gay kept insisting that someone from the outside could help relieve my frazzled state, I felt pushed to come up with something. It occurred to me that having someone else prepare meals might help. I remembered that Touching Hearts at Home (T.H.), which had provided transportation to radiology for John, listed meal preparation among its services.

On Monday, January 21, after John's discharge from the hospital with the "brain irritation" diagnosis, we engaged T.H. to come in for three hours twice a week to prepare lunch for John and dinner that I could reheat in the evening. Consulting numerous cookbooks, he and I would select menus. I would do the shopping and make the other meals. I would be able to go to yoga classes and to the library to write in my journal.

Later in the week, John had an appointment with Heyer, his first since being hospitalized. I assumed the chemo regimen would continue.

We were seated in straight-backed chairs waiting for him when the doctor walked in and took a seat on a stool facing us. "John, the cancer has progressed to the point that there is only one treatment option." He spoke in almost a monotone, much like Melanie when she had read the C.T. scan report.

The cancer has progressed? Just *one* option? I stopped breathing. I listened as if in a trance while Heyer talked about another type of chemo, one that might work although it would weaken John's immune system, increasing his susceptibility to infection.

His voice became more inflected. "A part of me wants to try this, but I think you should be aware of the downside." Heyer was scratching himself—arms, legs, shoulders. He must hate this, I thought, but not as much as I did. What he did not say was even more alarming. Nothing had stopped the cancer.

Clear-eyed John, his voice calm, looked directly at Heyer. "I would opt against the treatment."

"I want you to take a few days to think about it. If you're going to be treated, we would have to start right away." Heyer spoke as though he had not heard John.

The possibility of his being rehospitalized with an infection flashed through my mind. John had barely survived the last one, and now he was even weaker. If he got another infection, I could not imagine his surviving.

Acceding to Heyer's request, John made an appointment to return Tuesday afternoon, and we left the office. With John at the wheel, we drove home in silence.

"I don't want the treatment with its expected and untold side effects." John was in his leather chair; I was on the sofa across from him.

Tears stung my eyes. "I understand, darling, and I agree." I swallowed hard. "Is there *anything* I can do?" Determined not to cry, I stared at him, waiting for his response.

"Just be yourself."

I took a deep breath. He had never asked me to be anything other than myself. I would always love him for that. From the moment we met, I had tried to be real, withholding as little as possible from him. And John in his way had revealed himself willingly to me. We had confided not only our strengths but also our weaknesses and insecurities. We had shared our separate dreams and fantasies, and together, with confidence and daring, had forged new ones.

It seemed impossible, after all he had gone through since he was first diagnosed with Waldenstrom's, that the barest shred of hope was now beyond our grasp. He had fought and survived for eighteen years. For the last two, we had persevered together with determined optimism. John was just fifty-eight years old, on the verge of his fifty-ninth birthday, with so many dreams still to be realized, many of them involving me. I felt horribly cheated. Waldenstrom's had erased our future.

Without another word but fully aware of the enormity of the bridge we had just crossed, I got up to retrieve our collection of recipes and cookbooks and set them on the coffee table. T.H. would be here in the morning. We had work to do.

The next day, I sent an email update to friends:

> This is a very hard update to write. We found out yesterday that John's cancer is uncontrollable. We do not know the eventual prognosis, i.e., timing, but the deterioration in his condition is unavoidable now. The only treatment option is high risk with low probability of success, and it would be a few months' minimum before there would be any real indication of the results.
>
> Just keep us in your thoughts.

Despair

On Sunday morning, I was curled up on the sofa with the *Washington Post* when I glanced across the coffee table at John. He was sitting straight in his chair, his long fingers gripping the armrests. The *Times* lay heavy on his lap, untouched. He was staring at me, his face distorted in pain.

"What is it? What's wrong?"

"I feel as though I've gotten you into something that's collapsing, and there's *nothing* I can do." His voice was strained, raw with feeling. I had never heard this voice before. I had never heard him express remorse.

"You told me when we first met," I said, choking back tears. "I knew there was a risk. I didn't want to believe it could happen!"

Moved by his painful admission, I knelt down in front of his chair and wrapped my arms around him. He did not return my embrace. His arms and chest were rigid. I drew back, rebuffed and frightened.

"I'm overcome by the darkest thoughts. I can't dispel them." He was staring at a point beyond my head.

Alarmed, I stood up and went back to the edge of the sofa.

"I'm ready to lop off Santa Fe. That's how desperate I feel, just lop it off!"

What did he mean, "lop off Santa Fe?" He looked crazed. I had never seen him like this. Images of my schizophrenic mother flooded my brain. I sensed he was coming to grips with an awful truth, and I was afraid. I couldn't deal with it. I who had bombarded him with hundreds of probing questions when we first met was afraid to ask him anything.

Struggling to clear my head, I thought of Barbara. She would know how to talk with John, how to listen. She would not be intimidated. "Do you want to talk to someone? I could call my therapist and ask if her colleague Roger could see you."

"Yes."

In the morning, I accompanied him there. As soon as we walked into the waiting room, Roger appeared. White-haired and overweight, he had a rumpled look; his long-sleeved shirt hung out in places over his khaki pants, and on his feet were scuffed athletic shoes. He nodded at me and introduced himself to John, asking him to follow him into his office. I took a seat in an upholstered chair next to a potted schefflera and waited, full of misgivings. Could he help John? I had my doubts. There was no one else in the waiting room. I picked up an old *New Yorker* and put it back on the table. I crossed and uncrossed my legs.

I wanted John not to be in pain. What was he saying to Roger, I wondered. Would I ever know? I imagined him telling Roger how guilty he felt—guilty for marrying me, guilty for dying on me. And was he guilty? For the first time, I wondered. Yes, he had been open about having cancer, but he never warned me that he had had two nearly fatal infections. He didn't tell me about his two-inch-thick medical file. He didn't mention the likelihood of early death. No, on our first walk, he chatted with me easily about controlling the disease with a positive attitude and periodic infusions of Rituxan; he even mentioned a backup treatment waiting in the wings, a safety net that would provide more than a margin of protection. He was not like Joe who had given me fair warning *before* we were married, insisting on a trial visit to Washington, D.C., from my home in San Francisco (where we had met on a business trip of his) and forcing me to face the fact that, being twenty-one years younger, I might not like it when he was much older. No, John did not throw down any red flags when he said he wanted to marry me. Was he so intent on surviving that he could not entertain any doubts? Or was he afraid I would say no if I knew too much?

After fifty minutes, he came out. His face revealed nothing. He plopped down beside me, hunched over, elbows on knees.

"How did it go?" I tried to keep the uneasiness out of my voice.

"I think I depressed him."

"Do you want to see him again?" I was trying to judge where John was.

"I have to," he said haltingly, his voice low and raspy, "because I'm telling him things that I'm unable to tell anyone else."

He meant he couldn't tell *me!* I turned to look at him. He did not meet my gaze. He was staring down at the gray carpet. My brain was on fire. What was it he could not tell me? Without another word, we left the office and drove back to the condo.

The minute we got home, we went to different rooms. In the kitchen, I turned on the gas under the tea kettle and pulled open two packets of Earl Grey. Dropping the bags into a white teapot, I waited for the water to boil. What could I do? Knowing that John was keeping something from me, I felt shunned. A horrible wall of silence had come between us, and *I* was to blame. When he was opening up, I had closed down. By suggesting he might want to talk with Roger, I had told him I couldn't bear to hear what he was trying to tell me.

"Would you like a cup of tea?" I asked a few minutes later when John sat down in his chair.

"Yes."

Setting a cup on the coffee table in front of him, I took mine with me to the sofa. What more was there? What more was there for someone who was dying, whose disease had spiraled out of his control? Last night, I hadn't wanted to know, but now I had to. I couldn't leave him alone with it for another minute. He had always responded to my questions. If I could ask the right one, he might open up again.

"Are you thinking about suicide?" I looked right at him. It was as if I already knew.

"Yes." He held my gaze. His eyes bored into mine. I sensed there was something more.

"Are you thinking about double suicide?"

"Yes." He sat utterly still.

I could hear the rhythm of traffic outside moving with the stop light. Dying together might be a way out of this disaster. Was I ready to die?

"We need to talk about this. We need to know more. Is it even doable? Joe thought seriously about suicide if he had a painful or terminal illness. He had a number of books on the subject that I kept." I had envisioned using them myself if and when the time came. "They're in the bookcase. Let me get them." I pulled down two by Derek

Humphry, handed *Final Exit* to John, and took *Let Me Die Before I Wake* back to the sofa. Pulling my legs under me, I started to read.

For the next couple of hours, we both skimmed, reading aloud significant passages, several marked by Joe. We didn't talk much. John was intent on whether it was doable.

"Here we are," he said.

> This is the scenario: You are terminally ill, all medical treatments acceptable to you have been exhausted, and the suffering in its different forms is unbearable. Because the illness is so serious, you recognize that your life is drawing to a close. Euthanasia comes to mind as a way of release. The dilemma is awesome. But it has to be faced. Should you battle on, take the pain, endure the indignity, and await the inevitable end which may be weeks, or months, away? Or should you resort to euthanasia, which in its modern language definition has come to mean "help with a good death?"

"My grandfather committed suicide when he was eighty-four years old," I said. "He left a letter apologizing to his children, hoping they would understand that he did not want to live without my grandmother who had died some months earlier. He died of carbon monoxide poisoning in his garage." I picked up my cup of tea, more cold than hot. Was I like my grandfather? Would I not want to live without John? When I tried to imagine my life without him, I couldn't. How or why would I live? Without him, I would have nothing. Would I be able to bear the sadness?

Restless and uneasy, I got up and exchanged books with John. Thumbing through the chapter titles, I stopped at one that spoke to me. "Here's a passage about dying together. Let me read this one."

"All right," he said, closing his book over his thumb. He looked up, waiting for what I would say.

> Some couples choose to die together, regardless of whether both are in poor health or only one. It is more likely to happen when both are ailing. Such double exits should be neither promoted nor condemned. Who are we to look in the minds of others? That the couple would wish to die together is a tribute to the strength of a loving relationship.

For a devoted couple at the end of their lives, who are in physically degenerating conditions, a clearly thought out, mutually agreed, and justifiable double suicide is an option we should respect.

"But *how* would we do it?" I asked, looking at John.
"Here's something," he said. "It's about Seconal."

Sonia told her husband that she was going to take entire responsibility for her actions. A friend with some knowledge of drugs advised her that about two and a half grams or twenty-five 100-milligram tablets of Seconal would prove lethal for such a tiny, very ill person as she was . . . . All she wanted from her husband was to have him present in the house to give her peace and security.

"What about the dosage for someone who's not tiny and frail?" I asked.
"A few paragraphs later it gives the exact dosage."

Sonia consumed only about one and a half grams of Seconal, the minimum lethal dose, but it was quite sufficient to end the life of a very sick, frail person who wished to die. Most people should take about 40 Seconal to be certain of self-deliverance.

"We would have to get enough Seconal for both of us," I said. "Would Dr. Heyer agree to help us?"
"I don't know. He might think it went against the Hippocratic Oath."
"Here's one about timing," I said. "Listen to this."

I was Jean's safety device against a too-early self-deliverance. While I did not want her to die, I was willing to take my share of the responsibility of decision-making if it brought her peace. Assisting in difficult decisions is an essential responsibility of a loving relationship.

Secondly, there is often an underlying and healthy reason why people who are terminal are not taking steps to die at a certain point. Something is happening on the fringe of their lives and they want to be part of it: a wedding, a birth . . . .

The bottom line is that they really are not ready to die if they are questioning the advisability of it. My advice in this quandary is: If you are in any doubt, then don't do it. Make the most of the time you have left.

How much time did we have left? Would suicide be senselessly premature? John didn't say. Was he having doubts too?

"Here's something else," he said.

If you want personal control and choice over your destiny, it will require forethought, planning, documentation, friends, and decisive, courageous action from you. This book will help, but in the final analysis, whether you bring your life to an abrupt end, and how you achieve this, is entirely your responsibility, ethically and legally. The task of finding the right drugs, getting someone to help (if you wish that), carrying out your self-deliverance in a place and in a manner which is not upsetting to other people is your responsibility.

"My greatest concern would be the impact on Dick's children," I said. "They're so young, one just out of high school, the other still in college. I don't think they would understand."

"We can't do it." His voice was calm but regretful.

"Why not?" I wanted to know what had made him suddenly give it up.

"Because there is no certainty it would work. We would need a third person."

I heaved a sigh, the first full breath I'd taken since I started the conversation.

Without knowing why, I wanted to live. I did not want to die in a double suicide with John. I didn't want John to die either, but he was going to, and if he wanted to commit suicide, I would try to help him.

"We could go to Oregon. They have doctor-assisted suicide there."

"I wouldn't have the strength."

John was dying, suicide or not. He would have needed my help to carry it out, and I don't think he wanted to put me through that additional ordeal. He was not in physical pain. How could he justify it to himself?

Placing Joe's books back on the shelf, I turned to find John standing behind me. Without a word, we put our arms around each other and held on for a long time. That night after getting into bed, we kissed each other goodnight and slept.

The next morning, we kept our appointment with Heyer, and I listened to John confirm his decision not to undergo any further treatment. He sounded confident and relaxed. The anguish in his voice was gone. My breathing was easier, the tension of the last two days all but dissipated.

"Is this the time to consider hospice?" I asked.

"I will contact hospice today, and you should expect a call soon." Heyer also sounded relaxed. Was he more relieved than disappointed by John's decision? He did not try to talk him out of it.

"Now I want to know what to expect."

Heyer explained that the cancer would affect the brain and respiratory system, not necessarily at the same time: "Shirley will probably notice first because you'll say something nonsensical. You won't know it, but she will."

He was going to lose his mind, his beautiful mind.

I waited for Heyer to say something about the second area. Without another word, he stood up and reached for a pad. "I want to give you a prescription for steroids." Scribbling something on the pad, he tore off a small sheet and handed it to John. "This will help your appetite but could eventually weaken your thigh muscles."

"Thank you." John slipped the sheet into the tan leather-bound diary he took to medical appointments.

"You can call me any time, but you probably won't need to see me again. The hospice nurse will keep me informed." He was matter-of-fact, almost offhand.

I shuddered. It seemed shocking that this man we knew and trusted was cutting us off—not on purpose; it was how medical care worked. The system was compartmentalized. Heyer was in the business of trying to keep people alive. By opting against treatment, John had severed his ties to the doctor he'd relied on. Death was outside Heyer's purview.

We stood up to leave.

"It's not a science," Heyer said. "My worst guess resulted in someone living for more than a year after hospice had been ordered."

Absorbing his words, I filed them away under Hope. Maybe John could still defy the odds.

After our appointment with Heyer, John's physical therapist, Janine, was due for a session, so I went downstairs to the fitness room for a while. When I returned, he was standing at the kitchen sink holding a full glass of water.

"Where's Janine?"

"She ran out in tears when I told her I was terminal."

"Oh." Lithe Janine, her dark hair long and loose, had been seeing John twice a week since he came home. With her encouragement, he had discarded the walker and increased his ability to walk and go up and down stairs. I had thought she might have a crush on John.

"Do you think she'll come back?"

"No." John drank his water.

I was beginning to realize that when a patient is deemed "terminal," all vestiges of medical care disappear one by one.

"I'm going to freshen up before thinking about dinner." Walking out of the kitchen, I looked back. "Have you talked with Dick?"

"Yes. I called him. I told him I had been thinking about suicide."

"What did he say?"

"He said he understood. We engaged in a heartening exchange of gallows humor." John's grin was rueful.

I wondered how it would end. Of course, I knew, but what would start the avalanche? "Shirley will probably notice first," Heyer had said. And what then? I remembered the time John had struggled to tell me something important and couldn't. Would it be like that? I wanted him to be himself until the last moment, but that didn't seem to be in the cards. Would Waldenstrom's take the man I knew and slowly rob him of himself? I shuddered, remembering frightening episodes with my mother. Often, to save myself physically and emotionally, I had fled. I would not flee from John.

Later that week, I kept my standing appointment with Barbara. I assumed Roger had told her about his session with John. I waited while she pulled her legs under her and sat back in her large brown chair.

"Barbara, thank you for speaking to Roger."

"I'm glad he could see John."

"After meeting with him, John admitted to me that he was thinking about suicide, not just his but double suicide."

Barbara's brown eyes opened wide. "Shirley, how do you feel about that?"

"At first, I thought it wouldn't be a bad solution. I love him so much, so deeply. I would do almost anything for him." Pulling tissues from the small box on the table next to my chair, I wiped tears from my cheeks. "I can't believe he's dying, not after all we've gone through—the surgeries, the radiation, the chemo. He survived the infection. I can't believe it was all for nothing!"

"You said that at first, you thought suicide wouldn't be a bad solution. What do you think now?"

"We spent a long time reading books by Derek Humphry. They were Joe's. I'd never read them. As we read through them, I realized I didn't want to die. I don't know how I'll feel after John dies, but right now, I want to live."

"What about John?"

"He's not considering it now. That day I called you, I think he was in shock that he had lost control of his cancer and was consumed with remorse for getting me involved with him. He was and still may be afraid that I won't be able to live without him. Suicide would have given him back the feeling of control, but to what end? He's not in physical pain. We're both in emotional pain, but this may pass. We both know I'm going to be bereft, but maybe I'll be able to bear it. I don't know. I just know that when John said we couldn't do it because there was no certainty without involving a third person, I was relieved. Dr. Heyer said it's not a science. Maybe John will outlast the statistics."

"How did you leave things with Dr. Heyer?"

"You mean after John told him he didn't want any more treatment?"

"Yes, how did Dr. Heyer react to that?"

"He listened. He didn't try to persuade him to change his mind. When I asked him if it was time to involve hospice, he said he would contact hospice and that we should expect a call in the next couple of days." Having dried my tears, I started sobbing.

"You might want to ask Dr. Hong for an antidepressant, something that will keep you relatively even."

The next day, I was staring at Hong's print of the Yellow Mountains in China when he walked in. A hiking enthusiast, he radiated good health.

"What can I do for you, Shirley?" Until John became ill and I asked for something to help me sleep, he had been accustomed to seeing me only for my annual physical.

I looked up at a smooth, bespectacled face framed by straight black hair. He was a kind man. He had been happy for me when I told him I was remarrying.

"My husband is dying of cancer."

He stopped smiling. "I'm very sorry."

"My therapist thought you might prescribe an antidepressant to help me over the next few weeks or months."

"Of course. I'll write a prescription for Zoloft. Start taking it right away. It will take up to six weeks to take effect."

"What does it do?"

"It will keep you from sinking and allow you to function." He handed me the prescription.

"Thank you." I did not want to sink. I wanted to stay afloat, at least as long as John was alive.

Before the end of the week, Marco of Capital Hospice called and made an appointment to meet with us. On Saturday afternoon, I opened the door to a slender young man carrying a thick binder.

Perched on the edge of the sofa, Marco gave us the history of hospice and explained in-home hospice care. A team of nine caregivers would come to our condo, some more often than others. A hospice nurse would be John's regular contact, and in the days ahead, we would be meeting the others. "You'll receive a package of drugs by FedEx. Keep the package in your refrigerator." He paused and looked at John. "You don't need to register now for hospice, but if you choose to sign up, you can unenroll at any time."

"Give me the papers," John said without hesitating. "I'm ready to sign."

On Monday, we met Kim, the hospice nurse, and Leisa, a social worker. Exuding warmth and openness, they shook hands with John and sat on the sofa across from us. John started talking right away.

"I'm comfortable with my decision to stop treatment," he volunteered, "because I want to have as much good time with Shirley as possible." He was enlisting their help.

Tears stung my eyes. This was the first time I had heard him say that I was the reason he'd refused more treatment. There was something noble about John's decision. It took courage to let go of hope, to put his remaining energy into living rather than trying to control the uncontrollable.

"I plan to assemble a book of sorts, things Shirley should know to handle our affairs." He was commanding, upbeat, like a CEO at an annual meeting of stockholders.

A book? Hearing this, I knew he wanted to take care of me. He *wanted* me to survive his death. And he would help me survive it. By assembling this book, he would be helping me as much as he could to manage the business of living without him. How very kind, I thought. Now that he was no longer struggling to survive, he was putting my survival front and center. My eyes welling with tears, I moved my chair closer to John's and reached for his hand. I had never felt so loved and cared for.

The next day, my friend Rick from work stopped by to take me to lunch. Before he arrived, John went into the bedroom and returned holding his wedding ring between his thumb and forefinger. Since being hospitalized, he had worn neither his ring nor his watch. Looking at me unsmilingly, he pushed the gold band onto his ring finger. I said nothing. Why was he doing this now? Was it a reminder to me to be faithful? He knew he would be losing me as his mate. Already he could see that other men would be taking me to lunch, to dinner, and to bed. We had not made love in five months, since just before he was hospitalized in September. Occasionally, we talked about how much we would like to, but we didn't. Sensing that John did not have the energy, I didn't push him to try.

On Wednesday, I went to yoga, returning in time to meet the hospice chaplain. A tall husky African-American with a round face, he sat on the sofa while I sat in a chair next to John.

"Dying is a revelation," he boomed. "My good mother died a few years ago." He paused. "Before she passed, she told me she saw God and that he was welcoming her to heaven."

I glanced at John, who rolled his eyes. "Excuse me," I said, interrupting his monologue. "John is very much a scientist and not a believer per se."

"Yes," he said, seeming not to hear me. "She was a good woman, and at the end, she had a smile on her face. Dying and seeing God is something we can all look forward to." Hardly taking a breath, he ranted on without asking John a single question. John, ever polite, said nothing. He would not have wanted to upset this man whose beliefs were so contrary to his own.

"Well, I suppose I should be getting along," he said. He walked over and vigorously shook John's hand. "I'm here for you."

"Thank you for coming by," I said, ushering the chaplain out the door.

He looked back at me. "Call me any time."

"Thank you." This was one member of the team we would not be seeing again.

On Thursday, Kim Beach, who had married us, stopped by. He asked John a lot of questions about his life, which he answered forthrightly and thoughtfully. Kim would reflect on nuggets of this conversation at John's memorial service.

Over the weekend I picked up the folder left by Marco and forced myself to read the manual on how to care for someone who is dying. I found it daunting. "Sweetheart," I said from my seat on the sofa, "if you become bedridden as described in this manual, I know I'll have to have help." I could not imagine being able to care for John alone.

"Yes." John nodded his understanding. "But I would not want to be institutionalized."

"Of course not. You would be here, and I would hire help." I had no notion of John's being cared for anywhere but at home. But life had other plans for us.

Our Last Best Time

WHEN I AWOKE ONE MORNING IN LATE FEBRUARY, THE BEDROOM was bathed in pearly light. On the far wall, a watercolor of lavender-petaled desert flowers painted by my mother floated above the dresser. The white drapes were open, exposing the sliding glass doors to the balcony. In one corner stood a large green flowerpot, empty since the summer after our wedding when fuchsia petunias cascaded toward the floor. The sky was gray-white, a winter sky.

"I must have forgotten to close the drapes last night."

"Yes," John said, leaning over to kiss me. "While I've been lying here, waiting for you to wake up, I've been overcome by the feeling that I'm getting better. I'm not exhausted or even tired after wandering through the supermarkets yesterday." He sat up, his long bare arms resting on top of the white wool blanket. Never muscular, they looked thinner than ever despite his gaining weight.

John's words caught me by surprise. "Oh?" I shook my head awake and sat up, leaning back against the pillows. "How wonderful!"

"I think my fifteen-pound weight gain has strengthened me considerably. If I didn't know better, I'd think I was getting well."

My heart was flip-flopping.

"Darling," I said, reaching across the blanket for his hand. "Maybe you're going to be okay."

Squeezing my hand, he looked me in the eye. "I'm feeling better, but I'm not getting well. You must understand that."

My stomach tightened. Of course, I understood. It was just that when he looked and sounded good, I couldn't stop myself from hoping for a miracle. "I do," I said, caressing his arm, feeling its warmth and smoothness.

"I made my decision so that we could enjoy this time together, our last best time."

"I know. You gave us this gift, and that's what we'll do. We'll enjoy each day to the hilt, I promise."

"*I* promise," he said, pressing his long fingers into my hand.

That night, we had planned a special dinner at Il Fornaio with Dick and Kerry. As a Christmas gift, we had given them an IOU for "Dinner Out in Reston." John was delighted to be able to deliver on our debt.

"Tonight I'm going to wear dress pants and a good shirt," he said at breakfast.

"Wow! If you're going to look that good, I'm going to have to spruce up."

"This will be my first time out to a restaurant for dinner since August!" He sounded buoyant.

John now weighed a hundred sixty-five pounds. After the infection, he had gone down to a hundred fifty, but his normal weight was a hundred seventy-five. Although he had not put flesh on his arms, his thighs and buttocks were filling out. His appetite was back, much as it had been before the infection. I smiled, remembering his recent declaration. He had been at the kitchen sink, emptying the coffee pot while I stood nearby making up a grocery list.

"I want to eat whatever I have a craving for," he said, turning to look at me. His blue eyes were sparkling.

"So, what are you craving? Tell me what you want, and I'll get it," I said, my ballpoint hovering over the list.

"Saint-André cheese and double-cream Brie with water crackers."

"Is that it?"

"For your list, yes. One evening, I'd like to go to Morton's for a really good steak."

"I'm sure we can arrange that," I laughed, thinking of his upcoming birthday.

John was helping the way he used to—unloading the dishwasher in the mornings, defrosting and toasting bagels, emptying trash and wastebaskets, and setting the table for dinner. The previous week, he had driven to the Wine Cabinet and used a gift certificate to buy a variety of reds and whites, including a couple of bottles of Petit Chenin from South Africa which we had served at our Safari Show & Tell. Now before dinner, he was enjoying a glass of wine while I sipped single-malt scotch.

We were both reading—books as well as the daily papers. After completing *Predictable Irrationality*, he'd started *What the Gospels Meant* and *God's Problem: How the Bible Fails to Answer Our Most Important Question—Why We Suffer*, which he had ordered from Amazon after reading about them in the *Times* book review. I was reading Barack Obama's *Dreams From My Father*, struck by the angst of his search for self, his intelligence and sensitivity.

It was still February when I sent an email update:

John has decided to stop treatment. Our despair and disappointment have given way to an acceptance of what is, knowing that despite the outcome, we have considerable control on many levels. A few weeks ago, John enrolled in hospice without hesitation. Fortunately, he's feeling good right now—ambulatory, cognizant, and pain-free despite increasing numbness in his hands. It's comforting to know there's a structure in place that will provide support at home for each of us down the line. We've met four of the hospice team of nine, and the drug pac, complete with morphine, is in the fridge.

Each day that John feels okay is a gift. His appetite is good, enhanced by the steroid Decadron, and he's regained more than fifteen pounds. He attributes his feeling of well-being largely to being comfortable with his decision to stop treatment. We're seeing friends as possible. Some bring in dinner to share, others lunch. Now and again, I'll go out to lunch with friends. John's brother Dick has been a welcomed visitor, sometimes just dropping by for a couple of hours and other times staying a night or two. He's an excellent cook, so dinner and breakfast by Ricardo are a treat. Yesterday, John announced that the first Formula One Grand Prix race of the season will take place in Australia on March 15 close to midnight our time, and that he's looking forward to watching it on TV. One week later is John's fifty-ninth birthday, March 22, and we're planning to celebrate!

Reading this now, I wish I had made it clear that John's decision was as much about devotion as acceptance—unwavering devotion to me, and to us as a couple. He had survived the infection "because of you, because of us," he'd said, and now he seemed determined to make whatever time remained fulfilling for both of us.

John sent an email to Gwenael, president of Le Verre Fluoré, telling him that he had decided to stop treatment, and resigning as the optical fiber company's U.S. representative. Gwenael wrote back:

> Pierrette, Erwan, and Yann-Fanch Furic were deeply moved by your news. Yann-Fanch remembered your fine palate—for wine in particular—and Erwan our joyful cider-seeking tour of Brittany. Pierrette spoke of the wonderful time we had with you and Shirley last summer in the Aber, and asked about both of you facing the fate with courage. Your involvement as representative has been of primary importance for our company. It was for me a pleasure and a constant reward to work with you in full confidence all that time. I appreciate that in spite of your troubles, you continued up to the limit. I got your messages of 24 and 27 January, and the payment for the ANMH arrived. However sad it is, I understand and respect your decision.

In many ways, I began to feel that we had our life back. I took comfort in remembering Heyer's "It's not a science" comment. I liked imagining the moment when he would say that hospice was no longer medically necessary. My father's cancer had gone into remission for nine months after hospice had been summoned the first time. Why not John's?

My routine of going to the library with my journal for an hour or so after yoga continued. One afternoon, I took in a movie and didn't get back to the condo until close to dinnertime. A couple of weeks later, sipping tea in the living room, I scanned the newspaper listings. "I'm looking at these movies and nothing grabs me." I glanced across the coffee table at John, who looked up from reading the *Economist*.

"Unless you really want to go, I like for you to be here." His gaze held mine.

My heart melted. I never again considered leaving John to go to the movies.

One afternoon, Kim stopped by for her weekly hospice visit. I was in the kitchen putting away groceries and heard her talking with John.

"How are you feeling?" she asked.

"I'm feeling better than ever. Shirley and I are enjoying this time together."

"I'm glad to hear that."

"I've just ordered a book I want to read, about research showing that most people want to keep all options open." He had told me, and now was telling Kim. "I'm intrigued by the book's premise, especially since I closed the treatment option and feel good about it."

"I think you made the right decision, but it must have been difficult," she said, her voice registering empathy and concern.

"Knowing what I know and weighing the pros and cons, it was not a difficult decision." John sounded sure of himself, without the slightest trace of self-pity.

After all the anguish, we were relishing the respite. To me, it was worth everything I went through with John's infection to have this time with him. Looking back, I realize it would have been easier for John if the infection had killed him, but *I* wasn't ready. I think he knew that, and now he was doing whatever he could to make his death easier for me to bear. I was no longer in denial, but John's acceptance was more complete than mine. Understanding this, he was firm yet gentle with my faltering grasp on the reality that I would soon lose him.

A few days later, after shopping for groceries, I returned to the condo. Much to my surprise, John wasn't there. Minutes later, he walked in, a big grin on his face.

"I just drove to the optometrist to have my eyes checked. I ordered new glasses." He was joyous.

"Really?"

"Yes. The new prescription will let me see better than ever with the eye that was damaged years ago by steroids."

My jaw dropped. It was as though nothing was wrong, as if John, like any healthy person, needed a new prescription for glasses. You'd think he planned to live forever. He said nothing about the fact that he'd driven, for the first time since Dick's visit; I had planned to suggest he sell his car. Stunned and thrilled, I let myself toy with the possibility that he might beat the odds. After that excursion, hardly a day went by that he didn't drive somewhere in Reston, and one night a week or so later, he drove us half an hour to and from Arlington.

The next day after yoga, I called him before driving to the library. "How are things?"

"Good."

"Is Tracy preparing dinner?"

"Yes. The chicken dish with Indian spices already smells good!" Since hiring T.H. to prepare meals, John had served informally as the supervising chef. Once, when Tracy asked him which bottle of red wine she should use for a dish, he reminded her that the recipe called for white. On another occasion, he interceded in the nick of time to tell her she had left out the spices in a lamb ragù recipe he'd found in the *Times*. We found "Tracy moments" more amusing than aggravating. I was glad John had something to do while I was out at yoga.

That night after dinner, we watched the Lakers-Suns game—with Shaq newly traded from the Miami Heat. John rooted for Los Angeles, his hometown for twenty years, while I cheered on the Suns. The Lakers won.

A few minutes after 10, John went out on the balcony and stepped back in. "I'm going downstairs, out back, to check on the lunar eclipse." Earlier, the sky had been filled with snow flurries, and we had thought we would miss the total eclipse, but now the sky was clear.

"I'll go with you."

Grabbing our windbreakers, we went out into the dimly lit parking lot. Holding my hand, John led me through the cars into a wide open area. The air was cool and still. Standing there, hand-in-hand, we looked up. A red glow surrounded the blackened moon.

"The reddish orb is amazing," I said. "Why is there any light at all?"

"Can't be black," he explained, "because the sun's light refracts around the Earth's edges, hitting the moon."

I liked knowing that the moon could never be totally dark despite being eclipsed. John too was being eclipsed at the very moment of coming into his own fullness. And yet, despite the inexorable shadow moving across his life, he was touched with an undeniable radiance.

That day, like many others, felt remarkably normal. John's remembering and wanting to check on the lunar eclipse was something he would have done when he wasn't ill.

The next day's mail held two surprises. I was working at the computer when John walked into the office. "These are for you," he said, handing me two light, rectangular packages, one thicker than the other.

"But I haven't ordered anything," I said, getting up from my chair. I sat down on the living room sofa with the parcels while John stood watching me. Curious, I tore the wrapping from the thicker package to find a box of my favorite candy: See's Scotchmallows. Together we had finished the Valentine's batch. "You're too kind," I said, grinning. "I know you'll help me with these."

"You can count on it," he laughed, plucking one from the box I held out with a flourish.

Savoring the delicious chocolate-caramel concoction, I slipped the wrapping from the second package. "Oh my." In my hands lay a slender book with a gray linen cover; on it, wildebeest and zebra grazed under a cloud-streaked blue African sky. Beneath the photo was the title in charcoal lettering: *Another African Day: Botswanan Game Drive, November 2006.*

John had talked about assembling a book of his safari photos. But that was when he was well. I thought the plan had gone the way of so many others. And now he had done it.

Holding my breath, I opened the cover and found myself staring into the golden eyes of a magnificent one-eared lion. John had been the only one to capture a head-on shot of this male lazing in the shade of a cigar tree with his pride. Below the photo were the words, *Photography and Narrative by John Bessey,* 2008. Beneath the year, he had signed his name. I turned the page. In black lettering in the center of the blank page, I read the dedication:

To Shirley
The love of my life

Tears wetting my cheeks, I looked up at John. "When did you do this?" I choked.

"The last couple of weeks, when you were out for yoga or here practicing the piano."

Slowly I turned page after page, reliving our safari, remembering our Show & Tell and the program for George Mason University that we would never do. In the back of the book, John's captions told the story of each photo. I focused on the one for "Leader of the Pride": "The face of the leading male bears witness to the struggle to remain on top. Scars and a missing ear are only external signs of a life spent rebuffing challenges to his leadership." At the time, John had said he felt a connection with this lion who, according to our guide, would not live much longer. Now it struck me as prophetic. It was John who had selected the lion for his title page. My heart was aching.

"It's beautiful, darling. Thank you."

Two weeks later, I was playing the piano when John walked in with the mail and handed me a slender package.

"This looks familiar," I said, removing the outer wrapping.

"Yes, but there's one change on the dedication page."

Extracting *Another African Day* from the cellophane envelope, I opened it. Below the original dedication, four lines had been added:

> *Our time together*
> *has been more*
> *than I had any*
> *right to expect.*

Under it he had written in black ink in a shaky hand:

> *To Shirley*
> *All my love forever*
> *John*

My cheeks wet with tears, I stood up and wrapped my arms around him. He returned my embrace, his lips close to my ear.

"This is the book I want you to have," he said softly. "I'll give the other one to Dick and Kerry."

"Thank you," I said, overcome. Later, I wondered if those four lines were an apology. I hoped not.

Late the next afternoon, jacketed against the cool air, we lazed on the balcony sipping wine.

"I've decided to enter the Fairfax County Arts Council juried exhibition," he said, swiveling his chair toward mine.

"Oh? Where is it and when?"

"It'll be at GRACE in July. The registration deadline is March 28."

"Do you have something in mind?"

"Yes. I'll enter four photos, all taken in Brittany last spring. I'm going to submit a smaller-than-usual format." For the past two years, the jury had selected one or more of John's submissions. Why not again?

"What a great idea!" I was delighted by his enthusiasm and more than a little surprised. Just a few days earlier, Dee Ann had offered to help him have a one-man show of his photography at a gallery in Santa Fe. John had turned her down, saying he didn't have the energy to do it.

"Are you sure?" I'd asked, clueless about what might be involved.

"Yes. It would require a lot of printing and framing, not to mention hanging on gallery walls. I'd have to be in Santa Fe."

His no to Dee Ann had made me wince. A show of his own was one thing John had wanted to accomplish in life, and he had been working toward it for years.

"I have three new photo ideas," he said, setting his wine glass on the table between us.

"Yes?"

"I'd like to enter them in next year's Arts Council competition posthumously or give them to GRACE. I'm calling one *Ten Spaces,* inspired by the view from this balcony. From here, I can look down at Reston Town Center and see ten parking spaces on Market Street alongside the Hyatt Regency. Most of them are filled whenever I look, but given enough time, I figure I could capture a photo of each space empty. The last photo would be of all ten spaces filled."

"How would you display them?"

"It would be an interactive wall display. I'd mount the photos in a circle on something like a roulette wheel, allowing the viewer to spin the wheel. "

"I like it, and GRACE has the space for it."

Only now do I see that John, as an artist, was finding ways of dealing with his impending death through his photography. First was the photo of the failing lion on the title page of his safari album. Now with *Ten Spaces,* he was playing with absence and chance, making concrete how the spin of a wheel leaves one space empty—the space that would soon be his—while all the others remain filled.

"My second idea is to shoot those white candles on the dining room table, the ones that drip in all directions, against a solid-color background and call it *Straighten Up and Drip Right.*

I grimaced at the memory of those candles dripping all over the glass tabletop. "I guess I'd better not throw them out yet," I laughed. This tongue-in-cheek humor was John's way of refusing to give in to self-pity. "And the third idea?"

"A montage—a photo of blooming flowers with the blossoms blacked out on top of a simulated article on terror from the *Times* and a Freedom of Information Act printed release with nearly everything blacked out."

Here it was again: the eclipse. At the time, I thought it was merely a political statement. "Intriguing. Do you know what you'll call it?"

"No."

The word "posthumously" ricocheted in my brain. John was looking ahead, and he was not envisioning a miracle.

A few days later, I was heating a can of Progresso chicken noodle soup for lunch when John walked into the kitchen.

"I want to show you something." Turning down the gas under the saucepan, I followed him into the office. The door to the closet was open, the light on. He stepped in and placed a hand on a brown-paper-wrapped package tied with twine on the shelf above the hangers. "This package contains my four submissions for the juried exhibition I applied to online. They're framed and ready to hang. I wanted you to know where the actual ones were in case I'm not here."

"July's not that far off," I said, wishing John would stop forcing me to face reality.

That evening over chocolate ice cream, I asked him about the photo workshops he had taken. "Were they all related to landscape photography?"

"Yes. But if I were well, I would *really* want to take a portrait workshop and start photographing people."

"Really?" Early in our relationship, John had confided his difficulty in picking up on social cues. "I thought you were dedicated to photographing landscapes."

"I've been photographing landscapes for a long time. Now I wish I'd had the self-confidence to photograph people years ago."

John had taken wonderful portraits of our guides in Africa that he had matted and carefully packaged before mailing to Botswana. There were so many people without talent living to a ripe old age, so many people without John's kindness and zest for living. When we got married, I pictured us living out our dreams, growing old together, holding hands until the end. Even now, after all that had happened, that image still floated in my brain.

One afternoon a couple of weeks before his birthday, John walked into the living room from the office, carrying a copy of the *Economist*.

I looked up from my book. "Would you like a cup of tea?" It was too early for wine.

"Yes."

Setting a cup on the table in front of him, I sat back on the sofa and pulled my legs up. "I've been thinking about your birthday. How would you like to go to the Inn at Little Washington?" A two-hour drive or more from Reston, it was a highly touted destination restaurant and inn. I had gone there with Joe more than once for special celebrations, but John and I had never been there together.

His response took me by surprise. "No, I'm afraid it would only remind me of what I'm going to be missing." He sounded matter-of-fact, not regretful. Wasn't he going to be missing everything? Why would this, more than something else, remind him of what he would be missing? Was it because it was his last birthday, his last special time with me? Unlike his no to Northrop Grumman and Dee Ann, this one had nothing to do with waning energy. It was a self-protective no. He was closing a door to an experience he knew he would never be able to relive.

"Where would you like to go?" I asked.

"Morton's."

For his birthday, John received a batch of zany cards. Early in the day, I found purple irises, his favorite flower, at Whole Foods and placed them in the turquoise crystal vase on the coffee table next to my wrapped gifts. "These are for you," I said when John walked in from the office.

Sitting on the sofa, he carefully removed the paper from the larger one, a heavy book titled *Life* by famed nature photographer Frans Lanting. John admired Lanting's work; he'd ordered his book on Africa before our safari. He could not help but be intrigued by Lanting's concept of "a personal journey through time." At least I hoped so. Setting the tome on the coffee table, he picked up the smaller package. It was a C.D., *Return to Forever* by jazz great Chick Corea.

The irony of the two titles in the context of John's last birthday did not hit me until later. I see now that *Life* and *Return to Forever* were more about me than him. The Chick Corea C.D. was not new for John; he had one in Santa Fe. I wanted to hear it in Reston. "All my love forever" is what he'd written, and that's what I would remember when listening to *Return to Forever* without him.

That evening, we walked from the condo complex across the parkway and down Market Street to Morton's. John was not wearing the dress slacks he'd worn to dinner with Dick and Kerry a month earlier. "I can't close the waist," he said that morning, walking into the bedroom to show me the problem: A discernible pot on his slender frame kept the button and buttonhole inches apart. He now weighed a hundred eighty-three pounds.

"Your black microfiber pants should be just fine with the blue and white shirt; you'll look great." I was glad I'd ordered a couple of pair from REI before John came home. With an elasticized waist, they were easy to get in and out of.

Entering the low-ceilinged restaurant, we threaded our way through a crowd of bodies waiting to be seated. The din from the adjacent bar was inescapable. After a wait that felt too long, we were led into the quieter dining area. Seated side by side in a leather banquette, we took in the display of raw meats offered by our white-jacketed waiter and made our selection: filets, medium-rare, with sides of wild mushrooms and giant asparagus. Reviewing the wine list, John selected a French burgundy and told the sommelier, "We'll start with Kir Royales."

"Happy Birthday!" We clinked our flutes of berry-hued Kir Royale.

"Thank you," John said, smiling. "Here's to being together."

"Yes."

"It took us a while . . . as in years!" he said, shaking his head.

"I'm glad we've crammed in so much—but I think you've always crammed in a lot."

"Yes, but before I met you, it was solitary."

"What is this?" I asked the waiter as he placed small plates of tantalizing lobster in front of each of us.

"Our treat for making you wait so long to be seated."

"The wait was worth it," John said, picking up his fork. "Thank you."

The lobster appetizer was not the only treat by Morton's that evening. The lava cake with melted chocolate interior was outrageously delicious. John's arrived with a single flaming candle, which he snuffed out with thumb and forefinger.

That night, lying in bed, I thought about John's comment. Was he solitary before he met me? Despite his long marriage and brief engagement, he must have felt, in some sense, alone. I thought about how close we had become and how much pleasure we took in our many pursuits. We had so many plans—so many—and now, we were intentionally living in the moment because the future no longer existed for us.

My eyes were not welling up with tears. The Zoloft must be working.

The next morning, after a breakfast of toasted bagels slathered with cream cheese, John poured the last of the coffee into our cups and sat back down. "I'm going to ask Kim to visit every two weeks instead of weekly. I'm feeling well, and I don't need to see her every week." With that, he stood up and started clearing the table.

No, I thought to myself, but hospice protocol may require her seeing *you*.

"We should know soon whether I'm getting worse," John said, closing the dishwasher. "I'm tempted to ask Dr. Heyer to run another IgM test," which would determine the protein level in his blood.

"I'm not so sure we want to know. What good would it do?" John was feeling well. I didn't want to break that fragile spell with a reality I wasn't sure I could face.

A few minutes later, John reported that Kim had tried to dissuade him, then agreed to the schedule change if they could talk by phone the weeks she didn't visit.

That week, he proposed that we cancel T.H. "We could go out to dinner one night a week," he said.

"Maybe two," I replied.

"Yes. We're missing out on a lot of good meals because the recipes we have for T.H. don't take enough time to merit T.H. preparation. I'm talking about the casseroles."

"You know, sweetheart, we hired T.H. more for me than for you. I'd like to give it more thought. I'm going downstairs for a stint on the treadmill."

"All right."

John was sitting at the computer when I returned. I leaned into the office. "Although I'm not crazy about eating lots of casseroles because they're fattening, I simply can't envision cooking right now," I said.

"I could do the cooking."

"But," I reminded him, "you're the patient! Are you trying to save money?"

"No. Look, I'm comfortable with continuing T.H." He sounded unperturbed.

"Thank you."

"You know," John said the next day, "it's a good thing we didn't stop T.H. because after errands at three shopping centers today, I'm tired."

I had to smile. I was glad we'd been able to discuss the issue, and relieved that I hadn't agreed only to regret it later. Because of T.H., we had a ready supply of frozen leftovers. Granted, I found them tastier than John did. I would continue to make desserts. His favorite was the cranberry-apple crisp, with poppy seed cake and apple pie close behind.

In early April, John fell into the role of caregiver for a day when I was scheduled for a colonoscopy as part of my annual physical. He got up an hour earlier than usual that morning to fix breakfast for himself. At 8, I was awakened by a gentle caressing of my arm and shoulder. I opened my eyes to find John sitting on the edge of the bed, smiling down at me. He was fully dressed.

"It's time," he said. His voice was low and soft.

Feeling his touch and hearing his words warmed me through and through. He had told me the night before that he would get up early, letting me sleep in. He was true to his word. So thoughtful. He was taking care of me.

I smiled up at him. "All right. Have you had breakfast?"

"Yes."

"I'll take a shower and be ready to go in half an hour."

Shortly after the procedure, I was recovering in the post-op area when John walked in. Just seeing him, my heart skipped a beat.

"They say you can go home now."

"Good. I'm ready." Feeling somewhat unsteady on my feet, I held fast to John as he led me to the car. After arriving home, I still felt woozy.

"Do you want some soup?" he asked.

"I don't think I can eat anything right now."

"Why don't you lie down?"

I followed him into the bedroom where he turned down the bed and tucked me in. The feeling of being cared for was powerful. I wasn't used to being pampered. I couldn't remember ever being cared for like this.

That night at dinner, John toasted me. "I want to thank you for all the things you do, many of which I would do if I could. You do the shopping and the cleaning up after dinner, and you never complain. It's a joy to just sit together reading the newspapers in the morning. I like the routine we've developed—reading, doing things in the office, seeing friends now and then. I'm glad you've carved out time for yourself—yoga, the library, and other times for your hair, a facial, or a pedicure. By the way, I really like your new sassy haircut and highlights."

I was surprised and touched. Later, I remembered that the night before Joe died, he thanked me for all I had done. Weeks after his death, I wondered whether he'd had a premonition before he spoke. Hearing John's toast, I wasn't thinking about premonitions. I was relishing the warmth of his words.

In bed that night, John followed the ritual he had initiated early in our relationship. Even if I got into bed an hour or more later than he did, he would kiss me goodnight and place his hand over my hand closest to him, gently pressing his long smooth fingers into my palm before turning onto his left side away from me. It felt like an embrace. In the morning, after I had opened my eyes—he was usually awake first—he would lean over and kiss me good morning. Even now, after all he had endured, he continued the ritual. I could not imagine living without it.

In early April, I wrote in my journal: "The days, so very precious, are going too quickly." While we were consciously living in the moment with each other, there were all of these loose ends that John was addressing.

One morning, we were still in bed when he sat up and pushed himself against the pillows. "When Naomi and Tom get back from China, I want to take them to dinner at Il Fornaio."

"Sounds good to me, a reward for all the pecan pies Naomi's baked for you."

"And I want to take Rick to lunch one day soon to ask him to help you sell my car. He was looking at the far wall as though focused on a to-do list I couldn't see. The words "after I die" hung in the air unsaid.

"Do you want me to call him this week? He spends a lot of time at Dulles and could easily swing by for lunch."

"Yes."

"You're filling our social calendar to a fare-thee-well, and I'm all for it."

Rick agreed to meet us for lunch across the street at Clyde's. Bespectacled and dressed in a dark suit, he was waiting when we walked in. A young woman led us to a leather booth. Large models of racing yachts sat on a low wall dividing the area from one with airplanes suspended from the ceiling. After placing our orders, John put the question to Rick.

"I'd like for you to help Shirley sell my G-35 Infiniti when the time comes." Rick was the purchasing agent for the Airports Authority, and sold cars for friends as a hobby.

"I'd be glad to, John, and the car in Santa Fe if you want me to."

"Not so fast," I said. "I'm keeping the condo in Santa Fe; I'll need the Xterra."

"Oh?" Rick's brown eyes behind his glasses grew large.

"Yes, Shirley says she's keeping the condo."

A couple of nights earlier when Kathy and Jack had dropped by to visit, I'd gasped when John said, "Shirley will be selling the Santa Fe condo as soon as she's gone through my things."

"No," I said. "I'm *not* selling the condo; I have no desire to sell it. I'm going to spend time in Santa Fe because you love it there." John's eyes opened wide. I was annoyed that he had made such a major assumption without discussing it with me. I envisioned dividing my time between Santa Fe and Reston. More than that I didn't know.

One morning over breakfast, I shared my thoughts on Santa Fe. "I've been thinking, sweetheart. When I'm alone, I'd like to stay in Santa Fe for as long as three months at a time."

"You can't." John set his coffee cup down on the table.

"Why not?"

"Because the bills will be coming to Reston. Two weeks ago, I converted all the automatic electronic payments from my bank account to paper mailed to Reston so you would be able to see what's what."

"Oh no." I couldn't believe something so trivial would prevent me from staying in Santa Fe. First, John had told people I'd be selling the condo. Now, he said I couldn't stay there because of some clerical hitch. You'd think he didn't want me to go to Santa Fe! Later, I wondered if it was the expense of holding onto the condo that he didn't want me to incur.

"It'll be all right," he said after a silent moment. "I can arrange in a month or so to have the paper bills from Santa Fe automatically paid from your bank account."

"Thank you."

One afternoon, he told me he'd emailed Santa Fe photographer Carlan Tapp. "I explained my situation, telling Carlan I wanted to donate my photographic film equipment to a deserving organization and had been thinking of his foundation. It's a 501(c)3 that supports young Native Americans who've come out of prison and want to study photography."

"That sounds wonderful." I knew that John had put his film equipment, complete with darkroom, into storage when he switched to digital photography shortly before we met. He had taken photography courses led by Carlan, including the one to Canyon de Chelly after we married. He was impressed by Carlan, who had apprenticed with Ansel Adams.

That weekend, John spent hours in the office printing photographs of varying sizes. On Monday, he mailed a selection of Brittany prints to Gwenael and Pierrette. The next day he shipped a large print of *Dog Tracks* to Dee Ann, who had asked to buy it.

The good time and the end time. That's what we were living. I didn't ask John about the nuts-and-bolts book about his affairs that I knew he was assembling for me. As important as it would be, a part of me feared its completion. This, more than any other loose end he was tying up, was freighted with meaning. Completing the book would signal the end, the end of our last best time.

Giving Away a World

AFTER A SUNDAY MORNING BREAKFAST OF SCRAMBLED EGGS AND bacon, we moved from the kitchen into the living room to read the papers. Natural light filtered through the ficus in the bay windows. The baby grand gleamed cranberry red. I glanced at the headlines in the *Post* and looked across at John, partly hidden behind the pages of the *Times*. My thoughts were not on the day's news stories. I had awakened thinking about Santa Fe, wondering what I would find in the storage units there. Restless, I got up to fix some tea.

Placing a cup on the table in front of John, I returned to the sofa and sat back, pulling my legs under me. "Is there anything I might find in Santa Fe that you would rather I didn't?"

He lowered the paper to look at me, shaking his head no. "There's a locked cabinet in the garage that I don't have a key for. I think you can pick the lock pretty easily, but if not, ask Gary for help . . . with the lock, not the contents."

Oh? I was curious but not enough to ask then. I had other things on my mind. Sipping my tea, I held his gaze. "Tell me about your art collection. I want to know about your favorite pieces." During our first visit to Santa Fe, he had been eager for me to see the artwork in his air-conditioned storage unit. "I want us to go through it together when we have some time," he'd said. "You need to see it all so you can choose what you want to put in the condo." But we had never done it. And now, we had run out of time. I wanted to know which pieces were important to John.

"There are some Brett and Cole Weston photographs protected by plywood that you could bring back to Reston . . . ." He stopped for a moment, and when he spoke again, his words were halting. "There's so much . . . ." Suddenly, he was sobbing.

I knelt down in front of him, wrapping my arms around his shoulders, my head pressed against his heaving chest. I felt his arms come around me. I wanted to comfort him; tears were streaming down my cheeks. "I'm so sorry, my darling. I'm so sorry." When our tears subsided, we loosened our embrace and stood up. Without a word, we parted, each going toward a different bathroom, knowing we were on the edge of a precipice from which we dare not let ourselves fall.

A few days later, I awoke to find John sitting up in bed, his back pushed against the pillows.

"What are you doing?" I asked, my head foggy with sleep. "Are you reading?"

"I'm thinking. I've been awake since 4, trying to figure out how we could make a trip to Santa Fe."

"What? You want to go to Santa Fe?" I sat up, shaking sleep from my head, and listened.

"I want *us* to go to Santa Fe. I'm feeling stronger, and my hands are less numb now. My ankles too. If I can keep moving, walking and perhaps using the treadmill a bit downstairs, I should be in pretty good shape the end of April. By then, it'll be relatively warm in Santa Fe. If we go, we'll fly first class."

"What do you mean by 'if'?"

"We should know in a couple of weeks if I'm getting worse."

John was feeling good *now*—except for his hands. Despite the heat in the condo, his hands were often cold. In early February, he asked me for a pair of warm gloves. I'd bought black leather ones lined with cashmere. Sitting in his chair after breakfast, he would put them on before reading the paper. In the office, he'd take them off to use the computer. Walking by his empty chair, I would see the long-fingered gloves, one on top of the other, sitting on the armrest. Later, I realized that John envisioned our spending hours in unheated storage units in Santa Fe and may have feared being immobilized by the chill.

In early April, we met with Heyer whom we had not seen since John stopped treatment some eight weeks earlier. We were both sitting in straight-backed chairs when he walked in and sat on the stool opposite us. It was as though nothing had changed except that John was not sitting on the examining table.

"It's good to see you, John. How are you feeling?"

"My hands are a little numb, but I'm feeling good."

"I can see that you've gained weight. Your appetite must be good."

"Yes. We want to travel to Santa Fe the end of the month. I'm wondering whether I should be tested for the IgM level."

"I wouldn't advise it. Your CBC results show hemoglobin and other blood components little changed from the last time you were tested." When John made the appointment, Heyer had asked him to stop by for the blood test so he could have the results when he met with us. "I see no reason not to go to Santa Fe the end of April." Standing up, Heyer walked over and placed a hand on my shoulder. "However," he said, looking me in the eye, "if anything should happen, go to E.R. in Santa Fe."

I smiled ruefully, mindful of our last trip when I had not taken John to the E.R. I appreciated Heyer's concern, but that morning, I felt fairly confident nothing would go wrong.

"Kim suggested Ritalin to pep me up when I feel drowsy," John said.

"In some circumstances, I'd approve, but at the end, I don't. Ritalin can make you feel wired, and for what?"

Heyer's words caught me by surprise. Were we at the end? Apart from occasional drowsiness, John was alert, and he was still gaining weight. He was driving, even at night. And he hadn't said anything that didn't make sense. Heyer himself had said, "it's not a science," and that day in his office, I was still clinging to the hope that John could beat the odds. Driving home, we talked about Heyer's approval of the trip to Santa Fe. "I'll make our flight arrangements in a week or so." John did not refer to the doctor's comment about "the end," and neither did I. Looking back, I think he knew he was living out the final days or weeks of his life, while I was holding out for remission. My fevered desire for him to live blinded me to telltale signs: his flagging energy, the increasing numbness in his hands and ankles, and something else I saw as an indication: the ill-proportioned weight gain which showed up as a potbelly and filled his cheeks while leaving his arms stick-thin.

John made the reservations for our trip to Santa Fe, first class on American Airlines with wheelchair assistance in Dallas and Albuquerque. After Barbara, my therapist, suggested a limo from the airport in Albuquerque to the condo in Santa Fe, I reserved one.

Late one morning, I walked into the condo carrying a heavy bag of groceries. John, phone in hand, met me at the door. "Ron called," he said, following me into the kitchen and placing the phone in its cradle. "He and Karen want to visit us in Santa Fe."

"That would be great!" I knew it would mean a lot to John to see Ron and his wife, Karen. A few months after our wedding, we had met them in Sedona. Before parting, they had asked us to join them on a National Geographic trip to Antarctica in December 2008. At the time, 2008 seemed a long way off, but now, it was April 2008, and December was not on our calendar. Apart from the trip to Santa Fe, we were making no more plans.

Now focused on the trip, John was still tying up loose ends. "I want to keep my checking account in Santa Fe open a little longer, long enough to pay for our trip."

He was sitting on the edge of the bed one morning when I noticed a rash, a three-inch-wide swath of tiny black pinpoints between his broad, bony shoulders. How long had it been there? When he came home from Sunrise, I'd seen a rash on the back of his neck but given it little thought. Pulling on a well-worn green T-shirt, he said it didn't hurt, but he told Kim about it when they talked on the phone. He had started sweating at night the way he used to before Rituxan treatments. Making up the bed the past few mornings, I'd found his pillowcase damp to the touch. I noticed that he was now putting a towel under the sheet on his side of the bed.

"It's the buildup of the IgM protein," John told me after he'd talked with Kim.

My stomach churned. Between the rash and the night sweats, "the end" was visibly encroaching, and I couldn't ignore it. The fact of John's worsening condition seeped slowly into my pores. With pained reluctance, I gave up hope of remission and began to wonder whether we could make the trip to Santa Fe. With each passing day, my anxiety deepened over the decline I was seeing. I could not give voice to my doubts, not with John. He had determined he could make the trip, and we were going. But I didn't understand why. Later, Kim told me John was determined to make the trip so I wouldn't have to go through the storage units by myself. "He didn't want you to have to face all of that alone."

On the morning of my regularly scheduled appointment with Barbara, I left John in his chair with the daily papers and drove to the nearby office complex.

Following her into her office, I dropped my windbreaker and shoulder bag on the sofa and sat down in the upholstered chair opposite her.

"Are you sleeping?" she asked. "You look exhausted."

"Not very well. For the past two weeks, I've had a difficult time getting to sleep—sometimes not for three hours or more."

Crossing my legs, I shifted in my seat. "Two weeks ago, I was sure we could make the trip to Santa Fe, but now, I'm not so sure. John, who once wondered whether he'd be able to go, expresses no doubts. And yet he's dozing more during the day, even after napping for an hour or so. There's the rash on his back, and the night sweats—everything's getting worse. Yesterday, he told me he has a low-grade headache when he wakes up in the morning, but once he starts moving, he's not bothered by it—another sign, he thinks, of the increasing IgM level. There's no good news. Each morning, I wake up expecting another shoe to drop. I don't know what to say or do. I feel as though I'm a silent witness to the saddest days of my life.

"John has someone lined up to help empty one or more of the storage units the day after we arrive. My concern is once we're there, how will *he* be? On Sunday, he climbed the stone steps up to Naomi and Tom's front door very slowly, holding onto the railing. The next day, he said he was going to do stair-climbing exercises daily to try to strengthen his thigh muscles. These are the muscles that Heyer said the steroids could weaken. This morning, I asked him if he thought he'd be affected by the high altitude in Santa Fe, and he admitted it concerns him."

"How long will you be there?"

"Four full days and five nights. John wants to get everything done the first two days before Ron and his wife arrive on Saturday."

"Are you eating? You're starting to look a little gaunt, the way you looked when John was hospitalized."

"Yes, I think I am, although I've been more concerned about John's eating."

A week before our departure, I was back in Hong's office for the results of my first-ever EKG stress test, wrapping up my annual physical. He said I had passed at a high level and that he couldn't believe I was in my sixties. I couldn't believe, after these past eight months, that I could be taken for a day under eighty! I told him how much I hated taking Ambien to sleep, and asked him for a prescription for Ativan, which he gave me.

With our trip just a few days away, I felt my chest tightening like a vise. I couldn't concentrate or carry on a conversation. I knew we wouldn't have any trouble getting to Santa Fe—John had taken care of those logistics—but how would he fare once we were there? Would we end up in the E.R.? And if we did, would we ever get back to Reston? He'd decided that his headaches were related to congested sinuses, and had begun taking a nasal decongestant to flush out his sinus passages. He was breathing more easily, but his night sweats were growing worse. He was soaking through two pillowcases a night.

"It's the increasing IgM, and there's nothing to do about it," he said.

Looking back, I see that my fears were tied to the horrors of our last trip to Santa Fe. Oddly, I didn't consider the possibility of John's contracting another infection. My concern was focused solely on his obvious decline. As anxious as I was about making the trip, I wanted John to be able to do it because it was so important to him.

I started noticing our area rugs, particularly those between the bedroom and the office at the other end of the condo. The edges were turned up. I would straighten them, and the next time I looked, they'd be turned up again. And then it hit me: John was having trouble picking up his feet. Oh my god! His thigh muscles were giving out. I pictured the four steps going down from the photo studio to the living area in the Santa Fe condo. Fortunately, there was a handrail. And there were no rugs to trip over on the concrete floors.

Our flight April 29 to Dallas and then Albuquerque was uneventful. Wheelchair assistance at each stop worked well. It was late afternoon when we stepped out of the limo and into the condo.

Switching on the light, John rolled our suitcase across the photo studio to the steps leading down to the living area. He didn't try carrying it to the bedroom. With a hand on the rail, he planted both feet on one step, then the next. Once on the main floor, he walked easily to the leather sofa and sat down.

From the top step, I surveyed the condo. It had been eight months since our ill-starred departure. The walls, still bare except for the Naminghas and *Dog Park*, a very large painting by our friend Melinda Hall, reminded me of the projects now suspended in limbo: the valance over the solar shades that John had insisted he would build; the interior lighting, largely absent except for the builder's fixtures and a small black floor lamp donated by Pat and Philip. The furniture—John's walnut desk in one corner and his magnificent walnut coffee table gracing the space in front of the leather sofa—looked good if a bit stark against the concrete floors. My eyes fell on the leather chair next to the patio windows. It was where John had been sitting eight months before when the cab driver arrived to take us to the shuttle. I felt my breathing quicken. The memory of that morning and the specter of John's now-failing hold on life flooded my brain. Trying to clear my head, I looked at him sitting on the sofa, his back to me. Against all odds, we were back. And now that we'd made it, all I wanted was to get back home.

Carrying the suitcase down to the bedroom, I quickly unpacked our few items of clothing and asked John if he'd like a snack before going out to dinner. I'd brought Parrano cheese and crackers to munch on during the flights, but we hadn't eaten it all. He nodded yes. His jean-clad knees higher than his waist, he looked too large for the sofa.

I found a plate for the cheese and crackers and opened the pantry. Taking out a bottle of Glenlivet, I poured a couple of fingers into one of John's Riedel glasses meant for scotch and filled another glass with filtered water from the fridge for him. He had stopped drinking alcohol a couple of weeks earlier, saying it went to his head too fast.

That first night, John drove us to Tomasita's on Guadalupe Street where I had a tostada and he ordered beef tacos. Back at Zócalo, we went through John's collection of DVDs and watched the first two episodes of "Tinker Tailor Soldier Spy."

John did not sleep well. In the morning, he said he'd start taking Ativan before dinner rather than at bedtime to give it more time to take effect. He didn't think he was feeling any ill effects from the altitude.

That first morning in Santa Fe, we visited all three storage units so John could refresh his memory of what was where, returning to the condo for a lunch of PBJ sandwiches. While he napped, I started reading Annie Proulx's *That Old Ace in the Hole*. When John woke up, he drank two cups of coffee and a bottle of Ensure, then we went to meet Dale, the husband of Gary and Melinda's house cleaner, at the storage unit near the airport. With Dale's help, we cleaned out the unit, moving boxes of beautiful art books that I wanted to keep into the back of the Xterra and sending boxes of text books—mostly physics books—and the odd lamp or chair to the dump with Dale. Returning to the two in-town units, we made sizable piles consisting of photographic items for Carlan's program aiding Native American former prison inmates who want to study photography, and of outdoor gear for Santa Fe Search and Rescue, whose volunteers had found John in the mountains after he was lost overnight the summer before we met. This was John's thank-you to the group.

After a dinner of Mexican food at Maria's, we went home to watch more episodes of "Tinker Tailor Soldier Spy." Afterward, I huddled in the leather chair with my book while John sat at the desk sorting through a couple of boxes he'd brought back from a storage unit. "You're going to be surprised by some of the things you find here," he said. He was right. Later, when I found a revolver and a shotgun among his effects, I was stunned. I didn't want them to be there, and I couldn't imagine why he had them. That night, I suddenly remembered the locked cabinet. "I never asked you what was in the locked cabinet in the garage," I said, looking up from my book. "Oh, just some sex toys that didn't look very interesting after I bought them."

Later, when I returned to Santa Fe alone, I would find the cabinet empty and assume that John had spirited them away during our last trip together.

The next morning, Scott, from Santa Fe Search and Rescue, met us at the storage unit to pick up the outdoor gear, putting the sleeping bags, tents, cookware, and items I couldn't identify in the back of a pickup.

"Thank you, John." That was all he said. Had he told John on the phone how sorry he was? He didn't converse with either of us—probably didn't know what to say.

Dee Ann had invited us to meet her and her husband, Scotty, for lunch that day before they flew to Cedar Rapids. At Santacafé, a maître d' led us through a series of small dining rooms to their table in a white-walled alcove.

After we had ordered, Dee Ann handed John a check for *Dog Tracks,* which was at the framer. No mention was made of this being the last time she and Scotty would ever see John. He told them we were cleaning out his storage units. I was enjoying the moment, eating and drinking in a lovely restaurant, and I could tell that John was too. For the first time since we'd arrived in Santa Fe, I wasn't worrying about how we'd get back to Reston as John's condition declined.

After a delicious cappuccino, I excused myself to use the restroom. When I returned, John was not at the table. I assumed he was in the men's room. But after waiting ten minutes, I felt panic gripping my chest. "I wonder where John is," I said, getting up. "I'm going to look for him."

"We'll come with you." Dee Ann and Scotty followed me through the dining rooms to the entrance, where I spotted John. He was standing across the doorway at an odd angle, his feet planted behind him, his arms pressing against the door jamb in front of him.

"John, what are you doing?" I asked.

"I was trying to stay out of a photograph."

Glancing around, I saw no one with a camera; I knew John was in trouble. He seemed immobile. As I tried to help him straighten up, Dee Ann commandeered the maître d' who put his shoulder under John's armpit and led him to an empty chair. A quick-thinking waitress gave John a glass of orange juice, which he drank.

"Shirley, we're going home to get our collapsible wheelchair," Scotty said. It was something he rarely used but kept it at the ready because he had cerebral palsy.

"No, you've got a flight to catch," I said.

"The plane can wait. We're not leaving you and John here," Dee Ann said.

I looked at John, who suddenly stood up. "Can you walk?" I asked.

"Yes." He took a couple of steps toward the entrance.

Saying goodbyes, we left Dee Ann and Scotty watching as we made our way through the garden to the parking area.

"If you give me the key, I'll drive us home." Without hesitating, John gave it to me.

"What happened?" I asked, driving toward Zócalo.

"I knew I was tired, and when I stood up from the table, I felt unsteady."

"I'm glad the O.J. revived you."

Back at the condo, John lay down on the bed and fell asleep at once. I continued reading Annie Proulx before falling asleep for an hour. When I woke, he was still sleeping.

Fixing myself a cup of tea, I thought about the incident at Santacafé. Was John overly tired—we'd had an active day and a half—or feeling the effects of the steroid on his thigh muscles? Or was it the altitude? The fact that he seemed to be all right after drinking the juice was reassuring, but we had three days to go before flying back to Virginia. The day we arrived, John had called everyone he planned to see, firming up dinner dates with Carlan and Nancy for Friday, and Gary and Melinda for Sunday. Ron and his wife would arrive Saturday in time for dinner and stay at a lodge near Zócalo. We would treat them to breakfast at Cloud Cliff before they flew home on Sunday.

The next morning, Carlan met us at the storage unit. I remembered meeting him on our first trip to Santa Fe when John had stopped at the Santa Fe Photographic Workshops with a question for him. Well built and brown-eyed with a silver braid down his back, his Native

American heritage was clear. He had called before we left Reston and talked at length with John, asking him about his life, particularly his interest in photography. John had told him about his father's helping him take his first photo at age six.

That night, after dinner at Carlan's, the four of us were sitting around a large wooden coffee table. A crackling blaze in a kiva fireplace warmed the air while casting a subtle light through the darkened room. It was peaceful, and I felt more relaxed than I had in a long time. Carlan got up and said he would be right back. When he reappeared, he was carrying a long drawer.

"John, I want you to have one of my photographs," he said, setting the drawer on the coffee table in front of John. As many as fifty matted photographs, each in a clear protective envelope, filled the drawer. "Choose whichever one you'd like."

John leaned over the drawer, taking out one photograph and then another, admiring each in silence before putting it back. To me, they appeared to be sepia-toned landscapes. Holding one in his hand, he looked at Carlan. "I would like this one of Chaco Canyon because I've never been there."

"It's yours," Carlan said.

"Thank you."

On Saturday morning, John was unsteady on his feet. "I think I'm feeling the effects of the high altitude," he said over breakfast. I thought I'd seen him hold onto the door jamb as he walked into the bathroom. I cleared the table. The day before, John had printed *African Tapestry*, one of his safari photos, on the large floor printer, at my request. After he signed it in a shaky hand, we'd take it for shipping back to Reston. It would be the last photograph John printed.

Leaving for UPS, the air felt cool against my face. As we walked to the Xterra, John handed me the keys—the first time he had ever asked me to drive. Oh my god, could he hold on until Monday? Driving was the last thing John would opt to give up. Innately self-monitoring, he must have known that he could no longer depend on his legs to drive the stick shift Xterra. Visions of his being unable to walk, to get into his seat on the plane flooded my brain.

When we got out, I walked ahead of John.

"Do you want to walk behind me so you don't have to keep looking back to see if I've fallen?" His tone was acerbic. I hadn't realized my unease was so apparent.

"Do you think you can make it until our flight back Monday?" I asked.

"Yes. I think I'll be feeling better by next weekend when I'm back at a lower altitude. I have to be sure to eat enough."

It was an odd response. If his legs were giving out because of the steroid, altitude would make little difference. I really didn't understand what effect the high altitude was having on him, if any. Although he had said he thought he was feeling its effects, he did not complain of usual symptoms like dizziness, shortness of breath, or nausea. His strange response may have been the "nonsensical" signpost Heyer had predicted—but if it was, I missed it.

While I went to Albertson's to pick up cheese and crackers, John waited in the car.

"Ron called on my cell," he said when I got back. "They're on their way from the airport."

"Good. Damn, I was in such a hurry to get out of Albertson's with snacks for Ron and his wife, I forgot to get Ensure. I'll pick up some tomorrow." John's night sweats were continuing, but my biggest concern now was his control over his legs. Maybe Ensure would help. I didn't know.

Within minutes of our return, I opened the door to Ron and his wife, Karen. They followed me down to the living room where John was standing beside the sofa, smiling. Ron greeted him with a handshake and a warm embrace. Karen wrapped her arms around John, giving him a kiss on the cheek. They had known him longer than anyone else outside of his family. They had known him in his good days and bad. They had supported him through his divorce, his near-marriage to someone else, and then his marriage to me. Now they were here to say goodbye.

After an hour or so, I suggested they leave to give John a chance to nap before dinner. That meal with Ron and Karen would be our last outing in Santa Fe.

Early the next morning, I awoke first. "Darling, how are you feeling?" I asked when he opened his eyes.

"I'm too weak to take Ron and Karen to breakfast."

"Do you want me to call them?"

"No. I'll call."

After he talked with Ron, he called Gary and Melinda to cancel dinner. "I have to preserve my energy for the flight home tomorrow."

The next morning, the limo took us to the airport to catch our flight. Waiting for wheelchair assistance at the curbside check-in, I saw John's legs give out, just as they had the last time. Again, I called for help. Several men nearby kept him from hitting the ground. Seated in the wheelchair, he was alert, and we proceeded to check in for our uneventful flight home.

When the pilot announced our approach to Dulles, I exhaled deeply. We were almost home. My greatest fear—that John would give out before we could get back—had not come true. With tremendous effort, he had fulfilled his wish to return to Santa Fe to do what he did not want me to face doing alone. He had cleared out two of the three storage units and donated as he wished.

The wine, however, remained in the air conditioned unit. And also in storage were many boxes of books, some of which he had told me about—not just art books but also a collection of rare cookbooks, many of them signed; a collection of small quirky books on sports; and many others. We did not try to look at John's art collection. I think that would have been the saddest for him. The fine art photographs would have reminded him too acutely of his unattained dream of being a successful photographer.

Hearing the landing gear come down, I braced for touchdown and for the days that lay ahead.

Weekend Avalanche

WHEN I AWOKE EARLY SATURDAY MORNING, THE BED WAS COOL. Semi-dozing, I reached for John's arm, my fingers probing the smooth cotton sheets. There was no John. How long had he been up? Why hadn't he come back to bed? Blinking my eyes open, I looked across the room into the dark of the walk-in closet. An eerie stillness filled the air. Where *was* he? Panic gripping my chest, I bolted into the dimly lit living room. There he was—in his chair, fully dressed, his arms on top of the armrests. I took a deep breath. "How are you feeling?"

"I woke up with a headache."

Whew! He was talking. The night before, I'd invited our neighbors Kathy and Jack up for wine and cheese. Telling them about our trip to Santa Fe, I'd glanced across the coffee table at John. His eyes were closed. Occasionally, they would flutter open only to close again. He was mute. "I'm sorry, Shirley," Kathy said quietly, looking at John and shaking her head. "It's not a good sign." As soon as they left, I heated a casserole pulled earlier from the freezer and made a salad. John got up to eat in the dining room. Afterward, he excused himself. "I'm going to bed. I'm very tired." When I went also not long afterward, he was sound asleep.

Now he was awake, but something didn't feel right. I dressed quickly and walked into the kitchen. The dishes from the previous night were still in the dishwasher, clean but not put away. Usually John unloaded the dishwasher first thing in the morning and defrosted the bagels for toasting. That was his job. "Do you want me to defrost and toast the bagels?" I asked, peering over the kitchen counter.

"Yes."

"What should I set the microwave for?"

"Two minutes."

I thought that sounded too long, but it was my first time defrosting bagels. Two minutes later, they were rock-hard. "Maybe I should try twenty seconds instead of two minutes."

"It always worked for me." His tone was matter-of-fact.

Waiting for the second batch of bagels to toast, I spotted the new vial of steroid medication on the counter next to the toaster—unopened. "Sweetheart, you didn't take your steroid medication yesterday morning."

"Oh well," he said, shrugging his shoulders.

His reaction struck me as bizarre. Didn't he care? Was he giving up? Two days earlier, Heyer had confirmed the loss of thigh muscle and reduced John's dosage. I opened the vial, placed it on the kitchen table, and poured a glass of orange juice for each of us.

"You know, Diane and Arlie will be here tomorrow," I said when he sat down at the table. My college roommate Diane and her husband were flying in from Boulder for a meeting at the National Science Foundation. We'd stayed with them on our road trip the previous summer.

"Yes. I may not be able to see them tomorrow for dinner," he said, slathering his bagel with cream cheese. "I'll have to see how I feel."

"Of course," I answered, trying to cover my disappointment. Mentally, I canceled dinner. After breakfast, I called the weekend hospice nurse. "My husband seems a little confused. I don't know whether not taking his steroid meds yesterday has anything to do with it."

"Hard to say," she said.

When I awoke Sunday morning, the bed was warm. John leaned over to give me a kiss. Astonished, I felt my lips parting in a big smile. "How are you feeling?"

"Good. I'm looking forward to dinner with Diane and Arlie tonight."

"Wonderful!" What a difference from yesterday. Maybe it *was* the steroid meds. I didn't know. I was just grateful to have John back.

That evening, after predinner drinks at home, the four of us walked to Il Fornaio where we had a lively discussion about the merits of Hillary vs. Obama. Unlike the previous evening, John was thoroughly engaged and engaging. The next morning, when Diane picked me up to go to Wegmans' gigantic supermarket near Dulles Airport, John said, "I'd like some prosciutto if they carry it." I bought two kinds, thinly sliced. That afternoon, John finished off one of them with water crackers.

When Kim, his hospice nurse, called Wednesday, I told her about John's increasing weakness toward the end of our stay in Santa Fe and Heyer's cut in his dosage of Decadron. I mentioned that John had been a little disoriented Saturday morning but seemed to be all right now. "I want to see him, not just talk with him on the phone," she said. "I was going to come by today, but I'll wait until tomorrow. That will give us another day to observe how he's doing." With her use of the word "us," I became the onsite part of the team monitoring John. I would be vigilant.

On Thursday, I thought John was all right. Kim, however, after talking with him and taking his vital signs, said she would call the next day and arrange for the weekend hospice nurse to visit on Saturday. Kim's focused attention made me uneasy. What was she anticipating? Later, I would remember John's "two minutes" as his first nonsensical comment.

Looking back, I realize that the steroid—whether he took it or not—had no bearing on his apparent confusion. It was the IgM protein finally affecting his brain, and there was nothing to do. Kim must have known.

"I'll be back right after yoga," I told John on Friday morning. From there, I went straight home without my usual stop at the library. Opening the front door, I was relieved to find John standing in the hallway.

"I heard your key in the lock." He was smiling.

"I came straight back. Kim said she would call, and I wanted to be here."

"She called while you were out."

"Yes?"

"I told her I was all right."

I hoped so. Standing there, looking up at him, I thought he was. "Would you like some soup?"

"Yes."

After lunch, John took a nap. I was resting in the living room, working on a crossword puzzle, when he walked in and sat down across from me.

"I'm giving up the idea of photographing *Ten Spaces.*"

I looked up from my puzzle. "Why?" I asked, my shoulders tensing.

"There's not enough time." His voice was soft, cushioning the impact of his simple statement.

I closed my eyes, trying to blot out his words, and felt my brain spinning. I knew he was dying. Did he have to rub it in? I took a deep breath and sank back into the sofa. Of course, he was right. There would never be enough time—for John to photograph *Ten Spaces,* to take portraits, to become the renowned photographer he knew he could be. Never enough time for us to complete our move into the Santa Fe condo, to design our website, to visit Burgundy and spend a day at Versailles, to explore the natural beauty of the Southwest . . . to grow old together.

Earlier that week, I'd read something about "duality residing indissoluble at life's core" and copied bits of it into my journal. The author had written that "dawn is unimaginable without dusk," and "life without death would be miserable" since "its beauty is bound to its fragility." When the infection happened, I'd gotten a crash course in life's fragility. I didn't know about the rest. The feeling of abandonment kept getting in the way of my understanding.

For the past few weeks, I had felt utterly abandoned, not only by John but also by hope, that elusive feeling that had permeated my every pore after he survived the infection. Even after he had enrolled in hospice, I would wake up in the mornings hopeful. Now, more often than not, I woke up fearful. I despaired.

Looking back, I believe John's "not enough time" was more than a statement of fact. It was a warning to me that his hold on life was more tenuous than I could imagine. It started a bell tolling inside me. Yet in spite of it, I thought we still had some good time left.

The next morning after breakfast, I was loading the dishwasher when I heard an unusual sound. Startled, I glanced down the hallway toward the guest bathroom. The door was ajar. John was sprawled on the floor. Racing down the hallway, I heard myself scream, "Oh my god, John!" Conscious, he was struggling to rise to his hands and knees on the white-tiled floor. His rimless glasses lay next to the bathtub. The silver shower curtain was ripped and hung oddly. He must have grabbed it, trying to break his fall. "Darling, I'm going to help you up," I said, nudging my left shoulder under his right arm and planting both feet firmly on the floor. Heaving with all the strength I could muster, I was able to help him sit on the covered toilet seat. I hurried to the bedroom to get his walker, thinking he could use it for support to stand. But he couldn't. He was helpless, and so was I. Gripped by panic, I stood stock-still, trying to think.

"I'll be right back," I said, backing out of the bathroom. Finding the hospice manual on my desk, I dialed the number Kim had circled.

"Hello," a female voice answered.

"This is John Bessey's wife. My husband just fell, and I need help to get him up."

"I'll contact the weekend nurse. Expect a call from her shortly."

When the nurse called, she said she was helping a patient on the other side of Fairfax County, and it would be at least two hours before she could get to us.

I told John she was on her way. I couldn't think past getting him to stand up. If he could do that, he'd be fine. I tried again to help him stand but to no avail. He had no strength in his legs, and at a hundred eighty pounds, he was too heavy for me to lift. Those damn steroids! They'd given him an appetite and taken away his legs! Pacing between John and the front door, I lamented the loss of the shower curtain. It was one of a kind, and I had searched several bed-and-bath stores before finding it.

Opening the door for the nurse two hours later, I felt my shoulders drop with relief. She was tall, with short dark hair, and looked fit. Together we helped John stand, walk to his chair, and sit down. After taking his vital signs, she said she had a bedpan I might want in her car. A bedpan? I couldn't picture John using it or my helping him. Nonetheless, I followed her down to get it.

"What do you think of John's condition?" I asked.

She handed me the pink plastic bedpan. "Well, it's not positive."

My chest tightened. "The bedpan makes me think it would probably be good to have a hospital bed now. I understand that hospice can deliver one."

"Yes, but the beds are in the warehouse, and it's closed weekends."

Closed on the weekend? Why? Illness isn't nine to five Monday through Friday.

When I returned to the condo, John was reading. I walked past him to the linen closet where I stashed the bedpan on the floor beneath a shelf of stacked towels.

That evening, using the walker, John stood up from his chair and went into the dining room. After dinner, he undressed and got into bed without assistance.

The next morning when I awoke, John was lying on his back beside me. He did not move toward me. Leaning up on an elbow, I turned to look at him. He was staring at the ceiling. My fingers touched the sheet near his hip. Oh my god! He was lying on a sheet soaked with urine. He couldn't get up to use the bathroom. How embarrassing for him. I should have told him about the bedpan.

Leaping from bed, I threw on jeans and a long-sleeved orange shirt, a man's shirt I'd picked up at an outlet years earlier. After many washings, it was soft and felt like an old friend.

Returning to John's side of the bed, I looked him in the eye. "Can I help you get dressed?" I saw no point in mentioning the obvious.

"Yes."

Hanging his legs over the side, John sat up. I helped him pull on underwear, black microfiber pants, a dark blue T-shirt, and a long-sleeved blue cotton shirt over it. I pushed the Isotoner slippers onto his feet. Using the walker, he stood up and went into the bathroom. From there, he walked into the kitchen and sat down at the table.

"Would you like some orange juice?"

"Yes."

"I'll toast bagels for us in a moment."

Leaving John in the kitchen, I called hospice with an update and waited for the nurse to call.

"I'll be there as soon as I can," she said.

Pulling the sheets and mattress pad off the bed, I put everything in the washing machine and turned it on. Then I made breakfast as if nothing had happened. After drying the pad, I remade the bed, placing towels on top of it and between it and the mattress.

John was still sitting at the kitchen table when the nurse who had visited the day before arrived. He couldn't stand, even with the walker. Together we helped him to the bathroom, then into bed. I had a package of Depends, which John had suggested I buy as a precaution before he came home from Sunrise. Until now, it had never been opened.

"I'll have to find someone who can help John get to the bathroom and back to his chair because he's too heavy for me," I told the nurse when we were alone in the living room.

"Oh, no. He can't leave the bed."

"Then I've got to have a hospital bed immediately!" I looked at her intently. "You have to get me a hospital bed." I didn't want John to ruin our expensive Sleep Number bed! So far, the air-filled mattress was dry, but who knew for how long?

"Yes, but we can't get it to you until tomorrow after the warehouse opens."

"Please don't leave yet." My brain shifting gears, I hurried into the office and grabbed the hospice folder off my desk. Finding the list of home health aides, I thrust it into her hand. "Can you recommend any of these?"

"I'm sorry," she said, handing back the list. "Since I've started working only weekends, I'm not as familiar with the list as I once was."

After she left, I went into the bedroom and sat on the bed next to John. Holding his hand, I looked into his trusting eyes.

"Darling, I'm going to spend the next little while arranging for help for both of us."

Smiling, he nodded his understanding.

Back in the office, I flipped through the hospice manual to the page on respite care. It described an inpatient center where hospice patients could be taken care of for several days to give the caregiver a break. But when I called, I was told that all the respite care beds were taken.

Feeling despondent, I turned the gas on under the kettle. With a cup of hot tea in hand, I sat down at my desk and stared at the list of hospice home health aides. My jaw tensed. Figuring I would need three of them to cover twenty-four hours, I called the first name on the list. It didn't take long to learn that my assumption about the ease of hiring them was totally wrong. Some aides worked only certain days of the week, some only partial days, others only certain nights. Three hours later, I was still trying to arrange twenty-four-hour care for John. Looking at my calendar, I saw that we were supposed to have dinner with Kathy and Jack that evening. After calling Kathy to cancel, I left a message for Alice and Barney canceling our lunch on Tuesday. Late in the afternoon, a friend who had talked with Alice called. She gave me the name and number of a caregiver who had helped her after a car accident, describing her as "very kind." Desperate to fill the 8 a.m. time slot, I called Rosetta. When she told me she could take care of John in the mornings, beginning the next day, I breathed a sigh of relief.

On Monday morning, the doorbell rang on the dot at 8. Standing in the doorway in a crisp white uniform was a brown-skinned woman with full cheeks and a wide smile. I sensed that she was indeed kind.

"Please come in. My husband, John, is in the bedroom. I want you to meet him."

John smiled at her.

Now that I had her help, we could move him into the "transportation chair," a small-wheeled narrow chair that had been in the closet since he'd come home from Sunrise. Like the chair used to move John into the plane, it was not meant to be sat in for long but to move someone from one place to another. I had not thought to use it when the hospice nurse and I had helped him walk from the bathroom to the living room. Pushing the chair across the resistant short shag of the bedroom carpet, we crossed the threshold into the living room, where the chair rolled easily along the hardwood floor.

"What do you want me to do?" Rosetta asked, pushing the chair into the kitchen.

"Take care of John. Help him take his medications with juice and eat some cereal. I've got to change the bed."

I dashed back to the bedroom. Again, I tore off the sheets and mattress pad, as well as the urine-soaked towels, and threw the lot into the washer. The pink bedpan was still tucked out of sight in the linen closet. But John didn't have the motor control to use it, and the Depends obviously were not enough. With the washer going, I went back to the kitchen. Rosetta had put a pillow between John and the table, keeping him from leaning too far forward. She was talking with him, giving him a little orange juice with each pill.

I grabbed a pen and leaned over a small note pad on the counter. "Rosetta, please tell me what I have to buy."

Spooning a little cereal into John's mouth, she told me what I needed, and I listed them. "A rubber pad to go under the sheet is the most important."

"I'll go out for these as soon as we get John back into bed."

Rosetta was pushing him back to the bedroom when the phone rang.

"We have a bed for you," a woman said.

"How soon can you deliver it?"

"I'm talking about an inpatient bed at the hospice center in Arlington. I'm the director, and we'd like to transfer your husband here this morning. The nurse and social worker are on their way to you now. I'm hoping they arrive before the transport people who are scheduled to pick up your husband at 10:30."

I stopped breathing. An inpatient bed? It took me a moment to understand what she was saying. When I did, every muscle in my body relaxed. "Thank you." John would be cared for by people who knew what they were doing. Over the weekend, he had entered a phase over which he had little or no control. And now when he needed help the most, I felt utterly helpless as a caregiver. Joe had once said he would hate to be seriously ill around me. He was more right than I'd known. Dealing with illness, I was out of my element. I had no instinct for what someone who was bedridden might need, nor any experience to draw on. Growing up, I had never been exposed to anyone who was bedridden. Warm milk over toast was my mother's cure-all for whatever ailed my brother and me, from mumps and measles to chickenpox.

Helping Rosetta push the transportation chair over the carpeting in the bedroom and get John into the newly made bed, I knew I had to talk with him privately. "Rosetta, please wait for me in the living room. I'll be there in a moment."

Perched on the edge of the bed, I held John's hand in mine and looked into his eyes. "There's a bed available for you at the hospice center in Arlington. Would it be all right with you to go there?"

"Yes."

Tears of relief stinging my eyelids, I bent over and kissed him. I had promised him he would never be institutionalized, but that's what care at an inpatient hospice amounted to. Looking back, I think his "yes" was a gift, the generous gift of a dying man who wanted to ease my anxiety more than hold me to my promise.

I told Rosetta he would go to the hospice center.

"What do you want me to do?"

"Stay with John in the bedroom until he's picked up."

When the bell rang, I said a silent prayer—let it be Kim and Leisa—and opened the door.

Whew! "I'm so glad to see you two."

"We wanted to get here before the transport people," Leisa said as they walked in. Leading them into the bedroom, I watched Kim take John's vital signs. After giving him an injection, she pulled a clipboard from her large bag and completed an attached form.

When the phone rang again, it was the concierge telling me the transport people were on their way up. "I'm going down to ask him to open the door in the back of the building so John can be taken out that way," Leisa said, hurrying out of the condo.

Seconds later, the doorbell rang. I opened the door to a tough-looking woman in white pants and a short-sleeved white shirt. A timid-looking, dark-haired man in white followed her in, carrying a folded metal-framed bed.

"We're here for your husband," she said, not meeting my eyes.

"He's in the bedroom. Follow me."

When Leisa returned, John was lying under a sheet on the portable bed, being rolled toward the front door. "Wait," I said to the transport team. "It's cold outside. Let me get a blanket to put on the sheet."

"The concierge has opened the back door so you can take him out that way, to give him some privacy," Leisa told the woman leading the transport duo.

"Oh no. We go through the front door." Hands on hips, she stepped toward Leisa. "That's how we do it."

"But it's better to go out the back."

"We always go out the front, and that's how we're doing it." Her tone was defiant.

"Besides," the man with her said, "the truck is too high to get through the back door."

"The truck doesn't enter the building," Leisa said. The words "you idiot" hung in the air unspoken. "You just park it at the building's rear entrance."

"Don't you understand," I said, jumping into the fray, "that it's better for my husband to go out the back rather than through the reception area?" If I were in John's place, I knew, I wouldn't want people in the reception area watching and commenting, though now that I think about it, John probably didn't care one way or the other.

"I don't have time to discuss this. I've told you what we're doing, and that's it. We always go through the front entrance."

"I'm reporting them," Leisa said, watching the two wheel John out of the condo toward the elevator. "I don't know who they are or whether they have a contract with hospice. Their conduct is unacceptable. I apologize, Shirley, and I'm very sorry."

After the hullabaloo, I thanked Rosetta and paid her for a full day. Her caring presence had helped ease my pent-up anxiety. Now alone, I was overcome by the stillness. I shook my head, trying to rekindle the brain cells. There were things I had to do before I could follow John. I called and explained to the other caregivers I'd scheduled why I had to cancel; they were all gracious and sympathetic. After calling John's brother, Dick, in New York, I picked up my purse and paused. At the very least, I should brush my teeth. No time for makeup. A quick look in the bathroom mirror reminded me I was still wearing the wrinkled orange shirt I'd worn the day before. John wouldn't care. I looked at my watch. It was nearly two hours since he'd been picked up. He would be waiting for me.

Clutching the directions to the hospice that Leisa had pressed into my hand, I hurried toward the elevator to the garage. I needed to see John. He needed to see me, to know that I had not abandoned him. The hospice was in Arlington, a good forty minutes away. What kind of place was it? With all that had happened, I hadn't thought to ask. I remembered the rehab center where Joe had died—dark and drab. My chest tightened. I hoped better for John.

Looking back, I wonder why, if John was to die at home as he wished, hospice hadn't prepared me for his deterioration. Granted, I had the hospice manual, but that was all. Why didn't someone tell me in advance what to buy and actually help me find caregivers instead of just giving me a list of names and numbers. And why didn't the hospice people consult me before setting that sudden move in motion in response to what one of the nurses must have told them? I had counted on the hospice's support in helping John to have the death he wanted, at home with me. In the end, it failed us both.

Room with a View

WITHIN MINUTES OF LEAVING THE GARAGE, I PULLED ONTO THE toll road and sped east toward Arlington. It was early afternoon. Ahead of rush-hour traffic, I could make good time. With EZPass affixed to the windshield, the silver SUV eased through the toll stations without stopping. Merging onto I-66, I slowed for the inevitable bottleneck before exiting onto heavily trafficked North Glebe Road. Now I was in Arlington, but where was the hospice? Glancing at Leisa's directions, I followed Glebe to Fifteenth Street and turned left into a residential neighborhood with tall oaks lining both sides of the street. Could this be right? Ahead on the left was the address, 4715, a one-story brick building partly hidden behind trees. I noticed a vine-covered gazebo off to the side. Blooming fuchsia and white petunias filled pots along the sidewalk leading to a wide concrete staircase. There was no signage in sight.

At the top of the steps, I pushed open a large metal door and stepped into what appeared to be a spacious, high-ceilinged living room. Natural light filtered through an expanse of windows on two walls. On my right, a long sofa and chairs upholstered in a pale lavender print embraced a large glass-topped coffee table. Side tables of dark wood, some with tasteful lamps, skirted the room. A few people were milling about. Two were in deep conversation on the sofa. On my left, a well-dressed gray-haired woman stepped out from behind a desk. "Can I help you?"

"I'm looking for my husband, John Bessey. He was brought here nearly three hours ago."

"Yes," she said, glancing at a ledger on the desk. "He's in Room 2."

I followed her into a wide, dimly lit corridor. She stopped in front of an open doorway on the right. Above the entrance, the number 2 was painted in black on the wooden doorframe. "Your husband is in here, next to the windows."

"Thank you." Unaccompanied, I made my way into a room with six beds and walked through a blue-curtained passageway toward the window wall. There were no blaring TVs, no sounds of any sort. Glancing to my left and right, I glimpsed people in beds. Much older than John, they appeared to be sleeping. Would John be sleeping?

Nearing the windows, I peered around the end of the blue drape. On my right was an empty bed. I looked left. There was John, sitting up in bed against a pile of pillows. He was looking out the windows into tree branches and fluttering green leaves.

Once after driving cross-country from Santa Fe, he'd said, "I know when I'm in Virginia. I can't see anything."

"But there are beautiful trees," I'd protested.

"Yes. That's what I mean. There are so many trees I can't see anything!"

At his bedside, I bent over and kissed him softly on the lips. I set my purse and windbreaker on a chair and pulled another close to the bed. I leaned toward him, my fingers caressing his face and his thin, bare arms. Holding his left hand in mine, I looked at him intently. His eyes were clear. Despite the slight steroid fullness of his cheeks, he looked pretty much like himself. His hair had grown enough to cover the implant and fall across his forehead above the right eye, mostly hiding the craniotomy incision along the scalp line.

He opened his mouth as if to speak. No words came out, but I read his lips: "I love you forever."

"I love you forever," I said, tears welling up.

"Excuse me." A pleasant-looking dark-haired woman stepped from the passageway to the foot of the bed. "I'm the director of the center and wanted to introduce myself." She was smiling.

I smiled back. "Thank you for calling this morning. I must admit I was surprised to find the center in a residential neighborhood."

She said it had once been a school, which explained the high ceilings, wide corridor, and walls of windows. Long ago converted to a hospice, it had just fifteen beds. I had no idea how John had ended up in one of them, and didn't think to ask her.

While I was sitting with him, two other women came into our draped area and introduced themselves. One was a nurse, the other a volunteer. They said to let them know if they could do anything for either of us. As long as John was comfortable, that was all that mattered.

Later, stepping out of Room 2, my eyes fell on a cart draped in white linen not far from the doorway. A silver tea service, cups, saucers, and small plates sat next to a large cake.

"Would you and your husband like a cup of tea and a slice of cake?" a white-haired woman asked.

"Yes, I would. Thank you. Let me ask my husband."

John wanted the cake. I carried a small plate with a slice of carrot cake back to him while the volunteer brought in tea and cake for me. So this was inpatient hospice care. Who knew? Twenty-four hours ago, I had been scrambling to find care for John at home. And here I was now enjoying afternoon tea with him, my spirits buoyed by this home away from home, my heart melting with relief. Sipping from a porcelain cup, I watched him swallow forkful after forkful of cake and marveled at his persistent appetite.

The bed next to John was occupied, the one opposite him empty. The draping on two sides of his bed gave me a feeling of privacy, with room to breathe. The absence of medical paraphernalia—plastic bags suspended from metal skeletons, blood pressure and other monitors—was a stark reminder that there would be no Code Blue here. When John signed up for hospice, he had said goodbye to all that, not just to chemo but also to the "heroic" measures that hospitals often use to keep patients alive, the same measures that had enabled him to survive the infection. This was not a hospital, where survival was the watchword. This was a hospice, where dying was expected and the point was to make the dying comfortable. John would take his last breath in Room 2.

After months of hoping for remission, I found that I was at peace with the inevitability of John's death. My only concern now was his comfort. Finding him there in that peaceful setting with a window view, tended by kind-faced individuals, I felt reassured.

My acceptance had not come easily. Bit by bit, the reality of John's dying had penetrated my consciousness. The rash that began as a few pinpricks on the back of his neck when he came home from Sunrise had spread in a broad swath across his shoulders. The increasing night sweats, the waning energy and frequent dozing, the confusion—these were loud signals, screaming a warning.

But more powerful than any of them was John's telling me that he was giving up on *Ten Spaces*. Until that moment, I had been held hostage by his very existence, refusing to accept that he was dying. His quiet declaration of, "There's not enough time" had signaled the end. Had he sensed how imminent death was? I hadn't. But in that moment, I knew he spoke the truth, and I tried to accept it.

What had left me no choice was the weekend avalanche—his fall in the bathroom and the loss of speech and bladder control. John was the epitome of control, though it was subtle; to some people, he seemed laid back. Although he had once told me he liked it when I took the initiative "because I don't like to do all the driving," he did not give up control easily. John was daring but not foolish. He liked driving fast, playing poker, skiing black diamonds, and climbing vertical cracks in mountain walls, but he didn't do any of them without thinking about what could go wrong and taking steps to reduce the likelihood of disaster. That was how he had tried to control his cancer. His decision to refuse more treatment and register for hospice was a huge act of surrender. And when he told me he was giving up *Ten Spaces*, a project he was passionate about, I knew he must be sensing that death was near.

Late that afternoon, after John had been served dinner and eaten every bit of it, I went home. Dick arrived from New York a short time later. After a quick meal at Clyde's across the street, I drove him to see John, who was still sitting up, waiting for us. The room, indirectly lit, was in semi-darkness. Dick pulled up a chair next to the bed and moved in close to speak to John. Stepping out into the passageway, I glanced through the open drape into the space next to John's. A dozen people were standing around the bed. They were leaning over the person lying there, their voices muffled, their words indistinguishable.

By the time we said goodnight to John, Room 2 was quiet again.

Early the next morning before heading for Arlington, I called friends in the area to tell them where John was. I knew this would be the last chance for anyone who cared about him to see him. I imagined John might want to see them too, though I couldn't be sure. Returning to the hospice, Dick and I planted ourselves at John's bedside, our backs to the windows filling the area with light. I was holding John's hand when a bespectacled, white-haired man in a white jacket walked in. Extending a hand to Dick and me, he introduced himself as the hospice doctor.

"Please excuse us for just a moment," he said, looking at John. John nodded, and we followed the doctor out to the corridor. He turned to face us, and my shoulders tensed. "I've given John an injection that will allow him to be wakeful and responsive. We call this 'the honeymoon.' It might last for two or three days, after which he will start sleeping until the end."

All right, I thought, my shoulders relaxing. Surprised by his announcement of a honeymoon, I was grateful at once—grateful for the two-to-three-day reprieve and the forecasted ending. Dying while asleep would be a gentle way to go and, I presumed, pain-free. John had never complained of pain. But who knew when or how it might be felt in his waning days and hours? Hospice was geared to manage pain, to assure a pain-free leave-taking. Naively, I counted on that, not knowing how much could go wrong.

It was Tuesday. Kerry would arrive on Thursday, in time, I hoped, to see John awake. Returning to his bedside, Dick asked John if he'd like to have some good red wine. Smiling, John nodded yes. "I'll bring it in tomorrow," said Dick, who had already cleared this with the doctor.

My cell phone rang. It was Marilyn asking if she could see John before she caught a plane to L.A. for a Northrop Grumman meeting. "Of course. I'll wait inside the front door." I only found out later that I could have said, "Meet me in Room 2." Fourteen years earlier, her husband had died in that very same room.

"Shirley, it's May 20." Marilyn looked at me knowingly.

"May 20? Oh my god. I didn't realize." I could feel my face flush. It was our second wedding anniversary. Unlike the first, which we'd talked about and planned for months in advance, the second had never been mentioned. I didn't know when it dropped off our radar; maybe it had never been on it. Our last celebration had been John's birthday at the end of March, two months after he enrolled in hospice.

Sitting beside John, Marilyn reminisced about our wedding in the beautiful backyard on that perfect spring day … when our imaginations were afire with dreams I was sure we would realize. If John had harbored doubts about that, I never knew.

Other friends showed up. Giving John a break from the growing crowd, we all decamped to the hospice living room. We were seated around the coffee table when Marilyn excused herself. After a while, she returned and slid into the chair next to me. She leaned close. "I said goodbye to John," she half-whispered. "He knows exactly what's going on. I'll tell you later."

A couple of weeks later, she stopped by for wine and cheese.

"Marilyn, didn't you say before leaving the hospice that John knew what was going on?" I handed her a glass of La Crema chardonnay from John's old winery.

"Yes. But you should know that weeks earlier, he called me, concerned about how you would manage after he died. We must have talked for nearly an hour."

"What did you say?"

"I told him you were strong."

"Really? I remember John's telling me he'd been talking with you and that you'd said I was strong. I didn't know what he was talking about. And I had no idea he had called you. I assumed you had called me and talked with him because I was out."

"No, he called because he was worried about you. So when I came to the hospice center to say goodbye, I told him that I and others would look out for you, and that he shouldn't worry."

"He understood?"

"Yes. Tears ran down his cheeks."

Late that afternoon while Pat and Philip were at John's bedside, he pulled the sheet up over his face. "Do you want to be alone?" Dick asked. The sheet's movement made clear that John was nodding yes. After that, I made sure there were no more visitors.

On Wednesday, hospice staff members helped Dick transfer John from the bed onto a cushioned lounge chair with wheels. I draped a blanket over his shoulders, and Dick wheeled him outside to the gazebo. The air was cool but the sun was out, a lovely spring day. Jack and Kathy found us there as Dick was pouring red wine into small plastic glasses. For John who loved wine, this tasting was a fitting tribute. To see him smile as he swirled the wine before lifting the glass to his lips was a bittersweet pleasure. It was something I had seen him do many times. But never while wearing a hospital gown. "Ready for a refill?" Dick looked at John, who held out his empty glass in reply.

When Kerry arrived from New York on Thursday, John was alert and still eating everything the hospice served him. The three of us were seated at his bedside when a male nurse I hadn't seen before appeared at the foot of the bed. Pale-faced with narrowed eyes, he glared at me.

"You've got some decisions to make."

"What?" I blinked in puzzlement.

"You need to think about alternatives."

"What are you talking about?"

"This hospice is a short-term facility. Your husband is alert and eating well. You need to consider where he might go, to a nursing home or possibly home with you."

My jaw dropped. Was he kicking John out of the hospice? I looked at John. He had heard everything.

"What are you saying?" I wanted to scream, and it must have shown in my voice.

"Let's take this outside," Dick said.

In the corridor, I turned to face the nurse. "How dare you speak as you did in front of John," I sputtered before dashing into the rest-room across the way. Locking the stall door, I shook my head, trying to think, trying to quell the rage. What was going on? Didn't the hospice doctor tell us that John would be alert for two or three days? This was Day Three.

Was John overstaying the honeymoon?

When I came out, Kerry told me the nurse was "verbally assaulting" Dick in the living room, and that she had left because she couldn't take it. Together we found Dick alone on the sofa. "He was telling me that he had excellent reviews from other patient families." Dick raised his eyebrows in disbelief.

The hospice center's social worker, a young, pleasant, blonde woman, found the three of us standing outside Room 2. "I seriously doubt that John will have to be moved," she said in a consoling voice. "I'm taking the long Memorial Day weekend off and won't be back until Tuesday. I don't want you to worry." She placed a hand on my shoulder. "A lot can happen between now and Tuesday." My brain was on fire. First the nurse with his "you've got some decisions to make" and now the social worker and her "doubt" that John would have to be moved. Who was in charge? And why was John's presence an issue? I had assumed when the hospice director called with a bed for John that it would be a bed until the end. The hospice doctor himself had talked about John's sleeping "until the end." What was I supposed to do now?

That night I awoke with a stabbing pain in my left eye. I knew immediately what it was: herpes simplex virus-1, blisters on my cornea triggered by emotional stress. I had first received the diagnosis several years earlier when my parents were ill, and had suffered from it two or three times since. The condition requires immediate treatment with a refrigerated antiviral medication that pharmacies don't always have on hand. My ophthalmologist was in D.C. At 3 a.m., I called his number and left a message explaining why I couldn't possibly drive in to see him and asking him to call in a prescription to the CVS pharmacy in Reston.

On Friday morning, after sleeping fitfully with the blistering pain, I called the pharmacy. The prescription was ready for pickup. I told Kerry and Dick staying at the Hyatt across the street that I was running late because of the eye condition and would meet them at the hospice. Returning to the condo with the prescription, I called the hospice to see how John was doing. I waited for someone to find a nurse to talk to me.

"He's having a seizure." The woman's voice was matter-of-fact.

"Oh no!"

"His brother and his wife are here."

"Tell them I'm on my way."

Pulling into the hospice lot, I felt my heart racing. Half-running up the steps, I bolted into John's area and stared in disbelief. He was sitting slumped to one side, his head hanging toward a drooping shoulder. His eyes were closed. "Darling," I said, reaching for his right hand. There was no response. His hand was limp.

"They had to give him a lot of medication to calm him," Kerry said. Seated on the other side of the bed, she got up and handed me a small box of tissues.

Wiping tears from my cheeks, I stood as if in a trance.

By Saturday afternoon, John had been sleeping for more than twenty-four hours. A hushed silence had fallen over Room 2. No sounds from the other draped areas broke the stillness. Kerry and Dick were out for a walk. Sitting beside John's bed, I thought he looked peaceful. He was lying on his left side, the side he often slept on, his face illuminated by light filtering through the trees behind me. Suddenly, his eyes opened. He seemed to be looking up and beyond me, his pupils the size of pinpoints. "Oh, my darling," I whispered, "lower your gaze." I so wanted him to look at me one last time. Instantly, he lowered his head to meet my eyes. Now he was looking right at me, but he seemed more to be looking through me into some elsewhere I couldn't see. I wasn't sure if he was seeing me or not. I thought he was. I felt he had made a supreme effort to come back to me even though he was nearly gone. I wanted to know what it meant. A tiny hope flared inside me. Was this a reprieve?

Sparks going off in my head, I jumped up and ran out of the room to find a nurse. I found one in the corridor. "John opened his eyes!" I half-shouted.

"Consider it a gift," she said, hurrying into the room after me. When she called out John's name, his head moved slightly in her direction. "He's with you. Tell him how much you love him."

Overcome by a sense of urgency and wonder, I sat back down and reached for John's hand, holding his palm between both of my hands. Did he press my hand ever so gently in response? Or did I only imagine it? "I love you, my darling. I love you forever," I said again and again until his eyes closed. I felt that he heard me. Was it sheer luck I was with him when he opened his eyes—or did he somehow know we were alone together?

Late Sunday afternoon, I asked the doctor on duty to talk with the three of us about what we should expect. I knew Kerry would have to fly out Monday for a meeting the next morning at Time Inc. in New York. The doctor urged her to forego the meeting "if at all possible." I tried to persuade her to go and then come back; after all, the other patients who had been in Room 2 when John arrived were still alive. I felt sure that John would be sleeping for several more days. But Kerry remained in Virginia.

When the three of us arrived at the hospice on Monday, John was still sleeping. At noon, we went out for lunch at Tysons Corner. Afterward, Kerry wanted to shop for shoes, and bought a pair of sandals at Saks. But when we walked into Neiman Marcus, she held up a shoe and said, "I like these more."

"We can go right back to Saks to return the other pair."

"Shirley, it's not a question of either/or; I can get both. I'll take them," she told the saleswoman, handing her a credit card.

"We should probably get going," Dick said, his tone serious.

"Oh, yes," I looked at my watch. We'd been gone nearly three hours. Chagrin swept through my body. Away from the hospice in the bustling world of the living, I'd allowed the reality of John's dying to hang suspended in the back of my brain.

That evening, I told Kerry and Dick that I planned to keep an appointment with my therapist in the morning and would meet them afterward at the hospice.

On Tuesday morning, still wearing my wrinkled orange shirt, I sat down heavily in my usual seat opposite Barbara. "So much has happened. John had a seizure Friday morning. I wasn't there. Kerry and Dick were with him. I was picking up a prescription for my damn eye condition that erupted in the middle of the night. I speeded all the way there. I couldn't believe how he looked—slumped over, eyes closed, his hand completely limp. I felt awful—sad and guilty—that I wasn't with him, and that he would never see me again."

"I can understand why you felt sad, but why guilty?"

"If I had been there, even seconds before his seizure, he would have seen me, and I could have tried to comfort him. But I wasn't there. And then yesterday when I was out with Kerry and Dick, I almost forgot about John completely! What if he had died while we were shopping for shoes?"

"Sometimes it's hard for the worlds of the living and the dying to coexist in one's mind."

"Yes. That's how it is for me. When I'm in the hospice, that's the only world I'm conscious of. But once I'm out, especially in the hustle of Tysons Corner, the hospice seems unreal."

"Life goes on for the living, regardless of who's dying. Maybe because it does, it saves us."

"But the most amazing and wonderful thing happened on Saturday. I was alone with John, holding his hand, when he opened his eyes! This may sound crazy, but I sensed that he knew I was with him and he was saying goodbye to me."

"How do you feel about that?"

"Grateful, incredibly grateful. After the seizure, I didn't think John would ever open his eyes again. I feel it was a gift, John's last generous gift to me." Reaching for a tissue on a nearby table, I blotted my cheeks dry.

Returning to the condo, I heard the phone before I opened the door. It was the hospice social worker. "Shirley, John died this morning."

"Oh no," I said—stricken.

"It's all right," she said. "A volunteer was with him."

"A volunteer?"

"He's been moved into the Meditation Room."

Unable to speak, I lowered myself onto a kitchen chair. No, I wanted to scream, it was not all right. John had just died with a stranger at his bedside. *I* should have been there, not some stranger. I was so sure he'd be sleeping for a few more days. I was wrong. I had been less than vigilant. And now it was all over.

Motionless, I sat there. My eyes were dry. My body was empty. I felt nothing.

I don't know how long I sat in that blankness before I remembered Kerry and Dick. They should be told. Hoping they hadn't already left the hotel, I called.

Kerry answered the phone. "We'll pick you up, Shirley, and we'll go together." Together, we would see John one last time.

With Dick at the wheel driving us to Arlington, I huddled in the back seat, my mind a jumble of fragmented thoughts and feelings. Did John know I wasn't with him when he died? Guilt tightened around me. *I should have been there.* And yet, since the moment he had opened his eyes on Saturday when we were alone, I felt he had said goodbye to me and taken his leave on his own terms. Despite the phone call, a big part of me could not accept that he was gone. We had fought so hard for him to live. I needed to see him. I needed to see for myself that he was no longer sleeping.

Hurrying up the steps ahead of Dick and Kerry, I pushed open the front door. A crowd was milling around the desk. Excusing myself, I made my way through it.

"Where's the Meditation Room?

"Down the corridor, straight ahead."

I rushed ahead and flung open the door. What I saw stopped me in my tracks. There was John, sitting up in bed as though he were alive—except that he appeared to have been made up for a horror show. His skin was a bilious yellow, and one eye was half open, the other closed. With halting steps, I approached the bed. Reluctantly, I placed my hand on an exposed arm. It felt clammy to the touch. Sudden anger overcame my horror. He must have died hours earlier! When I'd left him the night before, he had been lying down, presumably asleep. Why was he now sitting up? And what had caused the shocking change in his appearance?

"Oh, Shirley," Kerry gasped, grabbing my arm.

Shuddering, I turned away from the bed and wrapped my arms around her. We were both trembling. I had thought I needed to see John in order to know he was really dead. But I had not imagined this. Could I ever erase this image from my mind?

Over Kerry's shoulder, I saw a row of chairs along the beige wall. "Let's sit down." We all sat, Kerry holding my hand, Dick holding Kerry's. With little furniture, the high-ceilinged room felt stark. I looked at John again and shook my head. This was not John. It was only a shell—and what a hideous shell to leave! I had to get away from it.

The door opened and in walked Philip. Before leaving the condo, I had left word on Pat's voicemail at her office. "Patricia got your message and called me. I was outside cleaning the koi pond." Philip was wearing faded black Levis and rubber-soled boots. He turned to look at John, and his jaw dropped. He took a seat with the rest of us.

I had to get myself out of there. "I should call the funeral home," I said, standing. Someone would have to pick up the body.

"I'll go with you," Dick said.

Without looking back, I walked out of the Meditation Room. "There must be a phone somewhere."

"Here's one." Dick led me to a small wooden table in the living room and pulled up two chairs. I rummaged through my purse for the piece of paper with the number I'd written down that morning. My hands were shaking. When the funeral home answered, my teeth were chattering.

John would be cremated. We had discussed it nearly two years earlier, when we were writing our wills that first summer after our wedding. At the time, death was simply a fact of life that one planned for—years in advance.

I did not see John again.

That night, back in the condo, Dick offered to open a bottle of wine and prepare pasta for the three of us. I stood in the kitchen, holding a glass half-filled with red wine, watching Dick saute garlic in olive oil. Kerry was prowling the living room. "Shirley, do you mind if I rearrange the furniture in here a bit?" (I had learned from her daughter that Kerry's typical response to stress was to feverishly redecorate.) It was an odd request, but I didn't mind. I didn't mind anything.

Then, looking into the living room, my eyes fell on the leather chair, the big, golden brown leather chair—John's chair. I had bought it from a Scandinavian furniture store before he came home from Sunrise nearly seven months earlier. At six-foot-four, he needed a large one that wasn't too low so he could get up from it easily. And I'd gotten an adjustable ottoman too for John to stretch out his long legs on as he recuperated. "I'm probably going to have to fight you for the chair," he'd said, smiling from the bed, when I told him of my purchase and extolled its wonders. He hadn't had to fight me for it. The chair had been his from the very start. I'd often look out from the kitchen to see

John sitting in the chair, usually reading, sometimes watching TV, and then, toward the end, dozing. Now empty, it was a stark reminder of John's absence. "Would you two help me move John's chair into the office?" I asked.

After they left to go to their hotel, I was alone for the first time since seeing John in the Meditation Room. It was nearly midnight. The condo seemed eerily quiet, the reverberating silence broken only by intermittent sounds from the air conditioning.

I walked into the bathroom and took my PJs from the hook on the back of the door—the flannel ones with faded roses, comfortingly soft and thin after innumerable washings. After putting them on and brushing my teeth, I walked into the bedroom, got into the unmade bed, and switched off the bedside lamp. I don't know how long I lay there, listening to the quiet and hearing nothing. The clock read 1:30. I closed my eyes but my mind remained filled with the hideous image of John. I turned on the light and got out of bed.

Purposefully, I walked across the shag carpet onto the cool wooden floors of the living room and down the narrow hallway to the office. I switched on the lamp on the bookcase. The light, directed toward the big Random House dictionary, was bright enough to illuminate the trunk across the room, its flat wooden top hidden by stacks of books and papers. And there it was, in plain view, our wedding album. I'd never put it away. I picked it up and carried it back to the bedroom. After piling pillows in front of the headboard, I got back in bed, pushed my back against the pliant mound, and slowly opened the album. The date on the title page was May 20, 2006—two years and seven days ago.

In the first photo, it was the night before our wedding, and the two of us were seated at a long table with some twenty out-of-town friends and family members at McCormick & Schmick's in Reston.

John is smiling broadly, the shock of brown hair streaked with silver falling over his high forehead. Through rimless glasses, he's looking at the camera, although I feel he's gazing directly at me, his eyes that distinctive blue, his expression open and engaging. He's wearing an open-collared linen shirt—one of my favorites—salmon-colored, under a blue blazer. How surprised I was when he stood up and offered a toast to all, thanking them for coming on such short notice to share the evening and the next day with us. I simply hadn't thought about a toast—so obviously appropriate—nor was I accustomed to seeing John, more reticent than talkative, address a group.

Slowly, I turned page after page, lingering over each photo of John, of us, reliving the joy we had given each other. We had been ecstatic the day of our wedding, pledging our love and committing ourselves to one another. It had felt so right.

After the ceremony, we walked down through the terraced garden. I remembered sitting on a stone bench under sun-dappled trees in front of a reflecting pond filled with koi. In the photo, John is standing behind me looking handsome in a dark blue suit, white shirt, and striped tie. On his lapel is a boutonniere of stephanotis. His index finger is touching my shoulder.

The wedding album spread its balm over my eyes and my heart. It did more than dull the memory of what I had seen in the Meditation Room. Looking at the photos brought John back to life as I wanted to remember him, as I wanted to remember us. I felt less forsaken.

I closed the album, placing it on the floor beside the bed. And then I opened the drawer of my bedside table where I knew I'd find the email John had sent me from Santa Fe three months before we were married, two months before I proposed:

> You are the center of my universe and occupy most of the rest of it as well. As long as I have you nothing else matters. My love for you is complete and unreserved and forever. It will keep me going when we are apart, until I can see you and hold you and kiss you again. The days until we are together again are too many. They will pass slowly, one by one, until finally they are gone. And then we will hold each other and express in words and deeds all of the feelings that we have had. I long for that time to come, so I shall think of you and my love for you will continue to grow without end. I love you with all my heart, John

As I read John's words, I wept. The loss was devastating. I felt that my heart was irreparably broken.

In Memoriam

THAT WEEK, AS IF JOE WERE SITTING ON MY SHOULDER INSTRUCT-
ing me, I sent John's obituary to the *Washington Post* and to newspapers
in California, Wyoming, and New Mexico. I had written it a couple of
weeks after he registered with hospice, and with a few minor changes,
he had approved it. Looking at the glossy black and white photos of
himself that he'd printed for me, I remembered the afternoon I first
broached the subject. John was reading in the living room when I interrupted.

"Darling, I learned from Joe, the P.R. ace, that if you want the
record to reflect the truth, you write your own obituary." Joe had written his years before he died, updating it every so often. The day he
died, I was in shock, unable to call anyone I knew to tell them, but I
was able to find his obituary and get it to the newspapers on his list.
"I'd like to take a stab at writing yours while we both have our wits
about us. Are you game?"

"Yes."

I had written my own obituary, so I wasn't mournful. I felt it was
part of life. If you want anyone to know that you've lived, this is what
you do. It's a great vehicle for that—the last vehicle. It was something I
wanted to do for John. I wanted to have the truth of his life on the record.

Sitting at the computer, my P.R. mindset in place, I drafted the
obituary, leaving some names and dates blank. I felt professional about
it. "Please, make any changes you want," I told John, handing him the

double-spaced draft. "I didn't know some of the places you worked or the dates. Just fill them in."

"All right." John put the draft on top of the *Economist* he'd been reading and pulled his Cross pen from a shirt pocket. In a matter of minutes, he did what he wanted and set the draft on the coffee table for me.

There were very few changes. I made them and handed him another piece of paper. "What do you think of this list of newspapers?" I'd listed half a dozen, including the *Washington Post, Reston Connection, Fairfax County Times, Laramie Boomerang, Santa Fe New Mexican,* and *Daily Breeze* in Torrance, California.

"I don't think most of them will care." He was matter-of-fact.

"I think the Laramie paper will, and probably the one in Torrance. But I wish I had a photo of you to send along."

"I can get some photos for you."

"Glossy black and white?"

"Yes. I have some glossy paper in the office. How many do you want?"

"Maybe ten or so."

The next day, he printed ten head shots of himself cropped from the wedding photo showing us standing behind the tiered cake. Transformed from color to black and white, his face is alight with happiness.

Within two weeks, John's obituary appeared in five of the six papers, and the sixth ran it June 18.

John Stewart Bessey (1949–2008)

John Stewart Bessey, 59, retired aerospace physicist-engineer and recognized landscape photographer, died of Waldenstrom's macroglobulinemia on May 27, 2008 at the Capital Hospice Inpatient Center in Arlington, VA.

Dr. Bessey was born in Norman, OK, and grew up in Laramie, WY, where his father was on the university physics faculty. He graduated from the University of California-San Diego in 1971 and studied astronomy at the University of Wyoming before receiving a Ph.D. in physics from the University of Arizona in Tucson in 1977.

Dr. Bessey began a career in aerospace in 1978 as an optical physicist with Optical Coating Laboratory in Santa Rosa, CA. While in northern CA, he received an MBA from the University of California-Berkeley and, with three friends, founded La Crema Winery in

Petaluma. In 1987, Dr. Bessey joined TRW, later acquired by Northrop Grumman, in Redondo Beach, working as a senior engineer in space technology and as a Six Sigma Black Belt, training colleagues in a statistically based methodology to increase efficiency. While working for TRW, Dr. Bessey became the U.S. representative for an optical fiber company, Le Verre Fluoré, in Rennes, France, and founded Seiche River Photonics.

A Formula One race car enthusiast, he attended a course for race car drivers in Magney Cours, France, where he determined that at age 38 he was too old and at 6'4" too tall to be a successful Formula One driver.

A love of classical music fostered by his father evolved into a wide-ranging collection of hundreds of records and C.D.s, from Bach's "Inventions"—one of which he taught himself to play despite not knowing how to play the piano—to the Jamaican jazz of Monty Alexander and the satire of folksinger Tom Lehrer.

An avid photographer since the age of six when his father introduced him to the wonders of photography, using an oatmeal box, Dr. Bessey retired from TRW/Northrop Grumman in 2004 and moved to Santa Fe, NM, to devote full time to landscape photography.

In 2006, he married Shirley Nagelschmidt of Reston, VA, where they lived while maintaining a residence in Santa Fe.

Dr. Bessey's great-grandfather, Charles Edwin Bessey, is widely considered to be the father of modern botany. His grandfather, Ernst A. Bessey, retired from Michigan State University as the chair of the Department of Botany and Plant Pathology in 1944.

Dr. Bessey's first marriage to Margot Gieselman ended in divorce. He is survived by his wife, Shirley (Nagelschmidt), of Reston, and a brother, Richard, of New York City and Raleigh, North Carolina.

New to me was the website legacy.com. A paid obituary in any of the hundreds of newspapers affiliated with it is sent automatically to the site, where readers can share memories or express condolences in an accompanying guestbook.

For weeks after the obit was printed, I would find messages about John on the site, some by people I knew and others by total strangers. A personal letter from John's Ph.D. adviser, Marlan Scully, touched me deeply. Of course, I knew how special John was, but these messages proved that he had not lived without making an impact on others. His courage and kindness had been appreciated as much as his talent and accomplishments by co-workers, friends, and relatives. This was important to me. The range of comments enlarged my understanding of John, whom I was still getting to know when he died. Their sincere appreciation affirmed the wisdom of my choice of a mate whom I had loved but known for too short a time.

Before our last trip to Santa Fe, I'd started pondering where to hold John's memorial service, and decided to ask his opinion. If he cared, I would try to carry out his wishes. Joe had decided long before he died that he didn't care one way or the other about a memorial service. But John seemed interested. "How about the social room downstairs?" He was into it.

"I don't know if it's large enough, but I'll ask Blake," the condo complex manager. "What do you think about live music?"

"Too fancy. Just play some of my favorite jazz C.D.s."

After clearing the date with Kim Beach, I reserved the room for a service in June, and engaged the caterer who had been with me on both the saddest and happiest occasions of my life—Joe's memorial service and my marriage to John.

It felt strange. My brother and his wife and some of my closest friends who had been at our wedding would be back in Reston for the service. As they had two years earlier, they would stay at the Hyatt across the street—a reunion of sorts, with Reverend Beach presiding, but this time, there would be no rehearsal dinner.

As she had when Joe died, my friend Barclay arrived a couple of days before the service.

"I'm going to speak," I said, driving her to Reston from Dulles International, "and I need your help cutting my remarks. When I timed myself last night, it was forty minutes!"

"Of course. We can do it tonight after dinner."

That evening we surveyed the social room. Tasteful drapes framed windows on one wall. A narrow white marble table with potted palms on either end divided the area. The caterer would be setting up food and wine on linen-covered tables to the left, where people would enter the room. The service would be held in the other half, where long sofas upholstered in a plush beige fabric anchored two walls. The space looked too small to accommodate fifty folding chairs, but Blake assured us it would after he took out a coffee table and a couple of large chairs.

Leading to the room was a marble-floored hallway flanked by antique credenzas.

"Shirley, we could display photos on the credenzas, some of John's and of him." Barclay's voice rang with enthusiasm.

Late the next morning, the doorbell rang and I opened the door to John's cousin, Karen, a pretty blue-eyed brunette with a computer bag hanging from one slender shoulder." She had offered to drive up from North Carolina a day early to burn a C.D. of photos stored in John's computer. She wanted to meld them with his favorite music for showing after the service.

I offered her lunch, but she was eager to get started. After introducing her to Barclay, "my longest friend," I led her to the office. "All of John's photos are on his computer, the ones he took in Africa and lots of landscapes of the Southwest."

"All right. I'll take a look. I'll make a selection and combine them with the music you said he liked." Karen, a media teacher, appeared to be totally comfortable with the task at hand.

That afternoon, a vase filled with beautiful blue hydrangeas arrived, sent by Karen's sister Barbara from California. Another magnificent bouquet, this one of white roses, arrived from my brother and his wife. I asked Barclay to take them downstairs the next morning.

It was late afternoon when Karen previewed her four-minute show of John's images for us on her laptop in the living room. Barclay and I sat on either side of her. With the first sound of a jazz saxophone interrupted by soft sounds of African chanting voices, I stopped breathing. Images of wildebeest, elephants, giraffes, and leopards filled the African savannah, punctuated by portraits of the one-eared lion and the lone cheetah. This was John—his images and his music. Tears spilling onto my cheeks, I sat mesmerized. The African chants gave way to the soulful desert sound of two recorders, one answering the other while images of the Southwest—Utah's Comb Ridge, a single tree erupting from Sedona's red rock, and a hauntingly beautiful series of aspen in the canyons of New Mexico—slid across the screen. The impressionistic production concluded with the reggae beat of Jamaican jazz pianist Monty Alexander.

"It's wonderful," I said, touched by Karen's sensitivity and talent. "I'm going to work on it a little more at the hotel tonight."

That night, I read my remarks aloud for the last time, making still more cuts. After printing out a copy, I said goodnight to Barclay and went to bed. With my eyes closed, I thought about what would happen the next day. Comforted by Barclay's calming presence, I told myself I should be able to relax. With Barclay and my helpful neighbor Lolly and now John's cousin engaged, I shouldn't be so anxious. They would handle the logistics, and the caterer was an ace. All I had to do was show up. Nonetheless, waves of tension rippled through my body.

I felt an overwhelming need to speak at John's service. Many who would be attending hadn't known him well or for long. I wanted them to know how wonderful he was, how important he had been to me. Others would speak, though I didn't know what they would say. I knew the readings that Reverend Beach would offer—I had selected them—but I didn't know what else he would say. John was multifaceted and deep. Getting to know him was like peeling an onion—there were so many layers. Would anyone be able to capture and convey his essence? As much as I might wish, it would not be me. Despite my pummeling questions, John had died before I'd gotten to really know him. He had died during what still seemed to be our honeymoon, and I felt cheated.

Late the next morning, after showering and washing my hair, I went downstairs. Barclay, who'd been up early, greeted me with a big smile. "Come, take a look. See what you think."

On top of the credenzas were photos of John, copies of his obituary, and the leather-bound book I'd bought for guests to sign. On the front cover, behind a square of clear cellophane, Barclay had slipped in a small photo of John on the *African Queen*. She was one for details, significant details. At her request, I'd printed it in my office the night before.

Walking into the social room, I spotted the vase of tall blue hydrangeas sitting majestically on a white linen-covered table. Silver trays strategically placed would remain empty until after the service. The white flowers graced the marble table dividing the room. The other half of the room was filled with multiple rows of cushioned white folding chairs.

"Barclay, you did a wonderful job. Everything looks great."

"Thank you. I had a lot of good help."

"Do you want to share a can of soup before we dress?"

"Yes."

After brushing my teeth and putting on makeup, I stepped into my charcoal gray pantsuit and medium-high black pumps. I fastened a single strand of pearls—a gift from John—just above the neckline of my cream-colored shell. On my jacket, above my heart, I pinned the silver roadrunner with the eye of turquoise. Clutching a manila folder with the program and my remarks, I headed for the elevator. The service wouldn't start for another half hour.

The first person to arrive was Joanne, the director of GRACE. Before taking a seat, she sought me out.

"Shirley," she said, her tone gentle but unwavering, "the board of directors just met and endorsed my recommendation to exhibit John's photography in the gallery this fall." Her gray-blue eyes held my gaze.

Blinking back tears, I gasped. "Thank you. What a wonderful tribute to John." This meant that he would, in a real sense, have his own show.

By 3 p.m., the sofas and nearly all the chairs were filled. My hairdresser slid into the last empty chair as the sounds of Schubert's *Trout Quintet* came to a close. This was the music that John had played—with a glass of red wine in his hand—when he learned that his father had died.

Focusing my eyes forward and taking a deep breath, I sat back in a folding chair. I was in the front row, wedged between my brother and Dick. When the music stopped, the Rev. Kim Beach stood and faced the guests. Wearing a dark suit with a white shirt and dark tie, he had a comforting, almost professorial demeanor, underscored by his short white beard and rimless glasses. He opened the service with words by Helen Keller, *We Bereaved.* He continued, in his well-modulated voice, with readings from Edward Abbey, Henry David Thoreau, and John Muir, "selected with the help of John's family, reflecting his love of nature and his sense of its beauty and power to nurture the human spirit."

When he read a selection from Anne Lamott's book, *Plan B,* I felt he was talking to me:

"If you haven't already, you will lose someone you can't live without, and your heart will be badly broken, and you will never completely get over the loss of a deeply beloved person. But this is also the good news. The person lives forever, in your broken heart that doesn't seal back up. And you come through, and you learn to dance with the banged-up heart. You dance to the absurdities of life, you dance to the minuet of old friendships."

Kim raised his eyes from the page and looked straight at me. "And, I will add, you dance to the minuet of a once and abiding love."

Dick stood up and turned to face the people behind us. Speaking eloquently and with feeling, he talked about John's fascination with photography, and marveled at his mastery of each new camera, one more complicated than the other. He explained that John was not fearless although he seemed to be. It was more that he had a knack for "anticipating what could go wrong—from rock-crack climbing to car racing to living with cancer—and mitigating against those possibilities while forging ahead, undaunted."

Kerry's heart-felt comments focused on John's attention to his mother after his father died. "He was attentive and concerned, including her in his travels here and abroad." John's roommate, Ron, mentioned John's academic brilliance but emphasized his "genius in being able to talk with anyone on any level. We bonded over weekend car racing and photography while freshmen at UC-San Diego."

Marilyn talked about the maze of connections and "six degrees of separation" between her life and mine with John, including the fact that "fourteen years ago, my husband died of cancer at the hospice center in Arlington, in Room 2." She also related a story from Hadley, who'd been a Six Sigma trainer with John at Northrop Grumman: "Part of the training for those selected for Six Sigma involved one full week of statistics. By the end of the week, most of the class was burned out and nodding off but not John. He sat there, bright-eyed and rapt. On the last day, he presented everyone in class with a handout showing how he'd used the concept of binary statistical regression to figure out which foods his cats preferred. Now, whenever I need to explain BSR to students, I whip out John's handout."

Hadley's story made me smile. Cats and statistics—John had loved both. He'd combined them in a singular way and shared his creation with the class. And now, four years later, Hadley was using it!

I heard what people said. As they spoke, John came alive. Everfluid images of him floated through my brain, but I was almost bursting with wanting to tell my story. As though clinging to a lifeboat, I had a profound need to share all the bits and pieces of our unexpected life together. Sharing these would make them real and permanent. He was a man who had mattered to me. As I told my story, everyone in the room would know how much. They would know my heartbreak. Deep down, I must have sensed that all too soon, the passage of time would obliterate, except for fading memories, the reality of our too-brief life together. For me and my captive audience, I would relive our life before the inevitable made of me, like John, mere ashes.

What I'd written and been unable to cut without Barclay's help was too long, way too long. And with each cut, my heart hurt. With each cut, I erased telling details, details I wanted to hang onto as if it would let me keep both of us alive. When Joe died, I'd felt a need to talk about who he really was because I felt I knew him better than anyone else, whereas with John, I didn't know him as well as I wished I had. But I needed to tell others about our two years together—how important he was to me, how he had transformed my life and helped me reclaim my adventurous spirit.

I stood up. Holding my remarks in one hand, I looked out at the crowd. So many people with faces upturned, waiting for what I would say. Glancing down at my first page, I took a deep breath and looked up.

"John was extraordinary all by himself, but together, we thought we were really something special," I said, choking back tears. "I once told him how lucky he was to have married me. 'Just think,' I said, 'I have no encumbrances for you to deal with such as parents [who would have loved him] or children. I'm perfect for you.' 'Even with encumbrances, you would be perfect for me,' he said."

Looking down at my blurring notes, I paused and took another breath. "We never would have imagined that the two of us, at our age, could have such a grand time of discovering each other, with the surprise bonus of rediscovering ourselves."

My eyes brimming, I launched into our story. I told it from the beginning—how we met in Raleigh on Christmas Eve when I was anticipating my first date after Joe's death with someone other than John—to the end.

I quoted his email proposing that we get together on Martin Luther King Day weekend and my response, verbatim. I described highlights of that weekend, from dinner at Les Halles to the Cézanne exhibit at the National Gallery, and missed nary a detail of his second visit and third, including our daily routine during the ten days that ended with my proposal.

I talked about the importance John placed on creativity. "During our time together, I witnessed his creativity, particularly in but not limited to photography. He was brimming with ideas. One of them was that, with my love of writing and his of photography, we could be great collaborators. He envisioned a multipronged website for displaying and selling his prints and my writings."

I even mentioned our show-and-tell "here in the social room" after our trip to Botswana, and in unrelenting detail, took the audience on our trip to Brittany.

I referred to Dick and Kerry. "John was quite taken by his brother Dick's bread-baking and loved to tell people about Dick's ventures building ovens and transporting loaves of bread from upstate New York down to the city for tastings at an upscale deli. Often, we'd be out for dinner and John might comment on the bread, saying, 'It's not up to Dick's standards.' He enjoyed his encounters with Kerry. He was highly amused by her admonition before he left Raleigh after we'd met: 'If your relationship with Shirley gets serious and then breaks up, don't count on coming back here for Christmas because I've known Shirley a lot longer than I've known you!' He loved the Southwest—the canyons, mesas, valleys, mountains, and star-studded nights. He was such a westerner. He enjoyed telling people that before he met me, he'd never lived east of the Rockies."

My tenuous composure broke when I told in detail of how Melanie had read to us the shocking results of John's C.T. scan: "I realized in that moment that our life as we knew it was over, and I think John did too." Crying, I talked through my tears, my voice getting louder.

I talked about learning the results of the MRIs, and how guilty I felt later when told of the infection and his fifty-fifty chance of survival, and that I was responsible for his not receiving medical attention in Santa Fe or Dallas.

I told how a few days after he was moved from the ICU into a regular room, I walked in and John announced: "There are three things in my life that I am the most happy about: meeting and marrying you, going to Africa, and taking early retirement." Two out of three involving me, I thought. Not bad.

"John's surviving the infection was, in a real sense, a gift to each of us. A gift of nine precious months together.

"Throughout all of this, I never heard John complain or express self-pity. He was ever hopeful but realistic. He used to say, 'life interferes with plans, but it's important to have plans.' As one friend so aptly put it, John lived his life until the end with grace, amazing grace. . . . He was the love of my life."

Still fighting tears, I sat down and tried to take a deep breath. Maybe now, some people would have a better idea of who John was and why his death had shattered my heart. I hoped so. I had talked about him the only way I could, as I'd come to know him. I had told our story, and despite the excessive detail, I had told it in bas-relief, so much of it still hidden in the stone. That was all I could see of it for now. The whole story, much of which I was hardly conscious of, was still churning deep inside me.

Looking back, I realize that I said too much about some things and not enough about others. I didn't talk about John's opening his eyes. It was a significant detail, one that I held close to my heart but one that did not alter the ending of the story. If I were speaking now, given distance and perspective, I would not give a blow-by-blow of our two years together. I might say it never occurred to me that John's battle against cancer was nearing an end. If I had known, if either of us had known, it's likely we would never have married. And that would have been a great loss, for each of us.

I might say that John was like a candle, lighting up my life when I had been blinded by darkness. Like a candle, he burned with a stunning intensity until snuffed out by an unrelenting wind. His legacy was manifold. Yes, he did far more than improve my palate for wine and coffee. He showed me how to live life with more courage than fear, to tame adversity with one's mind and heart, to not only dare to dream but also to delight in making dreams come true, to be open to experiences that stretch both our mind and our heart. More than all of these put together, he showed me that I could open my heart to love again.

While everyone who spoke revealed aspects of John, it was Kim Beach who captured the intrinsic paradox of his abbreviated life. His words resonated: "John was a renaissance man for our time who set out to do many things and who did them all with a flair. There is something thoroughly heroic in this life and something altogether tragic. We can see the tragic part: the dread illness—long endured without illusion and without surrender—but also the heroic part, how he held it off, year after year, as if at swords' points in a life-and-death duel, until finally, in a terrible rush, it overwhelmed him. John had no illusions and surrendered when he knew he must surrender—and in this very way, I think, remained master of his own soul, spiritually triumphant. No person can do more than this."

272

A Cairn in the Mountains

FIRST THERE WAS THE QUESTION OF THE ASHES.

"I'd like my ashes scattered in the mountains near Santa Fe," John had said.

"Oh? Not with your parents' in the Snowy Range?" When we'd visited Laramie the previous summer, John showed me where he and Dick had scattered their parents' ashes, and later, discussing the memorial service, he said something about scattering his own ashes in the Snowy Range.

"No. I've thought about it. I'd like them to be scattered near Santa Fe."

I had thought he might show me where during our last trip to Santa Fe, but it didn't happen.

In July, I flew west carrying John's ashes in a black plastic box, heavy in my Turkish tote bag. Dick would fly out from New York to meet me. Before he arrived, I shared my concern about where to scatter the ashes with Carlan and Nancy. "The only thing John told me was the mountains near Santa Fe. I've never set foot in or on any mountains here. Do you have any suggestions?"

They looked thoughtful. "How about Aspen Vista?" Nancy's voice rang with Eureka. She looked at Carlan.

"Yes! Once you get there, you can follow the dirt road up into the mountains. You'll see a lot of possible places off the road there, and no one will bother you."

"Where is this place?"

"It's on the ski basin road, near the top. I've taken my photography classes there. Take Artist Road to where it becomes Hyde Park Road and stay on it for about ten miles until you come to Aspen Vista on the right."

The next day, I drove up the curving mountain road to Aspen Vista and pulled off, parking in front of a billboard-like trail guide. There were four or five other cars, parked and empty. No one was around. It was quiet, with just the faintest rustle of wind through the leaves of tall aspens lining the length of the parking area. Locking the car, my purse stowed on the floor of the back seat, I set off toward the gate. Clad in gray hiking shoes, the ones I'd worn in Africa, I was on a mission, a mission to find a place for John before Dick arrived in Santa Fe.

It was mid-morning. The air was still cool. A bottle of water in one hand, my cell phone in the other, I stepped through an opening next to the gate onto a rough dirt road. Scattered wildflowers—scarlet paintbrush, evening primrose, and forget-me-nots—lined the wide road, which was closed to vehicles. I made my way uphill for a half-mile or so before spotting an arrow on a wooden plaque indicating a trail to the right. Without hesitating, I stepped down onto a narrow dirt path that led into a forest of aspen and fir.

Suddenly I felt hopeful. John had photographed aspen. He would like being near them, I thought, as long as there was a vista of some sort. The twisting trail was clear except for an occasional fallen tree or live root snaking across the path. Careful not to trip, I pressed on, hoping to find a spot that would feel right, something with air around it. The forest felt a bit claustrophobic, with spots of sunlight filtering through a dense canopy of tall trees.

Less than a mile in, I rounded a bend and came into a grassy clearing. The sun sitting high in the blue sky bathed the yellowing grasses in bright light. The sound of flowing water broke the stillness, and I veered left off the trail to find the source. On the far side of the clearing below a rocky outcropping, clear water rushed pell-mell along a wide bed, its course broken but not impeded by smooth white, gray, and black rocks. On top of the outcropping stood a single fir tree, sentinel-like although no more than six feet high, with branches close to the ground.

This would be the place.

Two days later, I drove Dick up to Aspen Vista. Wearing white sneakers and jeans with a pink polo shirt, he lifted John's blue backpack out of the back seat and slipped his arms through the straps, testing the weight of the black box against his back.

"It's a fairly long hike to the site," I said. "Are you going to be all right?"

Settling the pack on his shoulders, Dick looked at me and smiled. "He ain't heavy; he's my brother."

I laughed and shook my head. There was something so John about Dick's response.

"John would have liked that," Dick said, chuckling.

A small crowd of hikers with dogs was milling around the trailhead as I led Dick past the gate onto the dirt road. "Let me know if you get thirsty," I said, looking back at him. "I'm carrying a couple bottles of water."

Walking along ahead of Dick, I wondered how I would feel, scattering John's ashes. It was something he had wanted me to do—a final act. I remembered scattering Joe's ashes at the base of a tall oak in front of the house we'd built and loved. "It's fitting," Kerry had said when I told her. "Joe was a mighty oak." I thought this site would be fitting for John—in the mountains, which he'd wanted, in view of aspen but not suffocated by them, and near running water. My only misgiving was that the site was not on the top of a mountain with an unobstructed view. But that was *my* preference. John had said *"in* the mountains."

"We're almost there," I said to Dick, rounding the bend that opened onto the clearing. I led him to the fir tree overlooking the river below. "This is the spot I selected, under this tree. What do you think?"

"It's good." He slipped the backpack off and set it under the tree. "I'll have some water now." After a few swallows, he set the bottle down on a nearby rock. "Wait here. I'll be back in a few minutes."

Dick made his way down to the creek. Suddenly he was crossing it, jumping from one flattish rock to another. What was he doing? Within a few minutes, he had recrossed the creek and climbed back up to the outcropping. "These ought to work." He set several water-polished stones on the ground next to the tree. "After we scatter the ashes, I'll build a cairn."

What a great idea, I thought. A marker, a tombstone of stacked stones. "Dick, why don't you take the ashes out of the box."

"All righty, then." Lifting the black container from the backpack, he set it on the ground. From the box, he pulled a clear bag filled with ashes. It was fastened at the top with a twist-tie, which he undid. "I hope you don't mind if I take some of these to scatter in the Snowy Range." From his pants pocket, he pulled a Ziploc baggie.

"No, I don't mind." I was surprised—but I didn't mind. I watched Dick place the baggie under the lip of the larger bag and pour a handful of ashes into it. He closed it and placed it back in his pocket.

Gingerly, I reached my hand in to touch John's ashes. Like Joe's, they were a mix of ash and solid fragments, bone, I supposed, or maybe teeth. More like kitty litter than ashes. *This was it.* After all the hope and heartbreak of our human lives, this was our paltry leave-behind. We scattered handful after handful of John's ashes under the fir tree, finally releasing the finest particles by turning the bag upside down.

Dick placed a large dark rock on top of the ashes, and on top of that, increasingly small stones. Picking up a twig of fir needles, he pulled a book of matches from a pocket and set it afire. When it had burned completely, he dropped the charred remains on ashes of John's not covered by the rock. "Be at rest, brother."

Moved by Dick's actions and final words, I said nothing. As I stared at the cairn and ashes, no words came to me. I'll be back, I thought, alone.

After Dick returned to New York, I stayed in Santa Fe, thinking it might help clarify the present, and perhaps the future. I made several more trips to Aspen Vista.

On the first, I carried John's backpack with a bottle of water, a PBJ sandwich in his honor, tortilla chips, my small camera, and a copy of Kim's remarks at the memorial service. When I emerged from the forest into the clearing, my pulse quickened. I could see the tree but not the cairn. What if it wasn't there? What if some animal or insensitive person had destroyed it? I picked up my pace until I was standing next to the fir. The cairn was intact, some of the ashes still visible. Whew!

I set the pack down by a flat white stone near the tree. Taking out my camera, I photographed the cairn from different angles, not realizing that because of the shadows cast by low-hanging branches, none of the pictures would come out. I sat down on the white stone and stared at the rushing creek. The sound of water breaking against rocks was hypnotic. I took out the sandwich and chips. I would have a picnic, a picnic with John. In Laramie, we'd packed sandwiches, chips, and water before going on a day trip. In the Snowy Range, we'd found a picnic table at the base of a mountain that John had once climbed. From where we sat, we could see rock climbers ascending the walls in the distance.

Sitting cross-legged, I pulled out Kim's remarks and started reading—sometimes aloud—the words he had spoken at the service. Before I got to the end of the piece by Anne Lamott, I was sobbing.

"If you haven't already, you will lose someone you can't live without, and your heart will be badly broken, and you will never completely get over the loss of a deeply beloved person."

I closed my eyes, letting the sounds of the water flow through me. I would never get over it. How could I? The loss was too great.

My thoughts spoke out to John: With every breath, with every step I take, I feel you're with me. I can't differentiate between us. That comforts me, and it confuses me. Who am I? Am I nothing without you? If I'm nothing, how do I live? I thought I could—but now I'm not sure.

Dabbing my cheeks with the sodden tissue, I heard voices behind me. Three people and a yellow dog were on the trail. Let me be, I silently prayed, and they passed without a glance in my direction.

I continued reading aloud:

"But this is also the good news. The person lives forever, in your broken heart that doesn't seal back up. And you come through, and you learn to dance with the banged-up heart."

Yes, I thought, tears running down my cheeks, I would love John forever, but could I learn to dance again? Was it possible? Did I even want to?

I sat there, listening for I didn't know what, some sign from John. If he were present, wouldn't he make it known to me? But all I heard was the rushing water and the faint rustle of wind through the trees.

Finding My Way Alone

AFTER JOHN DIED, I FELT THE WEIGHT OF THE PLANS AND DREAMS that he would never realize resting on my shoulders. I would do what I could to complete these for him. It gave me a reason to go on when I wasn't sure if I wanted to.

One afternoon, doing some errands in Santa Fe, I parked near the Plaza. I wanted to walk where I'd walked with John and look in at the Niman gallery where we'd purchased the three paintings by Dan Namingha. On Lincoln, I paused in front of a small folk art shop. Through the windows, I could see painted animals carved from wood. The door was open, so I walked in—and within minutes, I walked out carrying a three-foot-long gray hare holding a dangle of green and red chile peppers. I went straight home and installed it on the ledge between the photo studio and the dining area below.

I was admiring the hare, with its legs and the string of chiles hanging over the ledge, when the phone rang.

"Hi, Shirley." My old friend Karen was calling from Topanga Canyon. "How are you doing?"

"I'm doing all right. I just bought a hare—not a real one, a piece of folk art. He's sitting here in the condo with me. Looking at him, I can't help but smile. He has long ears that point sky-high and wiry black eyebrows. He looks as if he's asking, 'What's going on?' I want to respond, but all I can say is, 'I don't know. I'm a little confused. I'll have to get back to you.' His boldness captivated me. I simply had to have him."

"I'd love to see him! Shirley, let's do something fun. Didn't you say that John had never been to Chaco Canyon and really wanted to go there?"

"Yes."

"Why don't the two of us go as a tribute to John? It would be my personal thank-you and farewell to the man who transformed my dear friend's life."

"What a wonderful idea! I'd like that. Have you been to Chaco?"

"Many years ago, I camped at Chaco. There's an energy there that felt spiritual to me."

A few weeks later, I picked Karen up at the airport in Albuquerque. She was still so tall and slender, with her shoulder-length blonde hair, that her high school art students called her Barbie. This was her first visit to the condo, still relatively unfurnished. Before she arrived, I borrowed a blowup bed from Pat that nearly filled the floor of the photo studio.

"Shirley, I love this gray hare! I love its wiry whiskers!"

"I was smitten when I spotted him. He lifted my spirits in a way I haven't felt in a very long time. But I think he needs company. After we get back from Chaco, I'll show you the folk art shop off the Plaza. Maybe we'll find a companion for him."

Although I didn't know it then, bringing the hare home with me that day was a turning point. It was my first baby step into a new life without John. Significantly, I never got to the Niman gallery; instead, something totally spontaneous happened. Buying the hare was the moment I started to trust myself again. My life force was bursting through the walls of grief. But the thought of seeking a companion for the hare took me by surprise. I suspected that the whimsical, bold hare was me, and I was very far from ready to seek a companion. It would be a long time before I made hesitant forays, aching for a passion as profound as John and I had had, into the world of the opposite sex.

Early the next morning, after consulting a map of New Mexico that I'd found in the car and picking up some bottled water, we headed toward Chaco. We figured it would take at least four hours to get there. Before leaving the condo, I remembered the turquoise necklace John had brought back to me from Canyon de Chelly and fastened it around my neck. I would carry this tangible reminder of his love for me on the journey I would make for him.

In hiking shoes, jeans, and long-sleeved cotton tops, we were dressed for the high desert. Karen was navigating; I was at the wheel. It was my first long trip driving John's stick shift Xterra. I liked sitting up high in the driver's seat. I liked the fact that I was sitting where John had sat when he drove to Canyon de Chelly. For a moment, it was almost as if I were John. As I'd seen him do, I shifted easily from one gear to the next to reach cruising speed, then sat back in the seat, eyes forward. Unlike John, who draped one hand on the steering wheel and the other atop the shift, I kept both on the wheel. That was how I had learned to drive, ever ready to turn the wheel one way or the other.

Driving across the open vistas of northern New Mexico with Karen, I felt a twinge of regret undercutting my eagerness to see Chaco. This was a trip I might have made with John. He would have been driving. He might have wanted to camp out, to experience Chaco at night under a star-studded sky. I didn't know. Karen and I would not be camping; friends had said we could find a motel in Farmington, the closest large town. On the way, I told her about the memorial service which she hadn't been able to attend and the cairn Dick had erected at Aspen Vista. Neither of us shed tears, but we talked with the intimacy of the old friends we were.

In Farmington, we stopped at a motel and made a reservation for the night. The clerk told us we were a good hour and a half from Chaco.

"Look, Shirley, there's where we can have dinner." Karen sounded ecstatic. Off to our right on the main street was a large sign: St. Clair Winery and Bistro.

"Great! John would have liked the idea of eating at a winery." I thought of all the delicious wine I had tasted with him, and looked forward to drinking some good wine in his memory over dinner.

An hour later, we left the paved highway and found ourselves on a washboard dirt road. Gut-beating! Finally, I corrected my speed to minimize the jarring.

"Leaving the highway is symbolic of going someplace uncharted," Karen said, "someplace off the grid, and we're taking John's spirit with us in our hearts to a place he wanted to experience."

It was late afternoon when we arrived at Chaco. We picked up brochures at the visitor center and decided to explore the most celebrated site in the canyon, Pueblo Bonito, a complex that once reached five stories high and contained as many as eight hundred rooms. Constructed in stages between AD 850 and 1150 by ancestral Puebloan people, this was the center of the Chacoan world, a world that once covered much of today's Southwest.

The visible ruins were stark. The reddish-brown hue of rock walls blended almost seamlessly with the floor and walls of the canyon. My limited exposure to canyons near Santa Fe had filled me with expectations of shrubs and trees that were nowhere to be seen here. I had not researched Chaco before making the trip with Karen.

For the next three hours, we walked through Pueblo Bonito, ducking low through doorway after doorway of chiseled rocks fitted together without a trace of mortar. With the incessant wind blowing dirt and dust in our faces, we stood on ledges, peering down into great round rock-lined kivas, trying to imagine the ceremonies that had attracted hundreds of people over the course of three hundred years.

It was not that long ago, yet no one knows why the Chacoan people left the canyon. I wondered what theories John might have come up with. Their disappearance was sudden like his. How does a culture bloom and die in a few centuries? How does a man burst into my life and disappear like that? As if struck by lightning, I knew that I had been meant to visit Chaco. I was standing in the ruins of this vanished world and my vanished marriage—desolation outside and inside. Like the baffling remnants of Chaco, I was a ruin that spawned more questions than answers. Could I emerge from the loss of John? From the loss of a marriage that had held so much promise? Would I ever dream that big again?

Tired, we left Chaco just before sunset. We got back on the awful dirt road—thirteen miles of it before we hit pavement—and headed north toward our Farmington motel.

Showered and refreshed, we made our way to the St. Clair Winery and Bistro where we tasted and rejected five red wines before settling on a so-so pinot noir to go with our pasta. How disappointed John would have been, and how disappointed I was. Life, even in small ways, was not playing along with my plans.

The next morning, we returned to Chaco to follow a flat trail lined on one side with rock walls covered by petroglyphs. After photographing the spirals and figures, we ascended another trail cut into rock high above the canyon, one that would lead to a mesa top with a bird's-eye view of Chaco.

Our ascent stopped when Karen's fear of heights paralyzed her in the middle of a blind curve. "Shirley, I can't move!" Her voice was shaking with terror. "There might be dropoffs ahead."

I looked back; she was frozen to the wall. "Don't move," I said. "It's going to be all right. I'll go on a bit to see what's around the curve." Rounding the bend, I met hikers coming our way who assured me we were within a few hundred feet of the mesa top, with no sheer drops en route. Reassured, Karen put one foot in front of the other until we reached our goal.

Standing there looking over the vast canyon punctuated by open kivas, I wished I had saved some of John's ashes. I would have scattered them on this mesa and watched the wind carry them away into the canyon he had so wanted to experience. Gazing across the vastness with the wind kissing my face, I did not feel anguished by his absence. Instead, from this great height above the ruins, I felt more free than I had in weeks, as though my soul were in flight. Without knowing why, I felt hopeful. Chaco was a piece of unfinished business I had completed for John, yet I sensed I had also done it for myself.

It was midafternoon when we made our way back to the car. We would spend the night in Santa Fe before Karen's flight to L.A.

The next morning, we got up early. I wanted her to see the other hares in the folk art shop. Spying one that I had admired on an earlier visit, I heard Karen say, "Shirley, why don't you consider two more, not just one?"

"Take two on approval." Owner Davis Mather's open invitation convinced me. I would never have bought them if John were still alive— the upper level of our condo would have been a serious photo studio.

"I don't know how I'm going to pay for all these hares," I said as Karen and I left the shop, each embracing a large hare.

"You can pay for them in wine!" Mather said in jest. Had I mentioned John's wine to him?

Karen stopped short. "Shirley has lots of good wine!"

Ultimately, I acquired two more long-eared hares and a six-foot red and black snake in a trade for some of John's wine. Later, a Santa Fe sculptor of square bronze sheep also swapped art for wine. John's wine collection was a gift that kept on giving. It gave me a way to turn the old life into the new.

Day by day, I gained clarity. Because of John, I was in Santa Fe, a place he had loved, and being there felt good. I decided to spend three months at a time in each place—spring and fall in Reston when the rhododendrons were in bloom and the weather was beautiful, and summer and winter in Santa Fe where my only tie, apart from Pat and Philip who had moved there after John died, was John. I was not ready to uproot from Reston or totally ready to embrace Santa Fe.

Increasingly resolute, I decided I would fully furnish the condo. The first step was to order a valance for the solar shades in the living room. Then I would devote a couple of days, maybe longer, to sorting through the paintings and photographs in John's collection which were now under protective blankets in the garage.

The rugs—a large rust-colored wool one woven in Mexico for the living room and two striped runners to warm the entryways—I found in Madrid, a one-time coal mining town turned hippie settlement some twenty-five miles south of Santa Fe.

From the art collection, I selected three landscape lithographs in earth tones for the photo studio. On the lower level I hung black and white photographs by Brett Weston and Paul Caponigro, along with a stunning print of the California coast by Cole Weston. I left the wall above the bookcases open, intending to fill it with some of John's own work from Reston, and commissioned a whimsical painting of African cats by our artist friend Melinda for the wall above the desk.

The overall look of the condo, once the lighting was installed, was sleek-modern with warmth. It expressed my taste, punctuated by reminders of John's artistic acumen. With John still very much on my mind, I was taking the first tentative steps of my own. I was beginning to put my own stamp on his condo.

The condo reflected a new me, different from the Reston me. My Santa Fe home was bolder, with touches of whimsy—the hares, sheep, and African cats. It was more colorful and casual. Unlike Reston with its oriental rugs, hardwood floors, and silk chandelier over the dining table, the Santa Fe condo conveyed warmth and a sense of risk-taking.

In the fall, I went back to Reston to work with GRACE on the promised show for John. After Santa Fe, Reston struck me as stifling. I loved my condo, but like the house I'd sold because it was so full of Joe I could hardly breathe, the condo and all the local eateries I'd frequented with John weighed me down with sadness. This was where we had spent most of our time together. More than that, this was where John had become increasingly ill. This was where I had been when he died. Back in Reston, I felt his absence acutely. Nonetheless, I wasn't ready to let go of the condo. Before meeting John, I had envisioned living in Reston for the rest of my life. I still thought it would probably be a good place to grow old, if I could ever shake the oppressive memories.

Soon after my return, Joanne came to the condo to review John's photographs. She wanted to display only his photos of trees, in keeping with the gallery's fall theme, "Sleeping Tree." From John's prints and computer archives, she selected five. Four were of aspen in New Mexico, two of them taken at Aspen Vista. The fifth, "Coconino Burn," John had taken from a car window on a rainy day driving from Sedona to Canyon de Chelly. It shows a burned out pine forest on a mountainside, and in the foreground, nascent grasses in brilliant yellow-green.

The evening of the opening, wearing the black top and long crinkly turquoise skirt I'd worn for our anniversary dinner in Paris, I walked down Market Street to the gallery. It was still early. A sizable L-shaped space—two white walls—displayed John's photographs. It had been a task to get them ready; a photographer friend from the Smithsonian had helped with the printing. Above the photographs in gray lettering on one wall: Photographs by John Bessey (1949–2008). I swallowed hard. How many times had I seen the birth and death of an artist denoted by the telling parentheses—often hundreds of years after the artist's death? John's absence from this honor his work was receiving made my heart ache. I would do my best to stand in for him.

I picked up the handout from a stack on the reception counter. "Coconino Burn" in black and white was the cover photo. I thought John would have been pleased with the selection. While Joanne introduced me, I stood looking out at the crowd—well-heeled couples, few of whom I recognized. I was as ready as I could be.

"Thank you, Joanne." I took a breath and began to speak. "I'd like to start by reading John's statement in the handout, which he wrote for juried competitions: 'My first pictures were star trails, using a camera consisting of an old clock face, an oatmeal box, and a piece of photographic paper developed in a makeshift darkroom. The technology has changed, but my fascination with capturing the natural world in a photographic image remains. My goal is to express in photographs my emotional response to the beauty of nature.'

"This exhibition of John's photographs is not the ambitious project he envisioned for GRACE, but it is a window into his sensitivity to the world around him and a testimony to his belief in the resilience and strength of nature. With his lifelong passion for photography, John had anticipated having his own show one day. I want to thank GRACE—the board of directors, Joanne, and Erica—for giving him this opportunity."

That was all I said. Standing in front of that anonymous crowd, most of whom had never heard of John, I was struck by how much he had lost—the solo show he wanted, his potential fame as a world-class photographer. I couldn't say what I wanted to say, that these five images hardly did justice to his talent, that he had died before he became what he'd dreamed of becoming. I couldn't tell them how conflicted I felt standing in for him when I knew this was not the show of his own that he had envisioned.

Walking home that night, my head abuzz, I felt light-shouldered. A weight had been lifted. Another piece of John's unfinished business was done. But my relief was bittersweet. He should have been there, not for this exhibit but for the project he'd enthusiastically discussed with Joanne: the provocative "Patterns" installation. That would have been an opening to celebrate. This exhibit, as meaningful as I had thought it would be when Joanne offered it, hardly touched his wide-ranging photographic interests and accomplishments. His posthumous opening, like his death, was a premature closing. His show was not a retrospective. He had died too soon for that, too soon to have built up a body of work. And that fact in itself made me face a heart-wrenching truth: Try as I might, I could not complete John's life for him.

Back in the condo, I fixed a cup of tea and opened the manila folder I'd carried with me to Santa Fe and back—seventeen pages of information titled NOTEBOOK. I looked at the date, May 20. John had completed it a week before he died, and had left it for me on top of his printer. Now, months later, I was finally able to really look at it. Until that moment, I hadn't been quiet enough inside. There was a page of odd personal information—where he and his brother were born, the birth and death of each parent, his residences from 1949 to the present, his education and work experience. Other pages addressed our finances: how things were billed and paid, account numbers, Reston and Santa Fe insurance policies, computer access to miscellaneous accounts, and his thoughts on our 2008 income taxes. He also listed camera contacts who could sell the floor printer and other equipment he hadn't donated. He shared details about his two cars—their original costs and service histories, even describing a dent in a fender as "cosmetic only." On one page, he listed friends' names and addresses. Despite his failing brain, he had gotten down a lot of good information. I remembered him working on it in front of the computer. I had been afraid he wouldn't finish it in time, but he did. It was a labor of love, and I was grateful.

Placing the notebook on the coffee table, I sipped my now-cold tea. So much information and so little direction. How like John to focus on the data and never talk with me about living on after him. Now I had to find my way alone. Would I let his death define me? Was

I more than John's widow? If not, I should clothe myself in black and be done with it. There was a heartening assumption in the notebook that I would keep going. Now, if I could just figure out how.

That winter back in Santa Fe, nudged by John's comment about the importance of plans, I researched trips to the Galapagos. There were few that didn't include an add-on visit to Machu Picchu or the Amazon. And then I found one that sounded perfect—ten days in the Galapagos on a boat, the *Endeavor,* with expert naturalist guides and a professional photographer, no add-ons.

While I was there, I didn't think about John, or rather, I didn't feel his absence. Each day from sunrise to sundown was physically demanding and absorbing. I was taken out of myself so completely that my story did not define me. I was not a woman who had been widowed twice but an adventurer, a world traveler, the girl I was before I married Joe. Waking early, I'd throw on safari clothes and amphibious shoes and head for the dining room. I wanted to eat early and listen for the day's itinerary. Twice a day, I'd stand in line to disembark from the *Endeavor,* climb down into a rubber dinghy-like Zodiac landing craft, and venture onto islands with a naturalist guide. I was using the Nikon, huddling over it to keep it dry during these small boat rides to and from the islands. In the evenings after dinner, a National Geographic photographer would show his day's worth of photos. Each night, after turning on the Nikon's battery charger, I would drop into my narrow bed beneath a porthole and sleep soundly until the next morning.

John was not connected energetically with this trip. He had asked me from his hospital bed to book it; he had done that for me. But it was a dream of mine long before I met him, and in the end, I realized it by myself.

A few months after my return, a Santa Fe photographer friend invited me to show my Galapagos prints with his images of the Southwest. It took me by surprise: "I can't imagine that mine are good enough."

"You've got some good ones, and they'll be an interesting contrast to mine. I'll show you how to use Photoshop if you want to alter any of them a bit." His blue eyes twinkled behind dark-rimmed glasses. "Are you game?"

"Yes!" Emboldened by his vote of confidence, I threw myself into the project. For days and nights leading up to the show, I drove to the camera store on Calle Lorca where computers equipped with Photoshop software sat on long tables upstairs alongside printers to produce the large images I'd show. I practiced under my friend's watchful eye. Learning Photoshop in zip time was a tall order, and a frustrating one. I thought about John and his mastery of all things related to photography, and felt like a fraud. My Galapagos photos had turned out. Pure luck! I vowed that once the exhibition was over, I'd take a week-long course in digital photography at the Santa Fe Photographic Workshops. Who knew? Maybe I'd develop a passion for photography after all.

When I sold some of my Galapagos prints and notecards at the show, I was elated. Wow! I held fast to my decision to immerse myself in a week-long class. It would be telling.

And it was. Once the immersion class was over, I put the Nikon aside. I had learned enough in a week to realize that, talent or no, for me to become an accomplished photographer would take untold amounts of time. And for months now, I had felt a tug on my heart and brain that had nothing to do with photography.

I wanted to get back to my true passion: writing.

I told Pat and Philip over dinner that I had decided to write about my life with John. "I can't explain why, but I need to do it. It might help give me perspective that I'm lacking. And maybe my experience, if I can understand it, would prove helpful to others. I don't know."

When I first met John, I'd told him I wanted to write a book and had a good idea for one, but once we embarked on our joint adventure, my book idea about women ages sixty to ninety took a backseat. Now, all I wanted to write about, as if my life depended on it, was him.

Once I started to write that second summer in Santa Fe, I couldn't stop. Like someone possessed, I wrote day and night, sitting in front of the computer at the long desk, taking little time out except for yoga and occasional dinners with friends. Through tears and sodden tissues, I kept hitting the computer keys. I was grieving intensely all over again, reliving our life together, but more than that, I was looking for answers. It was a drive that gripped every part of my being.

No sooner had I returned to Reston in the fall than I plunked myself down in front of the computer again and continued to write. Initially, I'd wanted to write about John—how wonderful he was, how wonderful we were together. But as time passed, it became more that I wanted to understand what had happened to me. I wanted to understand the choices I'd made. Writing helped me think. By writing, perhaps I would see the path ahead more clearly. Writing was my own form of expression. And it might also be my salvation.

Epilogue

"WOULD YOU LIKE TO HEAR SOME LIVE JAZZ?" FRANK WAS ON THE phone, telling me about the Tuesday night jam session at El Farol on Canyon Road. "We could grab a bite to eat before the music starts."

"Sounds like fun. I've never been to El Farol."

"Good. I'll pick you up at 7."

I hung up the phone and walked back into the studio, now converted into my writing area. Lowering myself into the black leather desk chair in front of the monitor, I stared at the screen: Chapter 26. I felt I was in the home stretch, but the ending was eluding me. Maybe I was writing too much?

The problem was that I kept interrupting myself. The photo exhibit of my Galapagos prints had taken weeks away from my writing. And now there was Frank, who kept calling me with invitations I couldn't say no to—first the Turner-Cézanne exhibition in Albuquerque and now live jazz.

I liked Frank. I liked his enthusiasm. A widower, he'd experienced similar tragedy, yet he was fully engaged in life. Certainly, he'd enriched my life in the short time we'd known each other. Though older than I, he was vigorously active, skiing black diamonds in the winter and golfing all summer. Interested in the world at large, he read the *Economist* and *New York Times*—déjà vu all over again. In a couple of weeks, he'd be traveling to Greece and Turkey. He'd asked me to go with him, but I declined; it was too soon. Clearly, if I didn't want to travel with him, he wasn't going to sit around and mope.

Tuesday night, Frank and I were sitting at a table in the crowded bar area of El Farol with a friend of Frank's who'd joined us for dinner. The air was filled with the sounds of guitar, piano, and drums—too loud for meaningful conversation. I looked out at a dance floor crowded with bodies gyrating to the jazz beat.

Frank leaned in close. "Would you like to dance?"

His question startled me. I'd thought we were just going to listen. "I don't know if I can. It's been a long time." I didn't know he danced.

"It's not so hard." His gaze was unwavering.

"All right," I said, standing up. "I'll give it a try."

I placed my fingers in Frank's hand, and he led me onto the dance floor. Almost immediately, he was moving with the rhythm of the music, his hand at my back subtly guiding me. I felt myself responding as though it were the most natural thing in the world.

Oh my god, I thought, I'm dancing!

About the Author

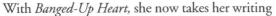

SHIRLEY MELIS IS A LONGTIME BUSINESS WRITER, travel writer, and newspaper columnist who traveled the world interviewing everyone from busboys to heads of international organizations before launching a career in public relations in Washington, D.C.

With *Banged-Up Heart,* she now takes her writing in a new direction, delving deeply into her own personal story of finding love late, losing it early, and discovering the strength to choose to love again. It is a fascinating odyssey, a journey both creative and erotic as Shirley and John work lovingly together to blend their dreams—until a mysterious bump on his forehead starts them on a tragic struggle against the dark hand of fate.

A graduate of Vassar, Shirley Melis has created an intimate memoir bearing eloquent witness to the kind of wild trust that can grow in the heart of an ordinary woman thrust into circumstances that few others must face. Her story will speak to anyone who has loved deeply and found the courage and strength to love again.

Now retired, she lives in Galisteo, New Mexico. She is a full-time writer and travels extensively, and also is active in local government.

Discussion Guide for Book Groups

1. A quote from Anne Lamott serves as an epigraph for *Banged-Up Heart*. Did it color your sense of Shirley's story before you read the book? Have you danced with a banged-up heart? And how might it have changed the way you acted or felt?

2. Early in the book, Shirley has a date with an old family friend that doesn't turn out well. What was your worst date ever? What did you learn from it?

3. When John visits Shirley for the first time, she tells him about the death of her husband. How do you feel about John's response? What do you find most helpful when you share your pain or vulnerability with a friend?

4. Before Shirley proposes to John, she's ambivalent about committing to him. What plays into her ambivalence? When you've been ambivalent about a relationship, what concerned you? How do you feel now about the choice—to stay or go—that you made? In late-life relationships, health can be a concern. Would you give up a relationship because of health concerns, yours or the other person's? Why or why not? Have you ever decided against a relationship because of health issues?

5. Shirley writes about her persistent hope that John will survive. What are the pros and cons of hope? How has hope helped or hindered you in dealing with risk?

6. At John's memorial service, an art gallery director offers to show his photographs in an upcoming exhibition. But Shirley's initial euphoria is not realized when the exhibition takes place. How invested should one be in a dying loved one's unfulfilled dreams? How do you carry your loved one's unlived life?

7. Did you ever doubt that Shirley would survive John's death? Have you survived the loss of someone deeply beloved? What helped you to go on?

8. Shirley finds herself pulled into a folk art shop displaying wood sculptures of wild hares. What does the purchase tell you about her? When have you done something like that? Have you ever had a similar impulse you didn't act on?

9. How does Shirley make a life for herself without John? When have you started over? How did you go about it? What helped you?

10. Did you think Shirley would open her heart to love again? Why or why not? In a similar situation, would you?

Q&A with Shirley Melis

How did you come to write *Banged-Up Heart*?

When my husband John died, I felt blindsided, and I needed to figure out what had happened to me. So often, writing helps me see more clearly. At first, I just wanted to relive the wonderful relationship I'd had with John. But once I got started, I became wiser, I think—more curious, more demanding. I was curious about John and his behavior toward me. Had he intentionally kept the severity of his illness a secret from me? I wasn't going to let him off the hook, which I had done all along. Now, I was determined to face the questions I had never asked him. In the end, celebrating the relationship was not nearly so important as getting as close to the truth as I could.

What challenges arose as you wrote the book?

It was really in the rewriting that I faced my biggest challenge. That's when I realized I had told only the outer visible story, whereas what I needed to tell was the inside story. It was my editor, Morgan Farley, who helped me get to the inner story by asking questions that guided me deep inside, into intense emotional places. Before I met Morgan, I wrote my story, but it wasn't the whole story. There was a lot missing—not only the emotional part, the feelings I experienced, but also my reflections on those past experiences from where I am now.

Did incorporating those missing elements change your voice or your writing style?

It certainly did. I had to learn the craft of fiction writing to make the memoir come alive—everything from scene-setting and character development to dialogue and pacing. My voice initially was pretty dispassionate. I was not used to writing about myself; I had done business writing for insurance associations and freelance travel writing for newspapers. In my kind of business writing, scenes were where meetings took place, and quotes by speakers didn't reveal much, if any, personality or character. In a nutshell, I had to learn the craft of novel writing, but I hadn't read many novels. In college, I was a history major, and I developed a high regard for the importance of original sources. Writing my memoir, I had a bushel of emails and a detailed journal. Those were my original sources.

Did your years of business and travel writing help or hinder you in writing a memoir?

In business writing, and even in travel writing, there's a need for accuracy, clarity, and a degree of balance that some call fairness. I had to use my training in objectivity to confront my story as I lived it: subjectively. I had to bring those values of clarity and accuracy to bear on expressing my deepest feelings and most intimate experiences. I had to drop the mask of objectivity to tell my own truth. "If you choose to do this, it will be transformative," Morgan said. I wondered how I would be transformed. All I could think of was butterflies and how they come from larvae in some hidden, mysterious process. It was a bit scary but more than that—inspiring.

And was she right? Did writing the memoir transform you?

It was this kind of writing that opened my eyes to parts of myself I didn't know. It became important to me to come face-to-face with myself, to tell the truth about my life, and to put it on paper—and it wasn't all positive either. I saw that I really fear abandonment, and that I tend to commit heart and soul. And yet I see myself now as much stronger than I knew. I am not done in by loss. I've lost a lot, but my heart is still open to other people. I've taken another risk to share my life with someone, and I'm not afraid. I don't fear the possible consequences of my decision to share my life again. There's something about renewal. When I committed myself to John, it was a new beginning, refreshing and heartwarming, and now that I've married Frank, there's a newness that energizes me. I see myself if not as a butterfly, then as someone who still has wings to spread.

Given the anguish you expressed, was it difficult to keep writing?

I couldn't stop writing. I felt compelled to write through it all. I re-experienced the pain and also the joys. When I was writing my first draft, the visible story, I was trying to get it right, so I put everything down. I did have emails and a journal documenting things, so in that sense, I re-lived much of it. But it was in the rewriting that I went below the surface of the journal and emails. I never resisted doing that. With the questions Morgan put to me, I had to do that, and it was liberating. Afterward I was able to breathe again, and open myself to another person.

Did you find the writing therapeutic?

Yes, in a real sense. I don't think I can say it saved my life—that may be too strong—but it helped me keep moving. I came away with a much more nuanced and complex understanding of John—who he was in himself and in his relationship with me. Just to be able to see that took me out of the blinding intensity of feelings that overwhelmed me at times. I saw eventually that I was not going to try to carry out his unfulfilled dreams. I couldn't. I needed to have dreams of my own. I took to heart his motto: "Life interferes with plans, but it's important to have plans." I was comfortable, finally, with myself as a survivor. And that allowed me to step out of the cocoon of grief and find joy in just being alive.

Do you have any advice for people suffering the loss of a loved one?

Allow yourself to grieve. Whether unexpected or anticipated, the loss is real. The absence of that person can be almost palpable, as though a part of you has been cut away and you're left bleeding. Your ability to think clearly may be distorted by the pain of loss. If you have a good friend who offers to help you—drive you to appointments, take you to dinner—accept. Friends who have never experienced the loss of someone beloved may not know what to say, but they want to ease your pain. Don't be afraid to ask for their help, and take comfort in their gifts of food, flowers, and cards.

If you're working when your partner dies, take some time off to do what needs to be done, but go back to work if you can. The structure of a job will give you something other than your loss on which to focus. You may find yourself tearing up at unexpected moments, but that's understandable.

If you can, join a grief group, and see a therapist. In a grief group, you learn empathy; hearing other people's stories is affecting, and you realize you're not alone. With a therapist, you can explore the roots of your anguish, something you might not be able to do alone, and perhaps shouldn't try to do with good friends since the burden of grief can be overwhelming for others.

I want to say something about closure—because I think it may be a myth. It just seems so accepted now that if you can talk about the loss and grief, then you can forget about it. I think you might put it aside, but I doubt you ever put it away. It's a part of your life experience that helps make you whoever you are. You don't keep talking about the people you've lost, but you keep them in your heart.

Do you have any advice for people who might be thinking of writing a memoir?

Be careful what you wish for. It's tough. To write a memoir, you have to have a lot of perseverance—to get at the truth—and courage to express it, letting the chips fall where they may. I'm reminded of a philosophy professor who wrote at the top of my paper on John Locke, "You might have come up with a more insightful analysis if you'd looked at the assumptions beneath his verbiage." You've got to go deep.

What helped you to persevere?

You need to take care of yourself while you're going through this. I took breaks to exercise—yoga, treadmill, weights. And there are the people close to you, people you don't want to shut out. Before I finished writing, I remarried, and I agonized over giving too little of myself to my new husband because I was giving so much to the book. I set boundaries for myself. I would write during the day, spending evenings and weekends with my husband. You can be sensitive to your loved one's need for time and attention without giving up your own need to write the memoir.

Would you encourage others to write a memoir?

I would—because for me, it was so rewarding. But people have to understand it's about unvarnished truth. It's difficult to get there if you're not introspective, but given the questions posed by my editor, I found that I could be.

So it was worth it?

Oh, yes. And not just because I can say I've done this—written a book—but to have landed an agent and a publisher makes me feel I've accomplished what I hoped to do. In the beginning, I was just writing for myself, but when friends read parts of it and said, "Shirley, other people will be interested in reading this," I thought, Really? Then I'd better see to it that I go the distance and make it worthwhile.